From Artisans to Paupers

To my parents, Shula and Joshua

From Artisans to Paupers:

Economic Change and Poverty in London, 1790–1870

DAVID R. GREEN

SCOLAR PRESS

Published by
SCOLAR PRESS
Gower House
Croft Road
Aldershot
Hants GU11 3HR
England

359.46
G79f

Ashgate Publishing Company
Old Post Road
Brookfield
Vermont 05036
USA

British Library Cataloguing in Publication Data

Green, David R.
    From Artisans to Paupers: Economic Change
    and Poverty in London, 1790–1870
    I. Title
TK339.4609421

Library of Congress Cataloging-in-Publication Data

Green, David R., 1954–
    From artisans to paupers: economic change and poverty in London,
    1790–1870/David R. Green
        p.   cm.
    Includes bibliographical references and index.
    ISBN 1–85928–033–1
    1. Poverty—England—London—History. 2. Poor—England—London—
    History. 3. London (England)—Economic conditions. I. Title.
    HC258.L6G73 1995   95–2702
    339.4'6'09421—dc20   CIP

ISBN 1 85928 033 1

Typeset in Sabon by Bournemouth Colour Press and printed in Great Britain by Biddles Ltd, Guildford.

Contents

List of figures

List of tables

List of plates

Between pages 180 and 181.

All published with the kind permission of the Mary Evans Picture Library.

Abbreviations

APRDM	Association for Promoting the Relief of Destitution in the Metropolis
GLRO	Greater London Record Office
GNCTU	Grand National Consolidated Trades Union
GSPDV	General Society for the Promotion of District Visiting
LCM	London City Mission
MCPF	Metropolitan Common Poor Fund
NS	*Northern Star*
PLB	Poor Law Board
Place Coll.	Place Collection, Newspapers
Place Coll. Add Ms.	Place Collection, Additional Manuscript
PLC	Poor Law Commission
PRO	Public Record Office
RC	Royal Commission
RN	*Reynolds Newspaper*
SC	Select Committee
SSM	Society for the Suppression of Mendicity
Webb Coll.	Webb Collection of Trade Union Manuscripts
ULMC	University of London Manuscript Collection

Preface

Throughout history cities have acted as a lens through which to view the dimensions of social life. By virtue of concentration they magnify the contrasts between wealth and poverty. In nineteenth-century Britain there was no city in which such contrasts were wider or posed more pressing problems than in London and it is that great metropolis which is the focus of this study. Nowhere were the contrasts between wealth and poverty drawn more clearly than in London and nowhere were the issues raised and the problems posed by such disparities more difficult to resolve.

In the first half of the nineteenth century, more so perhaps than in later decades, urban poverty was particularly widespread.[1] Over and above the qualitative evidence of impoverishment gleaned from contemporaries such as Engels, Faucher and Kay, more recent research has sought to outline the quantitative dimensions of the problem. Thus, John Foster has suggested that in 1849, 15 per cent of Oldham's, 23 per cent of South Shields' and 28 per cent of Northampton's families were malnourished.[2] For Preston, Michael Anderson has estimated that in 1851 about 20 per cent of families also lived in a state of chronic poverty, although this varied considerably depending on the stage of the family life cycle.[3] Both authors agree, however, that only a small minority of the working class were permanently free from primary poverty. In the second half of the century, notably from the 1870s, cheaper food and falling death rates helped to reduce the incidence of chronic poverty, although the work of Booth and Rowntree drew attention to the fact that large numbers of workers still suffered at various stages of their life cycle from the ravages of poverty.[4] It is to the first half of the century, then, that we should look to discover the greatest depth and widest extent of urban poverty in England.

My concern here is with exploring the relationships between economic change, poverty and the provision of welfare between the 1790s and 1870s, a theme that has as much significance for our own times as those of Londoners over two centuries ago. Inevitably, these concerns touch on a variety of issues not all of which can be explored here. I am less concerned with attitudes and discourses than with policies and practices. Thus, whilst I devote considerable attention to the pattern of economic change, little is said about political economy. I touch only tangentially on contemporary attitudes towards the poor in contrast to the more detailed discussion of the problems of providing poor relief. In focusing on the immediate problems posed by economic change and the incidence of poverty I do not wish to deny the importance of political and ideological discourses in understanding the issues raised. Indeed, it will become clear at various points that such considerations provide the basis for the creation and implementation of various policies and practices. None the less, my aim is directed more towards examining the relationships between economic change and poverty rather than an exploration of political and social discourses and as such I have left discussion of these issues to others.[5]

At the start of the century London's population stood at nearly one million; by the end it had reached over 4.5 million. In demographic terms it towered over all other nineteenth-century British cities and this in turn meant that the disorder and chaos associated with rapidly growing cities was magnified in the case of London. In this study I have tried to make sense of that disorder by following the many disparate strands that linked the economic, political, social and spatial structures of the capital. No doubt much has been ignored. I have said little, for example, about gender relations and working-class culture, though my omission is more than made up for by the excellence of other studies.[6] Although the metropolitan middle-class parade through these pages on many occasions, their lives and internal stratification are almost as obscure as the fog-laden atmosphere of the city in which they dwelt. Much more work needs to be done on this curiously neglected class. There are no doubt other gaps in this work that will appear to readers more perceptive than myself. However, to search for gaps is to miss the main point. Whilst the constituent disciplines of the social sciences labour long and hard to fragment the dimensions of social life into separate conceptual categories, here I have tried to map out the links between those categories, between the economy, society, geography and politics of nineteenth-century London. There was, perhaps, no other city in which those strands of human existence were more complex or more difficult to comprehend.

We invoke the past at our peril as a means of focusing attention on the present. None the less, and certainly without wishing to issue any emotive calls for a return to 'Victorian values', parallels exist between our own situation and that of early to mid-nineteenth century society. As the eighteenth century drew to a close, new belief and hope in the virtues of industrial capitalism and *laissez faire* political economy emerged. Dismemberment of the remaining vestiges of the mercantilist system, and a growing belief in the benign hand of the free market, was paralleled in the social sphere by an emphasis on the rights of the individual over and above the traditions, constraints and obligations of communal life. This new-found reverence for the liberties and rights of the individual were by no means universally welcomed. Those who feared that the ties which bound together the social order were threatened by the pursuit of individualism included both bourgeois and working-class critics. Thomas Arnold, for example, warned that 'the anarchical tendency of our worship of freedom in and of itself tends to anarchy.'[7] We continue to search for ways in which to reconcile the rights and obligations of the individual to those of the wider community.

The freeing of market forces and the unfettering of global capitalism posed challenges for the early nineteenth-century British economy no less than they do today. Improved transport lowered freight costs, thereby widening the market and heightening levels of competition between producers formerly separated by the barriers of distance. As markets widened, so opportunities emerged for extending the division of labour and introducing technological improvements. In this fashion, tried and tested methods of work and workplace organization were threatened with dissolution or swept away entirely, a situation that has parallels with that of today. Changes in the spatial framework of production ensued as manufacturers were brought into direct competition with others not only in Britain but also with those in Europe and even further afield. As the production of commodities assumed both national and global dimensions, so growing competition and falling prices provided further impetus for rapid technological and organizational changes in production. The precise forms taken by this transformation varied but were guided by the nature of work, the characteristics of localities and the relationships between capital and labour. Working-class resistance to those changes took various forms, including the defence of wages and conditions at the workplace, ideological opposition to the tenets of bourgeois political economy, and the call for wider political reform. The extent to which a balance was struck between transformation of the labour process and the welfare of workers thus depended on the relative power of capital and labour in particular places and we should therefore not underestimate the role of local practices in influencing the impact of global economic change in specific locations.[8]

In relation to the formal provision of welfare, the means of distributing relief, both then and now, were fundamentally restructured in response to changing political discourses and the demands imposed in the course of economic change. The Poor Law was transformed after 1834 to conform more closely to the principles of *laissez faire* political economy. However, this did little to prevent the recurrence of crises in the provision of poor relief, as happened in parts of London during the 1850s and 1860s and which ultimately led to the start of more centralized and redistributive welfare policies. Today, redistributive policies for the most part prevent the occurrence of localized breakdowns in the provision of welfare, although in the current process of redefining the relationships between localism and centralization, the strains and stresses on local government finance are only too evident. Clearly, differences as well as similarities exist between our own time and the early nineteenth century and it would be unwise to press a case for either too vigorously. Nevertheless, in terms of the relationships between economic change, political discourse and the provision of welfare, similarities exist simply because the problems of balancing economic change with social justice have still to be resolved under capitalism.

The work upon which this book is based originated as my doctoral thesis but has subsequently undergone substantial change. Several more years have passed and many new debts, far more than I could ever hope to repay, have been accrued. Through their constant enthusiasm for exploring nineteenth-century London, students at King's College and the London School of Economics have kept my own interests alive. The forbearance of my colleagues in the sabbatical year during which the writing was completed was much appreciated. A special word of thanks must go to John Thornes whose encouragement was unstinting and whose willingness to deal with the problems posed by my absence was at times sorely stretched. Gordon Reynell and Roma Beaumont drew the illustrations with their customary care. Not even as the number of maps and diagrams multiplied inversely to the time available did they lose their composure or sense of humour. To them I also owe a special word of thanks. Richard Dennis, Martin Gaskell, Paul Johnson and Ted Yates have at various times forced me to rethink my ideas. Humphrey Southall and Julian Hoppitt were extremely generous in allowing me to use their unpublished data. I have been most fortunate in having had at various times Dalia Magrill and Alastair Owens as my research assistants. Their willingness to stick to the task was exemplary. I am also grateful for the help provided by archivists in the Public Record Office, the British Library Newspaper Collection, the British Library, the Greater London Record Office, the Guildhall Library, the British Library for Political and Economic Science, the Office of Population and Census Surveys and the University of London manuscripts collection. Particular thanks go to Angela Whitelegge from the Goldsmith's Collection and Richard Knight from the Holborn Local History Library. I am also grateful to Alec McAulay of Scolar Press, who, despite the many delays, supported the work without reservation.

In the course of writing this book I have discovered that the main burden has been borne not by me but by those who had to put up with the antisocial hours that the task involved. Heather Magrill has listened to the arguments late into the night, clarified ideas and improved the text. She is not only my partner but also my most constructive critic. Her support and encouragement have helped see this book through to completion and her contribution is evident on every page. Finally, I owe more to my parents than I could ever hope to repay; to my father, whom I knew only as a young child, and to my mother whose interest in the world around her seems to grow as the years pass. My greatest pleasure is to dedicate this book to them.

Notes

1. Treble, 1979, p.17.
2. Foster, 1977, p.96.
3. Anderson, 1974, pp.30–2.
4. For a general discussion of urban poverty see Treble, 1979.
5. See, for example, Cowherd, 1977; Himmelfarb, 1984; Inglis, 1971.
6. In particular see Prothero, 1981; Taylor, 1983; Thompson, 1968.
7. Arnold, 1869, p.58.
8. This topic has been explored extensively by geographers such as Massey, 1984; Scott and Storper, 1984; Soja, 1989.

CHAPTER ONE

London: the fragmented metropolis

Introduction

Until the start of the nineteenth century, with the exception of capital cities, settlements in Europe remained small and the bases of social relations were perhaps little different between the town and the country. This was as true of England as it was of its continental neighbours. In the nineteenth century, however, circumstances changed. Fuelled by industrialization and demographic growth, villages mushroomed into towns and cities in just a few years. This process of urbanization, which was nowhere more rapid or widespread than in England, laid a new foundation for social life. As population densities multiplied, new problems emerged relating to the biological basis of urban living. Patterns of work were transformed as the division of labour intensified and as the factory system took root. Personal acquaintance became less as the urban crowd grew larger and the population more diverse. Traditional social relations, it seemed, were being replaced by a distinctive and peculiarly urban way of life. Nowhere was this more apparent than in London.

The weight of numbers

In the nineteenth-century world, London was a demographic colossus, yet figures alone can only hint at the immensity of the capital, both in terms of the size of its population and its geographical extent.[1] In the European context, no city came close to matching London: in 1850 Paris, its nearest rival, was only half its size.[2] At the national scale, London's position was even more dominant. In the early 1800s nearly one in nine people in England and Wales were Londoners, and by 1871 this had risen to one in seven. In 1801 the combined population of the next five largest British cities, Edinburgh, Liverpool, Glasgow, Manchester and Birmingham, was barely half that of the capital and, despite the rapid growth of northern and Midland industrial cities, matters had changed little by 1871. Even this, however, underestimates the real significance of the capital's size on the life of the nation. In the eighteenth century as many as one-sixth of the adult English population may have had direct experience of the capital.[3] By the nineteenth century, as the expanding transport network drew London and the nation into an even tighter embrace, this proportion may well have increased. Other cities may have grown at more spectacular rates. Manchester, for example, the 'shock city' of the 1840s as Asa Briggs once called it, immediately springs to mind, as does Glasgow. But in the age of great cities, to use Robert Vaughan's phrase, none was greater, or indeed more shocking to bourgeois sensibilities, than the unwieldy and overcrowded metropolis.[4]

What was true of numbers was also true of geographical size. In contrast to Paris, London's growth was outwards rather than upwards.[5] The early introduction of public transport encouraged the rapid spread of the built-up area along main routes to and from the city. From 1829, when the first omnibus was introduced between Paddington and the Bank, opportunities for middle-class commuting increased. For the working class, the 6d. fare was prohibitive and they remained tied to a residence close to their place of employment.[6] Profitability bred competition and by mid-century more than 1300 omnibuses touted for custom along the streets of the capital. By 1860, the London General Omnibus Company was carrying over 40 million passengers a year and web-like fingers of development stretched outwards in all directions along transportation routes.[7] Not until then did opportunities for working-class suburbanization present themselves. When the first commuter railway opened in 1836 between Deptford and London Bridge, later extended to Greenwich in 1838, further impetus was given to middle-class suburban expansion, although the main period of growth only occurred from the 1860s when cheaper fares began to attract significant numbers of lower middle-class and working-class commuters. Nevertheless, as omnibus routes and later railways began to appear on maps of London, the exodus from the overcrowded core gathered momentum and the city spilled outwards to engulf once separate communities in a seemingly endless tide of bricks and mortar. Writing in 1843, at the dawn of this period of urban transformation, John Burn likened the city's growth to ' ... a vessel brimful into which pours from above successive drops of human existence, while a continual stream is forced over the sides and a perpetual change, immigrative and emigrative, continuously goes on, leaving a capacious reservoir – ever receiving, ever discharging, and ever full'.[8]

Geographical growth proceeded at an astonishing pace. Writing in the 1880s, Henry James remarked, 'One has not the alternative of speaking of London as a whole, for the simple reason that there is no such thing as the whole of it. It is immeasurable – embracing arms never meet.'[9] Whilst central districts stagnated or declined from the 1830s onwards, the suburbs grew in leaps and bounds. The population of St Pancras, for example, increased from 31,779 in 1801 to 166,956 by 1851, at which time it was larger than either Bristol or Bradford and only slightly smaller than Leeds. Its neighbour, St Marylebone, was of similar size and if each was counted separately from London, they would have been the eighth and ninth largest British cities respectively. Indeed, of the 16 urban places at mid-century that contained a population of at least 100,000, seven were located in London. It was partly this speed and extent of growth that baffled contemporaries. Not until 1831 did the census provide a rudimentary enumeration of the metropolitan area and in the following census, only occupation tables were provided for the metropolitan districts of Middlesex, Surrey and Kent. London itself finally became a separate registration division in the 1851 census, the boundaries of which are shown in Figure 1.1, and this newly defined metropolitan area was to form the basic geographical framework for the remainder of the century.

If demographic growth and geographical expansion reinforced the impression of size, then the heterogeneity of the metropolitan population confirmed the capital's social complexity. Perhaps the most striking point was the youthfulness of the population.[10] At mid-century more than half the population was aged below 25 years, and nearly a third was less than 15 years old. Beyond that unifying characteristic, however, the similarities begin to fade. London's roles as the nation's capital and as a port of international significance ensured that its population was not only extremely large but also exceptionally diverse. A large number of the London crowd, it was true, had been born in the capital but nearly 40 per cent came from elsewhere. Rural migrants were the most numerous of this group, particularly from southern counties and from East Anglia.[11] Such were the attractions of the capital, however, that people were drawn from every county in the kingdom and many from further afield. About one in twenty of the population was Irish, although this proportion was much higher in the dock districts and in poorer quarters throughout the city, such as the rookery in St Giles.[12] Although foreigners were by no means absent they were relatively rare, often forming ethnic villages enmeshed within the larger urban fabric. In the central parts, Italians from around Saffron Hill were perhaps the most conspicuous of this group but foreigners were more numerous in eastern districts closer to the docks, especially Jewish migrants from Germany, Poland or Holland. Nor were all the faces of the London crowd white; the city's black population, as we have begun to realize, was by no means insubstantial.[13]

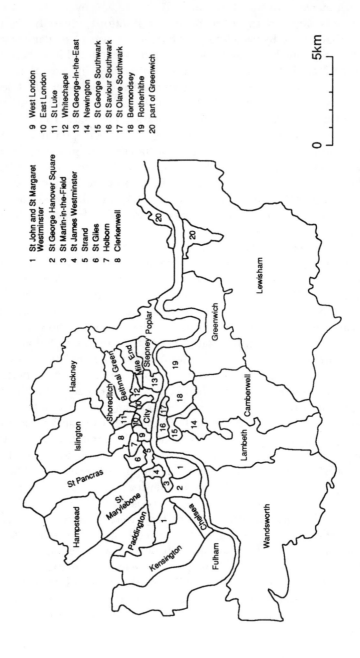

1 St John and St Margaret Westminster
2 St George Hanover Square
3 St Martin-in-the-Field
4 St James Westminster
5 Strand
6 St Giles
7 Holborn
8 Clerkenwell
9 West London
10 East London
11 St Luke
12 Whitechapel
13 St George-in-the-East
14 Newington
15 St George Southwark
16 St Saviour Southwark
17 St Olave Southwark
18 Bermondsey
19 Rotherhithe
20 part of Greenwich

Figure 1.1 London registration districts, 1851.

The division of labour

Social heterogeneity was paralleled in the economic sphere by the multiplicity of trades and the extraordinarily complex division of labour. When Adam Smith wrote that the division of labour was determined by the size of the market, he could well have had London in mind. Not only was it the largest city but it was also the wealthiest. According to Rubinstein, London possessed a larger total business income than all the chief provincial towns combined and its middle class was both richer and more numerous than elsewhere.[14] In turn, this wealthy élite provided the demand for a range of services and products in London fostered the specialization of trades and employment. In 1841 the census recorded at least 840 separate occupations in the capital, including some that were confined to London alone. Not only could one find gold beaters but also gold beaters' skin-makers. The demand for false eyes and scagliola – an artificial stone made from a mixture of plaster and glue – was small but was none the less catered for by a handful of workers in the capital and nowhere else. Even the census tables of occupations, however, fail to reflect the true extent of the minute division of labour. For example, in bespoke tailoring, artisans often specialized in coats, waistcoats or trousers, leaving shirts to those with less skill.[15] Even further down the economic scale, intense competition to earn a living amongst street traders ensured that each had their own specialized niche, from costermongers – the 'haristocracy of the streets' as Henry Mayhew called them – to 'pure finders' who scoured the pavements and sewers of London for canine excrement used in the tanning of soft Morocco leather. Competition even fostered specialization amongst beggars, each group of which was distinguished by their own 'larks', including amongst others 'naval and military', 'foreign', 'distressed operative' and 'disaster' beggars. Members of each category occupied a particular niche in the mendicant hierarchy.[16] From beggars to bespoke tailors, competition encouraged specialization and this in turn accounted for the multiplicity of occupations that appeared in the census tables and on the streets of London.

A second cause, however, flowed from the characteristics of London itself as a centre of manufacturing. Conditions in the capital were not conducive to the development of a factory system: high rents, distance from raw materials and coal, the seasonal nature of demand and the importance of fashion all militated against the development of factory production. The fact that many of London's industries were finishing trades, dependent on proximity to the market and on handicraft skills for working up semi-processed materials into the finished article, also hindered the spread of mechanized production.[17] Once railways had reduced the cost of freight, it was imperative for manufacturers to reduce their own costs, both in order to compete with cheaper provincial producers as well as to gain an edge over other competitors in London. In the finishing trades, wages were the largest proportion of production costs and the main means of implementing savings was to lower the element of skill and so employ cheaper forms of labour. In turn this depended on the ability to subdivide work and reduce manufacturing to a series of separate component tasks. Hence, the immense variety of occupations, which itself was a reflection of this intense division of labour, stemmed not just from the scale of demand, as Smith had argued, but also from the nature of metropolitan production itself.

The geographical distribution of trades mirrored the pattern of specialization and the division of labour. At one level, there were the obvious distinctions between the port area to the east and along the southern bank of the Thames, the commercial activities in the City itself, the manufacturing districts surrounding this commercial heartland, and the primarily residential outer suburbs. Within this broad economic geography, however, were numerous micro-geographies. First, in several of the larger manufacturing trades, notably tailoring, shoemaking and furniture making, there was the general division between skilled bespoke work in the more fashionable West End and the wholesale slop sector in eastern districts.[18] In addition, other more local differences existed. The need to share expensive tools and to be close to the sources of both supply and demand encouraged the further localization of trades. Within the manufacturing belt, specific trades were concentrated in particular districts: for example, silk weaving in Bethnal Green; watchmaking and the precision trades in Clerkenwell; tanning in Bermondsey and hat making in Southwark. Trades were even localized to a handful of streets, such as coach making around Long Acre and newspaper printing in Fleet Street. Just as the pressures to subdivide tasks and specialize in particular branches of production characterized the structure of employment, so the process of competition and specialization similarly resulted in a highly variegated and complex micro-geography of production.

Social transformations

Sociologists have long argued that the number and density of the urban population itself is an important factor influencing the nature of social relationships in cities.[19] Large numbers imply a loss of personal knowledge and mutual acquaintance. In the early decades of the nineteenth century, when urban growth and social change were particularly rapid, the breakdown of knowable communities in cities was of serious concern to the urban middle class.[20] Although subsequent research has shown that working-class communities were both more persistent and cohesive than bourgeois observers believed at the time, the feeling that quantitative growth had brought about a qualitative transformation of urban life was keenly felt, particularly in the rapidly expanding nineteenth-century metropolis.[21] The Association for Promoting the Relief of Destitution in the Metropolis expressed this most clearly in their annual report for 1858:

> The aggregation of large multitudes in our overgrown but still increasing cities, and especially in London, renders it a difficult task to establish those friendly relations and feelings of mutual regard by which the intercourse of rich and poor, in many a country village, is productive of the happiest results.[22]

Size alone was considered sufficient to ensure that urban life in the capital was qualitatively different from that experienced in other towns and cities of the time. Concern over the degree of social isolation experienced in the expanding metropolis was most frequently expressed by middle-class contemporaries. Writing in 1836, Robert Mudie noted in *London and Londoners, or a second judgement of 'Babylon the Great'*, 'The only thing that London supplies more than other places is a greater crowd and less individual acquaintance.'[23] Others shared his feelings of an atomized existence, as Raymond Williams has pointed out.[24] Speaking of London during the 1840s, Engels remarked, 'The dissolution of mankind into monads of which each one has a separate principle and a separate purpose, the world of atoms, is here carried out to its utmost extreme.'[25] Later in the century, Henry James spoke of London in similar fashion: on the one hand, 'the sense the place gives us of multitudinous life' was a source of fascination, while on the other, he felt overwhelmed by 'quantity and numbers', by 'the momentary concussion of a million of atoms'. 'There is really is too much of her', he remarked.[26]

Geography also had a part to play in fostering a sense of social isolation and class separation. From at least the middle of the eighteenth century, wealthy metropolitan families had begun to move westwards away from the overcrowded and insanitary inner core. From the 1770s, this exodus of wealth fuelled the development of large aristocratic estates, such as the Portman and Cavendish estates north of Oxford Street, the Bedford estate in Bloomsbury and, later on, the Grosvenor estate in Belgravia.[27] The centre, in the meantime, was left to commerce and to the working class who could not afford to move or who remained tied by the possibilities of finding employment. The exodus of wealth was less marked in eastern districts, there being fewer middle-class families in the first place. But even here suburban flight had commenced by the 1840s, leaving in its wake a mass of the poor that periodically threatened to overwhelm the capacity of both philanthropy and the poor law to provide adequate relief during periods of distress.

As the geographical separation of the classes gathered momentum, so individual acquaintance between rich and poor grew less frequent and more transitory. Early in the century it had still been possible to conceive of the poor in terms of individual or eccentric characters, as witnessed in Pierce Egan's *Life in London* (1821) or John T. Smith's *Vagabondiana, or anecdotes of the mendicant wanderers through the streets of London* (1817). But voicing what was to become a common concern, James Grant remarked in 1842 how 'Little do those in the more fashionable parts of the metropolis ... know the deep distress endured by myriads (sic) of the lower classes in the central and eastern districts'.[28] By mid-century, when Henry Mayhew's survey of the London poor appeared, what little personal knowledge remained had faded as distance further separated the classes. Even Mayhew himself, perhaps the most observant of nineteenth-century social reporters, struggled to comprehend the complexity of the 'monster city', as he called it. Much of the enormous public interest aroused by his letters to the *Morning Chronicle* in 1849 and 1850 lay in the fact that amidst the swirl of metropolitan life he managed to bring working-class individuals to the attention of an otherwise spatially segregated middle-class audience. Mayhew's skill in characterizing the poor by using their own words provided a personal point of contact for the middle class which had otherwise been lost by the geographical fact of residential separation. By the time of Charles Booth's survey later in the century, no such point of contact remained. Instead the poor were treated *en masse* merely as statistical categories, as classes A to D on the poverty scale.[29]

For the metropolitan working class, social fragmentation and geographical separation brought with it similar problems of coherence and identity. Heterogeneity and distance hindered efforts to organize the London trades. Different rates of pay, degrees of skill and levels of trade union organization, coupled with the logistical difficulties of coordinating workers separated by the friction of distance, combined to fragment the metropolitan working class. The diversity of experiences between and within trades further hampered attempts to foster any wider working-class consciousness. Support for Robert Owen's Grand National Consolidated Trades Union and Chartism, for example, was drawn primarily from those traditional trades, such as clothing and shoemaking, in which competition was felt most keenly. The so-called 'higher trades', such as engineering and printing, which were experiencing more rapid rates of growth, were less supportive of such broad working-class movements.[30] Nor was it easy, given the relative ease in several trades of becoming a small master, for artisans to identify clearly the separate interests of employers and workers. Indeed, in many cases the most important distinction was not between small masters and journeymen but between large firms and the rest. The overall effect of these various factors was that it was extremely difficult for the London working class to act in a cohesive manner. In geographical terms it was divided by distance and locality; it was similarly fragmented in economic, social and political terms. Although on occasion working-class leaders, such as the shipwrights' leader John Gast, or the committee of the London Working Men's Association, briefly managed to coordinate artisan politics, the forces of differentiation and fragmentation worked against collective political action.[31]

Laissez faire, local self-government and political fragmentation

Whilst social fragmentation and geographical separation hampered the ability of contemporaries to grasp the realities of urban expansion or to comprehend the complexities of the metropolitan economy, other factors were important in explaining the chaotic state of London's local government. Communities in the capital were linked by virtue of conglomeration rather than shared corporative sentiment. 'There is no sympathy, no congeniality of tastes, habits, feelings or pursuits between neighbourhoods', wrote John Murray. 'The inhabitants, for all they know of one another, are at as great a distance as the natives of China and Peru.'[32] Size had something to do with this: districts such as St Marylebone, St Pancras or Lambeth were large enough to be towns in their own right, let alone constituent parts of the capital, and until public transport became widely available it was not uncommon for people to live much of their lives within the confines of their own district.

Nevertheless, political fragmentation was not a function of size alone. Municipal government also came late to the capital for other reasons, notably the mutual suspicion of local vestries and the obdurate resistance of the City Corporation to any changes that threatened its own position.[33] The Municipal Corporations Act of 1835 excluded the City which steadfastly remained alone as the last great unreformed corporation. Nor was there much pressure from Parliament to reform metropolitan government. Although the number of London's MPs rose from 10 to 22 after the 1832 Reform Act, it was still grossly under-represented in relation to its population.[34] Not even the pressing needs of sanitary reform could persuade the vested interests of either the City Corporation or the collected powers of vestrydom of the need for concerted action. Consequently, London was exempted from the 1848

Public Health Act and had to wait until the formation of the Metropolitan Board of Works in 1855 before sanitary reform could start in earnest. For the remainder of the century the City Corporation soundly rebuffed threats to its independence.

Other forces, however, also militated against the emergence of municipal government in the capital. In an age of *laissez faire*, wide distrust of centralization also played a part in opposing moves that threatened the independence of local self-government. With few exceptions, local vestries resisted attempts to impose centralized control over expenditure. Against a background of rising rates for poor relief and sewerage, John Toulmin Smith echoed the views of ratepayers when in 1852 he wrote 'The system of centralization is demoralizing, degrading, and inconsistent with the spirit of freedom, and with the existence of free institutions.'[35] Parishes were like little commonwealths and no privilege was guarded more jealously in London than the right of local ratepayers to self-government.[36]

This firm belief in local autonomy partly accounts for the difficulties that the Poor Law Commissioners experienced in their efforts to persuade metropolitan districts to adopt the Poor Law Amendment Act. During the 1820s and early 1830s struggles against the lax, if not corrupt, government of select vestries had resulted in the formation of strong ratepayer groups in several central and western districts, notably St Marylebone and St Pancras. Ratepayers in several of these parishes had adopted the more democratic local franchise embodied in Hobhouse's Act and consequently it was these reformed vestries that proved most reluctant to implement the administrative changes introduced by the Poor Law Amendment Act. In several districts, notably St Pancras, local Directors of the Poor refused to elect boards of guardians until forced to do so in 1867.[37] Attempts by Edwin Chadwick in 1846 to create metropolitan asylum districts for the relief of the casual poor also foundered on the rock of local self-interest. Even the creation of the indirectly elected Metropolitan Board of Works in reality represented victory for the vestries. Not until the system of poor relief teetered on the verge of collapse in the 1860s did necessity force an acceptance of change. Until then, each district clung tenaciously to the principle of local self-government as a means of retaining control over expenditure. Only with the Metropolitan Poor Act of 1867, which established a common fund for poor relief based on the rateable values of districts, could it be said, in relation to expenditure, that the principle of local self-government was weakened *vis-à-vis* the forces of centralization.

Thus, during the first half of the nineteenth century, London failed to develop any corporate identity. Whether this was because the capital was merely an agglomeration of neighbourhoods with little in common other than the tie of proximity, as the Royal Commission into the City Corporation concluded in 1853, or whether subdivided administration was to blame, as John Stuart Mill believed, is open to debate.[38]

Although the structures of urban life in London may have given the appearance of stability, the reality was different. No place, least of all a capital city and port of international importance, exists in isolation from the wider national and global currents of social, economic and political change. Those currents that flowed most strongly, and proved to be most disruptive to the structures of metropolitan life, concerned the economy and consequently we start from that perspective. Chapter 2 explores the nature of the metropolitan economy and examines the processes of change. Although much economic activity in the city was self-generated, driven forward by the weight of numbers, much also depended on external factors. Indeed, this could hardly have been otherwise. As a major port and centre of an expanding global empire, interruptions to trade through warfare, climate or political upheaval always threatened to disrupt the smooth, and normally profitable, flow of commerce. From there the ripples spread outwards, engulfing those who depended on the demand from London's mercantile elite for their livelihood. 'In "panics" I have always found trade very bad in the City', an East End shoemaker told Henry Mayhew in 1850, and many other workers in the finishing trades, not to mention commerce and transport, would have felt likewise.[39]

Chapter 3 draws on existing research on prices and real wages together with the testimony of Henry Mayhew to examine the impact of trade fluctuations on London's manufacturing industries. The fact that real wages were rising for much of the period after the Napoleonic Wars sits uneasily with Mayhew's more pessimistic analysis of working-class fortunes. In part, this was the result of his focus on traditional London trades that were in the throes of decline. However, it also reflected a situation in which the labour process in several trades was undergoing significant restructuring. Such changes at the workplace did not occur in an ideological vacuum but were embedded in a set of social relationships and structures within which active resistance was organized and these are examined in Chapter 4. In order to assess the impact of change, we need to be aware of the conflicts that were generated in the workplace and the outcomes that ensued. Charting these lines of working-class resistance in London as a whole is the task undertaken in Chapter 5. Economic change and workplace conflict, however, were spatially mediated and it is therefore important to appreciate the geographical context of industrial restructuring. These issues are dealt with in Chapter

6 which seeks to map out the spatial dimensions of conflict and economic change in several of the capital's larger and more important manufacturing trades.

In Chapter 7 attention shifts to an exploration of the geography of poverty at mid-century and the problems that the map of impoverishment posed for social relations between the classes. From mid-century, bourgeois concern mounted over the problems of 'outcast' London, a term first used in 1858 by Revd Frederick Meyrick to describe the urban poor. At the root of this concern was the growing geographical gulf between the classes that had emerged within the living memory of contemporaries. A particular problem that arose concerned the provision of poor relief, and this is dealt with in Chapter 8. The political fragmentation of the capital, discussed above, was thrown into sharpest relief as a result of the localized crises of pauperism that erupted with growing frequency and rising intensity during the 1850s and 1860s.

While administrative and political histories are able to delineate sharp breaks in the continuity of policy or government, no such claims can be made in relation to the study of economic or social change. The start of our period coincides roughly with the outbreak of the Napoleonic Wars and the steep rise in prices that ensued. Labour shortages, coupled with the rapidity and extent of the price rises, altered the framework of industrial relations and set the scene for workplace struggles that proved to be so important for the fortunes of the London trades. The end of our period is similarly indistinct. However, in the last thirty or so years of the century significant changes occurred in London such that 1870 provides a convenient, though rough, break in the study. In terms of the Poor Law, efforts to establish a broader-based metropolitan system of relief bore fruit in 1867 with the establishment of the Metropolitan Common Poor Fund. Though borne of necessity, this measure represented a significant victory for the forces of centralization over the vested interests of localism. In political terms, changes were also taking place in both national and municipal contexts. The widening of the franchise in 1867 to include adult male householders was followed in London in 1870 by the establishment of the London School Board, the first directly elected municipal authority in the capital. The days of political fragmentation in the capital were clearly numbered. Working-class organization was also changing. The London Trades Council, founded in the aftermath of the builders' dispute in 1861, aimed to coordinate the activities of the London trades. Even before the mass unionism of the unskilled in the 1880s, craft workers in the capital had begun to recognize the need to incorporate the unskilled within trade unions. Women and East End Jewish clothing workers, for example, were recruited by the tailors' union during their 1867 strike, and similar efforts to establish broader unions were made by the other London trades.

Subtle shifts also occurred in the metropolitan economy from the 1870s.[40] The London money market gained at the expense of Paris, its main international rival, as well as against the provinces; wealth generated by trade, commerce and by British imperial expansion flowed increasingly through the capital. Though London lacked the grand processional routes and architecture of other European capitals, that growing wealth was manifested in the commercial rebuilding of much of the City. When set against this accumulation of wealth, conditions amongst the urban poor, most vividly and salaciously described in 1883 by Revd Andrew Mearns in *The Bitter Cry of Outcast London*, seemed the more shocking. That story, however, refers to a second generation of outcast Londoners. Our concern here is with the first.

Notes

1. The geographical definition of London is that used in the 1851 census and shown in Figure 1.1. The constituent districts are enumerated in Appendix 1.1.
2. Hohenberg and Lees, 1985, p.227.
3. Wrigley, 1967, p.49. London's population was 2.3 million compared with 1.3 million for Paris.
4. Vaughan, 1843; see Briggs, 1968, p.56.
5. Rasmussen, 1960, p.15.
6. See Green, 1988.
7. Dyos and Aldcroft, 1974, p.234.
8. Murray, 1843, p.167.
9. James, 1989, p.258.
10. The following figures refer to the London Division in the 1851 census.
11. Friedlander and Roshier, 1966, p.252, 263; Shannon, 1935, p.84.
12. Lees, 1979, pp.56–8.
13. Linebaugh, 1993, pp.414–15.
14. Rubinstein, 1977a, pp.616–18; *idem.*, 1981, pp.106–10.
15. Murray, 1843, p.191.
16. Mayhew, 1968, vol. 4, pp.393–448.
17. Hall, 1962b, p.119; Jones, 1971, pp.26–30; Spate, 1938, pp.431–2.
18. See Hall, 1962b, pp.37–95; see also Chapter 6, pp.160–8.
19. This argument is closely associated with the Chicago school of urban sociology, notably Park, Burgess and Mackenzie, 1967, and Wirth, 1964. For critiques of this approach see Fischer, 1984, pp.27–38 and Saunders, 1981, pp.62–79.
20. See, for example, Chalmers, 1821, pp.126–7; *idem.*, 1823, pp.39-40-26. See also Chapter 7, pp.200–2.
21. Anderson, 1974, pp.56–67; Dennis, 1984, pp.270–85; Green and Parton, 1990, pp.76–82.
22. *Association for Promoting the Relief of Destitution in the Metropolis*, 1858, p.15.

23. Mudie, 1836, vol. 2, p.262.
24. Williams, 1975, pp.259–87.
25. Engels, 1973, p.58.
26. James, 1989, pp.267, 269.
27. Summerson, 1945, p.146.
28. Grant, 1842a, p.157.
29. Booth divided the population into several classes according to economic circumstances. The chronically and intermittently poor were categorized as Classes A to D. See Booth, 1902, First series, *Poverty*, vol. 1, pp.33–50.
30. This is the argument outlined in Oliver, W.H., 1964; Prothero, 1966, *idem.*, 1971. For Chartism see also Goodway, 1982.
31. For John Gast's involvement in London radicalism see Prothero, 1981.
32. Murray, 1843, p.20
33. This topic is dealt with in more detail by Davis, 1988; Owen, 1982.
34. Sheppard, 1985, p.56. The total number of MPs was 658.
35. Smith, 1852, p.13.
36. Knight, 1854, pp.19–24.
37. Following the Poor Law Amendment Act, eleven London vestries remained under local acts for the relief of the poor: St George Hanover Square, St Giles, St James Clerkenwell, St Leonard Shoreditch, St Luke's, St Mary Islington, St Mary Newington, St Marylebone, St Margaret and St John Westminster and St Pancras. *Poor Law Commission*, 1836, p. 13; *idem*, 1837, p.5. See Brooke, 1839, for a discussion of parochial reform in St Marylebone and St Pancras.
38. Waller, 1983, p.58.
39. Mayhew, 1981, vol. 3, p.149.
40. See Harris, 1994, pp.19–22.

CHAPTER TWO

Engine of growth: the metropolitan economy

Introduction

In the seventeenth and eighteenth centuries London was the pivot around which the British economy revolved.[1] Its merchants were at the centre of an expanding network of national and international trade whilst its bankers lubricated the channels of commerce. Government bonds and company stocks, including many ill-judged ventures that preyed on the London bourgeoisie's thirst for profits, were floated in the City. The reputation of London's manufacturers was held in high esteem not only in the capital itself but throughout the country, and goods made in the city found their way to all corners of the nation. In return, London's demand for food and raw materials influenced patterns of production throughout the country. As Defoe remarked ' ... all the people, and all the lands in England, seem to be at work for, or employed by, or on account of this overgrown city'.[2]

As the nineteenth century dawned, however, the pathways of economic progress seemed to lead away from the capital. The growing pace of industrialization shifted attention from London towards towns in the Midlands and north; to Birmingham, Leeds, Liverpool and Manchester. In these new industrial cities, the power of steam-driven machinery and the development of the factory system persuaded contemporaries that the seat of progress had moved from the metropolis to the provinces. There was, indeed, some truth in this belief, although we now know that in many trades handicraft work rather than mechanization remained the basis of production for much of the period.[3]

Whilst manufacturing captured the contemporary imagination, other sectors of the economy were of equal if not greater significance in terms of their contribution to overall patterns of growth. Recent work has emphasized the contribution of commerce and banking to economic growth, particularly in relation to international trade, and these sectors were overwhelmingly concentrated in London.[4] Indeed, the metropolitan economy relied heavily on services, notably commerce, banking and insurance. Merely moving and storing the goods that passed through the capital required armies of casual labourers and clerks alike. Profits generated in the course of trade helped to create a particularly wealthy urban bourgeoisie, whose subsequent demand for domestic servants, entertainment, news, clothing, shoes and furniture laid the basis for much employment elsewhere in the city, let alone in the country at large. Yet the path of economic growth in the capital was by no means smooth. In an age of poor communications and inadequate information, trade and commerce were among the riskiest of ventures and many merchants found themselves listed as debtors in the *London Gazette*. Size and heterogeneity, therefore, were not enough to ensure that the metropolitan economy sailed through the century untouched by the shocks and cyclical fluctuations of the national and international economy.

Economic structure

The metropolitan economy was structured around three interconnected functions. First, and foremost, London was the commercial, financial and political centre of the nation. It was an international as well as national emporium of trade and commerce. Vast quantities of goods were conveyed through its port and it was not until the 1860s that its position as the largest docks in the kingdom was usurped by Liverpool. Furthermore, the channelling of both domestic and foreign government credit through London's banks ensured its dominant position not only as the pivot of national finance but also that of the world.[5] Allied to this commercial and financial function was London's role as the seat of government and political focus of the country. Indeed, commerce and politics were closely linked. Government and institutional contracts were important for London entrepreneurs who buzzed attentively around government offices and eagerly followed the publication of tenders in the *London Gazette*. Similarly, the fortunes, and indeed misfortunes, of commercial ventures and financial speculations, were shaped to a considerable degree by political events at home and abroad. It was little wonder that the pages of London newspapers were so filled with foreign news, for the outbreak of war or unfavourable developments overseas could spell ruin for thousands in the City.

The second function concerned London's position as the social focus of the nation. As the country's political and commercial core, London not only attracted the aristocracy for the Parliamentary Season, but also contained a far higher proportion of resident professional and commercial households than other cities.[6] Though relatively small in number compared with the population as a whole, the presence of these élite groups, together with a middle class that was both more numerous and relatively wealthier than elsewhere in the country, exerted an influence greater than their numbers would suggest.[7] As leaders of fashion, they were the focus of social emulation for the growing number of white collar workers and members of the lower middle class who aspired to a position in society. For this group, appearance was, if anything, more important than substance. In the same way that opulence of construction was emblematic of commercial success, so extravagant dress was *de rigueur* for young bloods in the city. 'Eccentricity of costume', remarked Evans in 1845, 'shows itself more in the city than in any other part of the metropolis. The sights afforded to the loungers of Regent Street and Bond Street are nothing to those that can be witnessed in Cornhill, Fenchurch Street or near the Bank.'[8] Nor was the role of fashion and social emulation restricted to clothes alone, but spread from there to encompass shoes, furniture, hats and even buildings. Though the coming of the mass market from the middle decades of the century lessened manufacturers' dependence on this social élite, nevertheless the influence they exerted in terms of fashion should not be underestimated.

Finally, size and geographical growth played their own part in generating demand for goods and services. Expansion of the built-up area had been marked since the Great Fire but from the late 1820s and 1830s the introduction of public transport added impetus to the process of suburbanization. As London literally marched out towards the suburbs, so the numbers involved in transport and distribution rose in proportion. The number of street traders, for example, was in part a function of the spread of the city. Population growth and rising incomes also generated a demand for goods and services. Whilst many working-class families could manage with second-hand clothes, cast-off shoes and minimal furniture, they still required other necessities of life: food, drink, warmth and entertainment. Rising real wages, particularly after mid-century, allowed an increasing number of workers, in addition to the expanding middle-class, to purchase new articles and in turn the coming of this mass market for cheap goods was a significant factor in further transforming the nature of manufacturing in the capital. Quantitative growth and geographical expansion, in addition to the wealth of London's social élite, thus provided the metropolitan economy with its own internal dynamic.

Employment structure 1831–1861

This complex economic mosaic of interdependent functions was reflected in the occupational structure outlined in the census figures. From 1831, the census provides data on adult male employment –

women had to wait a further decade until their occupations were included. Information was recorded for seven employment categories, one of which, retail trade and handicraft, can be further subdivided into those primarily engaged in production and those whose occupations mainly involved dealing or retailing.[9] From 1841 the census listed all occupations and not just those relating to handicraft production. However, two main problems remain: first, although female occupations were enumerated the coverage was very incomplete; secondly, general labourers were not distinguished from the trades in which they were employed. Improvements were made in 1851, particularly in relation to women, and the following census of 1861 probably provides the most accurate picture of employment for the period.

The breakdown of employment in 1861, shown in Table 2.1, suggests that in terms of specific categories, manufacturing was the major source of employment, followed by transport and building. However, by amalgamating the categories into broader groupings it becomes clear that services and commercial occupations accounted for about the same

Table 2.1   Employment structure, 1861

	Male		Female		Total	
	Number	Per cent	Number	Per cent	Number	Per cent
Government	43,587	3.1	427	0.1	44,014	2.5
Army	32,597	2.3	–	0.0	32,597	1.8
Professional	66,954	4.8	15,567	4.0	82,521	4.6
Commercial/ financial	34,075	2.4	726	0.2	34,801	2.0
Clerical	28,873	2.1	–	0.0	28,873	1.6
Dealing	37,479	2.7	5,754	1.5	43,233	2.4
Total	243,565	17.4	22,474	5.8	266,039	14.9
Transport, distribution, storage	260,826	18.7	546	0.1	261,372	14.7
Service	22,664	1.6	10,724	2.8	33,388	1.9
Domestic service	42,107	3.0	155,821	40.3	197,928	11.1
Food	108,533	7.8	10,258	2.7	118,791	6.7
Total	173,304	12.4	176,803	45.8	350,107	19.7
Manufacturing	435,578	31.2	184,029	47.6	619,607	34.7
Building	159,068	11.4	–	0.0	159,068	8.9
Total	594,646	42.6	184,029	47.6	778,675	43.6
Labour	84,452	6.0	172	0.0	84,624	4.7
Agriculture	40,260	2.9	2,540	0.7	42,800	2.4
Total	1,397,053	100.0	386,564	100.0	1,783,617	100.0

Source: Census, 1861

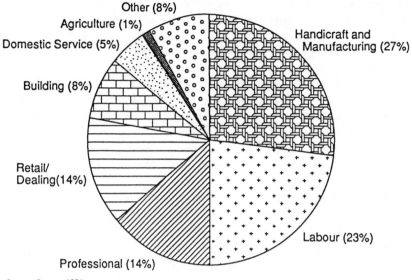

Other (8%)

Agriculture (1%)

Domestic Service (5%)

Handicraft and
Manufacturing (27%)

Building (8%)

Retail/
Dealing(14%)

Labour (23%)

Professional (14%)

Source: Census 1831

Figure 2.1   Male employment, 1831.

proportion of the workforce as the manufacturing trades, reflecting the overall importance of trade within the metropolitan economy and the derived demand for services generated by the London bourgeoisie.

Male employment

As far as male employment is concerned, direct comparison between the 1831 and 1861 census is problematic because of the different methods of enumerating labourers. Nevertheless, comparisons between the two years can still yield important insights into the economic structure of London. The evidence presented in Figure 2.1 confirms the image of London as a centre of the handicraft trades.[10] In 1831 over a quarter of the adult male workforce was employed in handicraft production.[11] To this number we should add those employed in 'manufacture or the making of manufacturing machinery', which elsewhere in the country referred primarily to factory employment but in London mainly concerned silk weaving in Bethnal Green.[12] The building trades, which in 1831 occupied about one in twelve of the workforce, shared many of the characteristics of handicraft production and can thus be included under that category. By including these categories, over a third of the male workforce was employed in one form or another in handicraft trades. Furthermore, in 1831, labourers were enumerated under a separate category but many would undoubtedly have worked alongside artisans and in terms of employment should also be incorporated together with those in the handicraft trades. The total figure of those employed in handicraft work was therefore likely to have been even higher.

The importance of manufacturing and construction is confirmed by the figures for 1861, illustrated in Figure 2.2, although we should note that difficulties relating to the enumeration of labourers means that direct comparison with 1831 is impossible. Nevertheless, over 40 per cent of the male workforce was employed in these two sectors. Within this broad grouping of handicraft employment, a handful of trades accounted for the majority of workers. As Figure 2.3 shows, in 1831 six trades accounted for nearly 70 per cent of the adult male workforce: building, clothing, shoemaking, wood and furniture making, metalwork and engineering, and printing. In 1861, although important changes had taken place, the basic structure of handicraft employment remained intact. The traditional London trades of clothing, shoemaking and furniture making had declined in importance, whilst engineering had increased. The numbers of trades has also increased, reflecting a more accurate enumeration of occupations as well as the increasing diversity characteristic of a maturing urban economy.

Each of the major trades was primarily concerned with finishing semi-

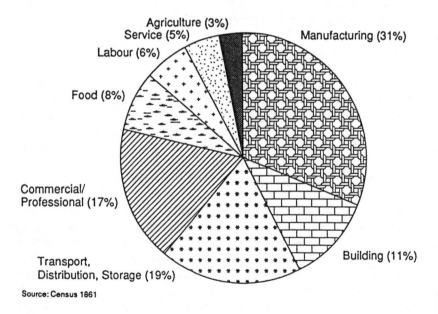

Source: Census 1861

Figure 2.2   Male employment, 1861.

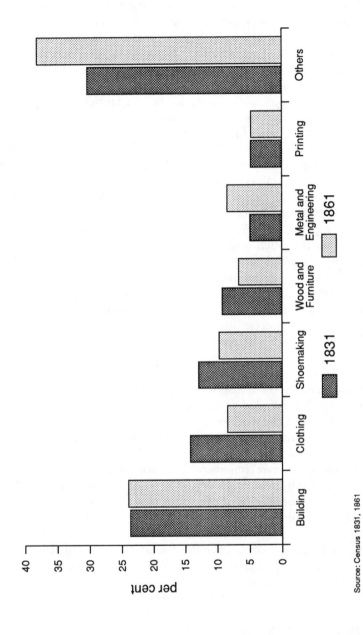

Source: Census 1831, 1861

Figure 2.3 Male employment in manufacturing and building, 1831–1861.

processed raw materials, such as leather, wood or textiles, and was oriented towards the local market, although some of the cheaper branches of production were also geared towards export. Thus, as Hall has noted, London was deficient in textiles but not clothing, in woodworking but not furniture, in paper making but not printing, and in iron making but not engineering.[13] Typically, the products themselves bore a high value in relation to weight, a fact accounted for by the significance of labour costs in the total cost of manufacture. In silk weaving, for example, labour costs for fancier fabrics, such as figured velvets, accounted for three-quarters of the total cost of production, although they were closer to half on plainer silks.[14] In the building trades, labour costs for carpentry and bricklaying also comprised about half the final cost, but were proportionately higher in the more labour-intensive work of masonry, joinery and plastering.[15] With wages in London typically higher than in the rest of the country, this cost structure of production presented serious problems for many trades. Improvements in transport, particularly the spread of the railways during the 1830s and 1840s, meant that such trades were increasingly vulnerable to cheaper foreign and provincial competition. In some cases, such as silk weaving and watchmaking, entire trades left the capital; in others, such as clothing, shoemaking and furniture making, production was restructured to take advantage of cheaper forms of labour. In particular, this restructuring process involved a greater division of labour, the significance of which was recognized by both Adam Smith and Marx alike.

Before leaving manufacturing, mention must be made of labourers and those involved in transport, distribution and storage. The large number of males recorded as labourers in the 1831 census, comprising nearly a quarter of the workforce, reflected three sets of influences. The first was the enormous significance of the casual labour market in the capital, as others have already emphasized.[16] As the main port and largest city, there were innumerable opportunities to earn an albeit precarious living by dock work or just by hauling goods through the city streets, and the importance of this sector should not be underestimated. Secondly, large numbers worked outside the handicraft trades, such as the rubbish carters, crossing sweepers, and street traders interviewed by Henry Mayhew. In contrast, the third influence reflected the fact that many labourers worked alongside artisans but in 1831 were enumerated separately. In 1861 labourers were included together with the trades in which they were employed and therefore do not appear as a separate category. In this one respect, the 1831 census probably provides a more accurate picture of the true size of the casual labour market than that of later censuses.

In considering the service and commercial sectors of employment, we move closer to the engine that powered the London economy. The city's pre-eminent role as the centre of world finance and trade was one that developed in tandem with the geographical spread of capitalism. From the mid-eighteenth century vast new zones in India, Africa, Russia, the Ottoman Empire and both North and South America were incorporated into the European-, and above all the British-, dominated world economy. As the web of commerce stretched outwards, so London merchants, insurers and bankers reaped the spoils. Londoners stood at the apex of the pyramid of wealth holding. In 1812 the Schedule D income tax returns show that the City of London, Westminster and Middlesex together accounted for nearly 39 per cent of the nation's taxable income, and if metropolitan Kent and Surrey were to be included this figure would be nearer a half. In total, between 1800 and 1839 nearly three-quarters of non-landed wealth holders lived in London and derived their income primarily from commerce and trade.[17]

The significance of this commercial and professional sector, or to use the 1831 census definition 'capitalists, bankers, professional and other educated men', is only partially reflected in the numbers involved in such forms of employment. In 1831 this category, together with retailing and dealing, accounted for over a quarter of the male workforce. The census categories in 1861 preclude direct comparison, but in that year over 17 per cent of the workforce was directly employed in commerce and the professions, including government, the armed forces, the legal profession, banking, insurance and trade. Indeed, Schwarz has shown that for each of these categories London's share was disproportionately large compared with the rest of the country.[18] So too was its share of domestic servants, demand for which was generated largely by those employed in the commercial and professional sector. The fact that the capital's middle class, not to mention the ranks of the very rich, was larger and relatively wealthier than elsewhere merely confirms the census figures. London was, as Rubinstein notes, 'the fixed point around which the Victorian middle classes revolve'.[19]

Female employment

In terms of female employment, the census is seriously flawed and the figures must therefore be treated with caution. Much female work was casual or intermittent and this posed particular problems in relation to the recording of occupations. Similarly, much employment in domestic service, washing and needlework represented an extension of women's domestic duties and thus often passed unnoticed.[20] The 1861 census, for example, records that over half the women aged 20 years or above were not employed. Of course, large numbers of working-class women worked in domestic industry either independently or alongside men, a fact recognized explicitly in 1851 when for the first time the census authorities included a separate category for 'shoemaker's wife'. Female earnings were vital in many trades, both in their own right and as a supplement to household income. In 1838, for example, married male bootclosers earned nearly 7s. more per week than their single counterparts as a result of the additional income gained by other family members.[21] Indeed, in the poorer trades, the employment of wives and children alongside their husbands and fathers was often an absolute necessity although the fact of their occupation may not have been recorded in the census.

Setting these well-known problems aside, Figure 2.4 shows that women were typically employed either in manufacturing or domestic service, which in 1861 together accounted for 90 per cent of female employment in London. Whilst the domestic servant may have been the epitome of women's work in the Victorian period, a more accurate picture as far as London is concerned was the seamstress or 'shoemaker's wife'. In reality, however, the two sectors reflected distinct labour markets differentiated by age and location. Figure 2.5 suggests that domestic service was heavily weighted towards younger, and usually single women. However, service normally ended with pregnancy or marriage, and at that point women turned to other sources of

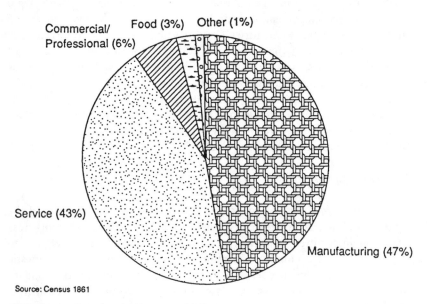

Source: Census 1861

Figure 2.4   Female employment, 1861.

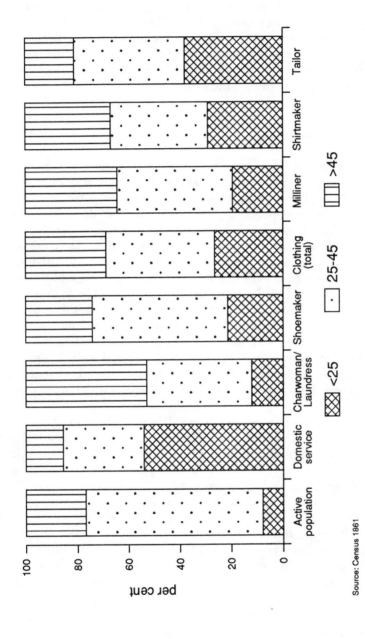

Source: Census 1861

Figure 2.5   Age structure of female employment, 1861.

employment, notably shoemaking, clothing and, above all, charring and washing – often a haven for retired servants and for those who through old age were unable to make a living by other means. In terms of geography, as we shall explore later, the labour market for women was equally constrained, with a marked spatial distinction between the importance of domestic service in wealthier, western districts and manufacturing in the poorer, eastern areas. For the time being, however, it is sufficient merely to note these differences.

Structure of production

It has frequently been argued that nineteenth-century London was overwhelmingly a city of small masters, the main centre of workshop manufacturing in the country.[22] By mid-century, when balloon views of the capital became popular, the city skyline was dominated not by factory chimneys but by church spires. To a certain extent the census figures confirm what the onlooker's gaze revealed. In 1851 the census attempted to distinguish journeymen from employers, and although the returns were far from complete, nevertheless the ensuing tables provided a broad indication of the structure of production. The figures suggest that nearly three-quarters of London firms employed less than five men, whilst over 86 per cent employed less than ten men. In contrast, only 80 firms were recorded with workforces of at least a hundred men whilst only 12 firms employed more than three hundred men. If the census figures are to be believed, the most impressive feature of industry in London was not that a few firms were so large, but that many were so small.

Circumstances in London conspired against the development of a large-scale factory system. Until mid-century, when the railways broke the northeastern monopoly of the coal supply for London, the price of fuel in the capital was relatively high. Land was similarly costly, particularly in central locations, and industries that required large amounts of space tended to locate in more peripheral districts. Large works in central locations were therefore relatively rare. At the time of the 1852 engineering strike, for example, the two largest engineering works in London were those of Maudslay and Field in Lambeth, and John Penn in Greenwich which employed 800 and 700 men respectively.[23] In the consumer trades seasonal variations in demand and frequent changes in fashion meant that stockpiling goods was a risky undertaking. Instead, employers in the bespoke sector of trade preferred to tailor production to meet existing demand rather than in anticipation of future needs. In the wholesale slop sector, where the dictates of fashion were less important, matters were different and large warehouses were more common. Coupled with these difficulties, other factors encouraged the 'vertical disintegration' of manufacturing into small units of production, as Hall has termed the process.[24] In several of the finishing trades, barriers to entry were low. In clothing, for example, it was also relatively easy to set up as a sweater, the only requirement being security of between £5 and £50 in order to receive orders from wholesalers.[25] It was little different in furniture making where between £3 or £4 was sufficient for cabinet makers to start work on their own account.[26] As Henry Mayhew was told in relation to the furniture trade, 'It's the small bit of money it takes to start with in our line that brings many into the trade, who wouldn't be there if more tin was wanted to begin upon.'[27]

To focus entirely on the proliferation of small masters, however, is to present a misleading picture of manufacturing in the capital. In fact, two separate processes were at work resulting in a bipolar structure of production with small masters at one end of the continuum and very sizeable firms at the other. Where production required little fixed capital, such as in making clothes, shoes and furniture, the spread of outwork became increasingly important, resulting in the proliferation of small scale units of employment. By shifting production to the home, employers were able to make considerable savings in heat, light and rent. It was claimed, for example, that Nicholls and Co., one of the largest clothing wholesalers in London, employed as many as 1200 sweated outworkers thereby saving about £19,500 each year by having the work done off the premises.[28] In those trades, such as engineering or printing, that required large amounts of fixed capital no such savings were possible. This was also true where the production process itself depended on the coordination of large numbers of workers, as was the case with major building projects. In these trades the main emphasis was on achieving economies of scale, thereby providing large employers with a competitive advantage over smaller firms. Therefore, it is important to recognize two distinct processes in relation to firm size: the first relating to cost cutting and resulting in an increase in the number of small units of production, the second to greater efficiency and leading to the growth of large firms.

The fact that this bipolar structure has often been ignored is due largely to the misleading impression created by the 1851 census tables of employment size. In the first place, the census seriously underestimates, perhaps by as much as half, the true number of firms in the capital. Whilst 1841 shoemakers and 1782 tailors were recorded as employers in the census, 2555 and 3207 masters respectively were included in *Watkins' London Directory* for 1853. Similarly, whilst 168 engineering firms appeared in the census, 334 were listed in the 1852 *London Post*

Office Directory. Secondly, the census dealt mainly with manufacturing and construction. No reference is made to other sources of employment, such as the gasworks, railways or docks, each of which employed large numbers of men. Thirdly, the enumeration of female employment was characteristically imperfect, as the census authorities themselves acknowledged. Firms employing women were listed separately to those for men. In those trades in which large numbers of women were employed either alongside men or on their own account, such as bookbinding or dressmaking, it is likely that the true size of the employment unit was understated. The figures also fail to take account of large wholesalers, such as Nicholls and Co. mentioned above, who organized production through sometimes very extensive webs of subcontracting. Subcontractors and sweaters themselves may even have been relatively large employers in their own right. In 1841, for example, about fifty female shirt makers were employed by Mrs Rowlandson, who acted as a subcontractor for Silver and Co., whose concerns included several shops in the City and a factory at Portsea near Liverpool in which 1400 women were employed.[29] Though not necessarily involved directly in the production of goods, such firms clearly were extremely important in the overall structure of production and need to be taken into account alongside manufacturing employers *per se*.

These shortcomings alone should be reason enough to be cautious about accepting too hastily the importance of small-scale production suggested by the census figures. A further reason for treading warily is demonstrated in Figure 2.6, which shows the breakdown of employment units in 1851 including the number of masters who either worked alone or who failed to state the number of journeymen employed. It is clear from these figures that it was the significance of this latter category that set London apart from other industrial regions and not simply the number of small masters. Over 43 per cent of London employers fell into this category, compared with 28 and 38 per cent for the North West and Yorkshire respectively. Indeed, in comparison with the other regions, London had relatively fewer masters who employed between one and four journeymen. If London was overwhelmingly a city of small masters, then so too were many other regions of the country.

At the other end of the scale, whilst it was true that large manufacturing employers with a hundred or more workers were more common outside the capital, particularly in Yorkshire and Lancashire, it would be wrong to infer from this that large firms were absent from London. Indeed, many of the largest companies in the land were concentrated there, as the examples in George Dodd's *Days at the Factories* confirm.[30] In printing, for example, six of the eleven largest firms were located in the capital. At mid-century, over 3000 workers

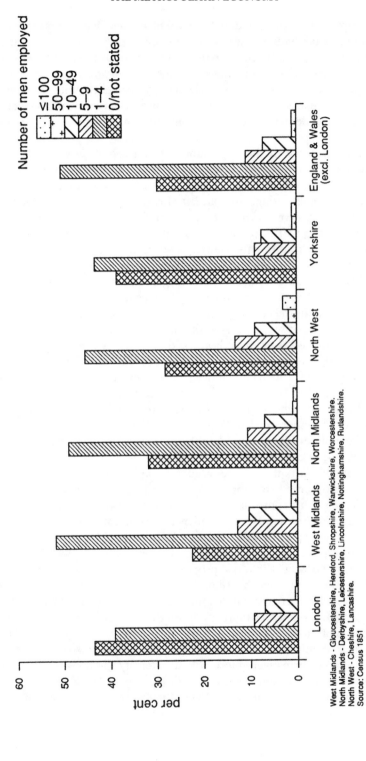

West Midlands - Gloucestershire, Hereford, Shropshire, Warwickshire, Worcestershire.
North Midlands - Derbyshire, Leicestershire, Lincolnshire, Nottinghamshire, Rutlandshire.
North West - Cheshire, Lancashire.
Source: Census 1851

Figure 2.6   Firm size, 1851.

were employed at the London Docks whilst the West and East India Docks may have had as many as 4000 employees.[31] In 1851 the census recorded six engineering firms with workforces of at least 100 men, but during the strike of the following year the *Northern Star* reported at least ten engineering firms that employed over 100 men each, with six having workforces in excess of 200.[32] Large firms were clearly much in evidence and we must be wary of underestimating their significance in the metropolitan economy.

Further evidence of the importance of large employers comes from considering the census figures in Table 2. 2. In engineering, printing and most notably building, medium and large firms were of considerable importance. In printing, the largest firms were those involved in newspapers and government stationery, and four alone accounted for 13 per cent of the workforce and over 30 per cent of the output.[33] In building, a trade traditionally viewed as one dominated by small masters, large firms were also commonplace, particularly in the City and West End where building projects were larger and the need for greater coordination of tasks more apparent.[34] Indeed, in 1851 22 of the 52 largest builders in the country were located in London. During the 1859 builders' dispute, it was estimated that between 18,000 and 20,000 men had been locked out by about sixty firms. Even allowing for exaggeration, this implied that the average workforce of each firm was well in excess of 200 men.[35] Indeed, a further account of the dispute recorded a total of 103 large building firms with workforces in excess of a hundred, 18 of which employed more than 500 men each.[36] The 1851 census, which only recorded 22 firms with comparable size workforces, therefore underestimates considerably the number of large builders.

Moreover, in certain trades, particularly those in which economies of scale were important and the need for capital investment high, the importance of large firms appeared to be growing. In type founding, for example, ten firms controlled production at the start of the century, but by the 1830s this number had fallen to about four or five, with the largest employing over 200 workers.[37] Similarly, Matthias notes that whilst the twelve largest breweries in London accounted for about half the output of beer in 1780, this proportion had risen to over 77 per cent by 1815 and 85 per cent by 1830.[38] Clearly, the growing concentration of capital within metropolitan manufacturing suggested by the growth of these large firms deserves more attention than it has hitherto received.

If the quantitative significance of large firms is recognized, so too must their qualitative influence on the transformation of the labour process. Larger firms were more able to intensify the division of labour and were thus in a better position both to employ less skilled workers and to introduce machinery. In 1814, for example, steam-driven saws

Table 2.2 Scale of employment, 1851 (per cent of masters)

Number of men employed	Baker	Carpenter	Cabinetmaker	Shoemaker	Tailor	Printer	Engine maker	Builder	All
1–4	96.6	78.7	72.3	70.6	70.1	46.3	41.7	23.9	69.5
5–9	2.9	15.1	17.5	17.8	15.4	18.8	22.2	27.2	16.6
10–49	0.5	5.5	9.3	10.3	13.8	29.4	28.7	40.2	12.4
50–99	0	0.6	0.7	0.7	0.6	3.7	1.9	5.4	1.0
100+	0	0.1	0.2	0.6	0.1	1.8	5.5	3.4	0.5
	100.0	100.0	100.0	100.0	100.0	100.0	100.0	100.0	100.0
Total	1,131	705	538	1,841	1,782	272	108	654	13,729

Source: Census, 1851

were introduced in the government shipyards at Woolwich.[39] In the same year *The Times* became the first newspaper to use steam presses.[40] In mid-century, large slopsellers, such as Nicholls and Hyams, were the first clothing firms to introduce sewing machines.[41] Similarly, the division of labour was most pronounced in the larger bookbinding firms and it was in these that machinery was introduced earliest.[42] Although mechanization and an intensification of the division of labour was not confined to major employers, nevertheless access to capital and large-scale production provided them with incentives to introduce these changes at an early stage and as such they tended to be at the forefront of transformations in the labour process.

In several London trades, particularly those that required heavy capital investment, large firms were sufficiently few in number to exert a degree of oligopolistic control over employment practices, wages and prices. In 1799, for example, large engineering employers colluded to bring forward the first Combination Act. This situation was repeated in 1813 when five of the largest companies pressed for reform of the laws concerning friendly societies and, in conjunction with large employers in other trades, successfully petitioned for the repeal of the apprenticeship laws.[43] In shipbuilding, a committee of 15 of the largest concerns agreed in 1825 not to employ shipwrights who belonged to the union, thereby precipitating an exceptionally bitter general strike in the trade.[44] A similarly close-knit group of employers existed in type founding where, by the 1830s, no more than a handful of firms controlled production. During a dispute in 1843 it was alleged that the largest founders had colluded to reduce prices by 25 per cent in order to drive smaller competitors out of business.[45] Pressures to reduce costs had mounted from the time that Wilson's, one of the largest firms, had started to employ cheaper Scottish workers at its foundry.[46] Although the type founders were somewhat unusual in the extent to which large companies controlled the trade, nevertheless their situation was not unique, as the other examples testify. Whilst this should not distract our attention from the continuing importance of small-scale production, it is clear that in similar fashion we should not underestimate the role of large firms in restructuring the labour process and transforming significantly the terrain of industrial relations in the capital.

Seasonal fluctuations

The ebb and flow of economic life in the capital were influenced by two broad sets of factors, the one relating to the pattern of seasonality and the other to the deeper cyclical rhythms of a maturing industrial economy. Of the two, seasonal variations relating to patterns of demand, levels of supply and the vagaries of the weather itself, affected the lives of workers most directly.[47] In terms of demand, the bespoke trades were most affected by the comings and goings associated with the London Season. Variations in supply of raw materials were mainly concerned with the pattern of arrivals and departures from the docks which not only affected the dockers themselves but also a variety of ancillary workers and trades such as sugar coopers, lodging-house keepers, biscuit bakers and shipwrights. Finally, the vagaries of the weather and the amount of daylight affected large numbers of outdoor workers. Rain and fog, for example, affected the barrel organs of itinerant Italian street musicians whilst frosts prevented market gardeners from working. Builders were probably the largest group affected by the weather and seasonal differences in daylight and rates of pay varied accordingly between summer and winter. Few trades, however, escaped some period of seasonal slack, and most experienced a lengthy period of enforced idleness.

Whilst seasonal fluctuations were thus an important aspect of economic activity, they were by no means an unchanging feature of the London scene. For various reasons, as Schwarz has noted, the impact of seasonality may have peaked during the first half of the nineteenth century.[48] First, improved communications made travelling to town easier and so allowed the Season to commence later. This had the effect of compressing bespoke demand into a shorter period resulting in a more intense pressure on production. Until the growth of a mass market in the second half of the century provided an additional and more stable source of demand, many workers relied entirely on this demand for their livelihood. Secondly, seasonal variations in employment were generally more pronounced during downturns and in the second quarter of the century recession years were more common than those of upturn.[49] Thirdly, the proliferation of small units of production, notably in the consumer trades, itself encouraged greater seasonal fluctuations in employment. Small masters had relatively limited opportunities for switching tasks according to seasonal demand. In contrast, larger firms were more able to switch separate tasks and so tailor output according to the state of demand. The outcome was that seasonality was far more pronounced in trades or branches of trade dominated by smaller employers.

One factor that has often been ignored in relation to the impact of seasonality refers to skill and the strength of trade unionism. It was common for the most skilled artisans to be retained during seasonal slack periods whilst less skilled or unskilled workers were dismissed.[50] Similarly, where trade unions were strong, the impact of seasonal variations could be mitigated by restricting hours of work during the busiest period and thus extending the length of employment. In both cases, as discussed later, pressures mounted in the first half of the century to reduce levels of skill and weaken the position of trade unions, thereby undermining the barriers which to some extent protected workers from the full impact of seasonal fluctuations in employment. Finally, climate itself was by no means constant. During this period winters were exceptionally long and severe, reflecting the final phase of the 'Little Ice Age' in Europe. Taken as a whole, there are strong grounds for suggesting that in terms of the metropolitan economy, the impact of seasonality peaked in the first half of the century.

Fluctuations in demand: the London Season

During the spring and summer months the West End filled with aristocratic families for the hectic round of soirées, parties and social engagements that accompanied the opening of Parliament and the onset of the London Season. During such times the demand for luxury products was at its height and shoemakers, dressmakers and tailors, not to mention the retinues of domestic servants and builders who cleaned and repaired the houses of the wealthy, were kept fully employed. For the remainder of the year, this social élite retreated to their country houses and demand fell accordingly. For the bespoke trades dependent on this wealthy demand, the Season was of crucial importance. In Mayfair, for example, the wealthy comprised 10 per cent of the population whilst the remaining 90 per cent consisted of those who served their needs: artisans and retailers who made and sold luxury goods, servants who catered for the daily needs of the family, and builders and decorators who repaired their houses.[51] For those who made the goods so conspicuously consumed by the West End élite – tailors, dressmakers, milliners, hatters, glovers, bonnet makers and shoemakers – the Season similarly marked the peak period of employment. Some idea of the significance of this pattern is provided by Figure 2.7 which plots the earnings of a West End tailor in 1848 and 1849. The spring rush as the Season swung into life is clearly marked, as is the second peak of demand as families returned to London after the Parliamentary summer recess. Others also benefited from higher demand during the Season. When wealthy families were in town washerwomen found employment easier to come by, as did those who built the carriages, made the harnesses and cared for the horses.[52] The preliminary spring clean of houses and the subsequent summer alterations provided work for carpenters, plumbers, painters and decorators.[53]

At such times the intensity of work was immense. During the spring

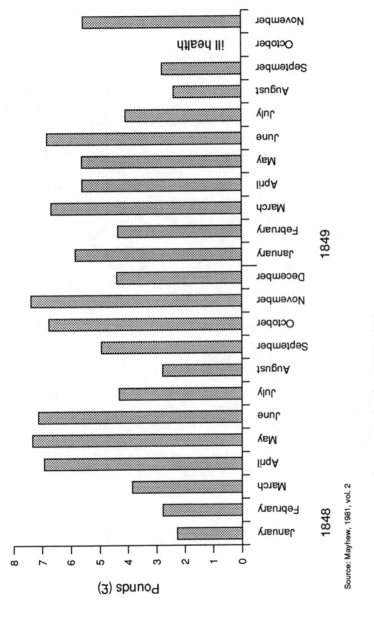

Source: Mayhew, 1981, vol. 2

Figure 2.7   Average earnings of a West End tailor, 1848–1849.

season, dressmakers not infrequently worked through the night to complete an order, whilst 15-hour days were considered normal.[54] Such intensity, however, whilst not unusual, needs to be set in both its historical and geographical context. During the eighteenth century, the Season extended from January until July, when Parliament commenced its summer recess, and resumed again in September until early December. Improvements in road transport later in the century, notably the spread of the turnpike system and the introduction of better carriages, meant that families could arrive in London later. As a result, from that period, the Season started later, only gathering pace in late February and March before getting into full swing from April till mid-July.

This temporal focusing of activity was also matched by an equivalent spatial concentration of wealthy families in élite West End districts.[55] In the eighteenth century, aristocratic landlords started developing estates to the west of the City. Between the 1720s and 1780s the Grosvenor estate was built up in Mayfair, and others, such as the Cadogan estate in Chelsea, the Portland in Marylebone and the Bedford estate in Bloomsbury, followed soon after. In the early decades of the nineteenth century, as the City and central districts emptied of wealthy families, other West End districts, such as Belgravia and parts of Kensington, were built up.[56] 'A dwelling in the City is a thing not now considered desirable', wrote D. M. Evans in 1845, 'all move either towards the west or emigrate to the suburbs – the one for fashion, the other for economy and fresh air.'[57] By the 1890s, when Charles Booth surveyed this part of town for his poverty survey, his maps show an overwhelming concentration of gold and deep red, the colours used to represent the location of luxury in the capital.

Such residential clustering was both a cause and effect of the shorter but more concentrated London Season. Packed into the few weeks from late April to July, the hectic social round of balls, parties, and social visits could not have functioned effectively unless wealthy families lived in close proximity. At the same time, such residential clustering encouraged the almost frenetic pace of engagements, attracting not only those aristocratic families attached to the Court but also the mercantile élite who aspired to enter the ranks of the nobility. Spatial clustering, as well as temporal, thus went hand-in-hand and both served to accentuate the seasonal press of demand on those workers who served the needs of the wealthy.

Fluctuations in supply: the docks

In terms of supply, the flow of trade through the Port of London was the main source of variation. It was not the only form of variation in the supply of goods: harvest and delivery of produce to the capital affected all those who depended on the sale of fruit, flowers and vegetables, including large numbers of street traders; fellmongers were busiest after the annual slaughter of animals at Michaelmas; winter was also the busiest time for undertakers. However, by virtue of the numbers directly and indirectly dependent on employment at the docks, coupled with the concentration of such employment in eastern and riverside districts, the flow of trade was probably the most important source of seasonal fluctuation in the supply of goods and the level of employment.

Although trade itself was highly diversified, the broad pattern of shipping was fairly predictable, depending primarily on the circulation of wind and ocean currents. The busiest period lasted from May to October as ships arrived from the West Indies, North America and the East Indies.[58] Figures of tonnage arriving in the Port of London for 1835 show two peaks in May and August, with arrivals slowing thereafter. In fact, the pattern was rather more complex than this, as Figure 2.8 shows, and depended to a large extent on the specific cargoes unloaded at individual docks. Trade entering the London Docks, and to a lesser extent St Katharine's, was more diverse than that arriving at the West or East India Docks and the seasonal pattern of unloading was therefore less pronounced. In the Commercial Docks on the Surrey side, timber was the main cargo and the busiest period there lasted from late summer to January, after which time very little work was done. The earnings of a rafter who unloaded timber at the Commercial Docks is shown in Figure 2.9 and illustrates clearly how this seasonal pattern of trade affected employment and wages. From about August until January work was fairly steady but tailed off during the rest of the year. In February 1850, in contrast to the previous year, the rafter in question was employed on contract work on the river, hence his wages were considerably higher. In all other respects, however, his earnings and employment followed closely the seasonal flow of trade through the docks. Though some mobility between docks and other river work was possible, as this example illustrates, in practice the unpredictability of arrivals and the distances between docks hampered attempts to dovetail employment. Furthermore, the hiring practices of both companies and middlemen contractors demanded that workers be close at hand and thus precluded much possibility of evening out daily or seasonal fluctuations of employment.[59] Although variations in the pattern of trade existed, therefore, the organization of employment and the friction of distance reduced opportunities to smooth out any fluctuations in employment between the different sets of docks.

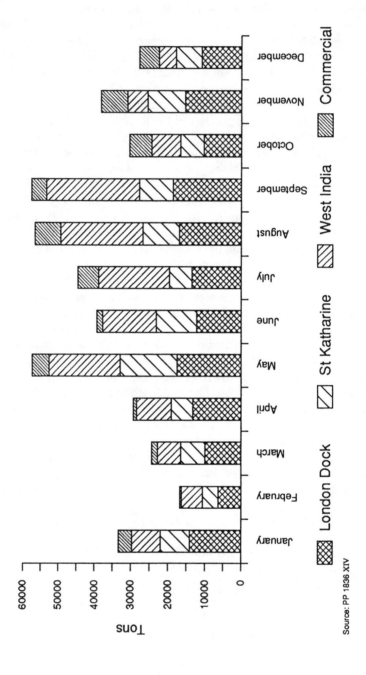

Source: PP 1836 XIV

Figure 2.8   Trade entering London docks, 1835.

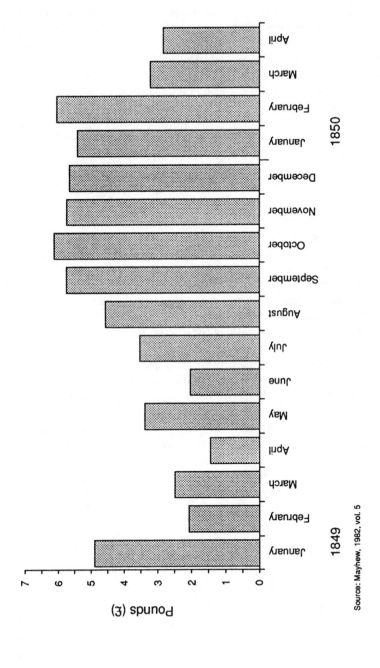

Source: Mayhew, 1982, vol. 5

Figure 2.9   Average earnings of a rafter at the Commercial Docks, 1849–1850.

The weather

For many outdoor workers the weather was the single most important influence on their levels of earnings. Builders felt this more keenly than most and for this reason rates of pay varied: bricklayers and plasterers received 6s. per day between Lady Day to Lord Mayor's Day compared with 5s.6d. for the rest of the year, with similar differentials recorded for other branches of the trade.[60] In general, during the winter months, lower earnings, higher unemployment and the cost of extra heat and light, forced many working-class households towards the unwelcoming embrace of the workhouse. Across London as a whole, rates of pauperism during January were between 10 and 30 per cent higher than in July. In St Giles, for example, the number of applications for poor relief doubled during the winter months, with the able-bodied poor accounting for most of this rise.[61] In general, workhouses throughout the capital filled and emptied with monotonous regularity as winter came and went. Mortality increased in similar fashion, and death rates were between 10 and 20 per cent higher in winter than at other times of the year.[62] Not surprisingly, undertakers were one of the few groups of workers to profit at this time. All this was quite normal, of course, and the seasonal rhythm of poverty tapped out by the lives of the poor was recorded in countless other places.

In the first half of the century the effects of climate on the pattern of seasonality was exacerbated by the onset of the last phase of the 'Little Ice Age' and the occurrence of a series of extremely cold winters. With the exception of 1796, relatively mild winters had prevailed between 1790 and 1813. The winter of 1814, however, was the coldest of the century and heralded the start of a lengthy period of cooler and wetter weather. Between 1790 and 1870 thirteen winter months had mean temperatures below freezing, all but two of which occurred between 1814 and 1855.[63] Figure 2.10 shows that between 1814 and 1855 severe winters, during which temperatures averaged between 34 and 36 degrees Fahrenheit (1–2.2 degrees centigrade), occurred in one out of four years, with exceptionally cold conditions prevailing in 1814, 1830, 1838, 1841, 1847 and 1855.

During such periods of extreme cold, unemployment rose sharply and working-class distress was acute. When the Thames froze over, which happened on at least four occasions, in 1814, 1830, 1855 and 1861, distress was exceptionally severe. Mayhew noted that an easterly wind, which was also associated with cold weather, disrupted shipping on the Thames, throwing up to 30,000 people out of work.[64] In those instances the line of the thermometer and the soup kitchen moved in opposite directions: whilst the one fell, the other rose. In 1830 the number of

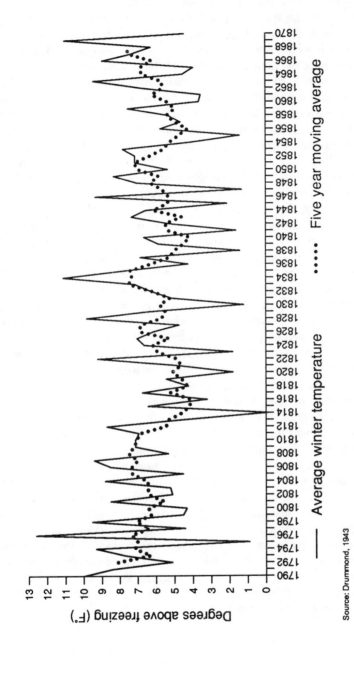

Source: Drummond, 1943

Figure 2.10 Cold winters in London, 1790–1870.

meals provided in January and February by the Society for the Suppression of Mendicity rose to 45,219 compared with 5571 for the same period in the previous year.[65] In 1838 and again in 1841 a severe frost resulted in a flood of applicants for the Society's dole of soup: over 89,000 bowls were dispensed in the first two months of 1838 and more than 104,000 in the same period in 1841.[66] On these occasions Poor Law authorities were hard pressed to keep pace with demand and when sharp frosts forced closure of the docks in 1855 and 1861, food riots broke out in several eastern and riverside districts as boards of guardians were unable to provide sufficient supplies of bread to applicants for relief.

Harsh as the distress was, the effects of the weather and seasonal variations in supply and demand operated within the social context of the relations of production and we need to be aware of how differing circumstances affected levels of employment. In particular, we need to take account of the strength of labour and the level of skill, both of which had an important influence on patterns of employment. For workers, various strategies existed with which to even out seasonal unemployment or underemployment. Work could be shared out, as was the practice amongst goldsmiths and jewellers, or jobs could be dovetailed so as to minimize the disjuncture between winter and summer employment. During the summer, for example, when the demand for gas lighting was low, stokers often worked in the brickfields. Similarly, during winter unemployed dockers often took to street selling.

The need to smooth out seasonal variations in demand also posed problems for employers. In some trades the work could vary according to the season. In food manufacturing, for example, large employers alternated jam making in the summer with the manufacture of sweets and potting of meat at other times.[67] In other trades, the main problem for employers was the need to establish flexible working practices that, on the one hand, would allow them to meet peak demand without running up against the barrier of labour shortages, and, on the other, to reduce their workforce during slack periods. Skilled artisans, therefore, were often retained during periods of slack demand, whilst less skilled workers were dismissed. Without the barriers of skill or trade unions, this latter group consequently bore the brunt of seasonal fluctuations in employment. The experience of seasonality, therefore, varied in more complex ways than just the simple ebb and flow of supply and demand, or the vagaries of the weather would suggest. Skill, the strength of trade unionism, the scale of production and the requirements of employers were also part of the equation.

Economic cycles and the London economy

Just as the significance of seasonality needs to be set in its historical and social context, so, too, must the deeper rhythms of economic life which emanated from the ebb and flow of the trade cycle. Here, although the tones were more muted, and the impact on daily life therefore more difficult to discern, none the less cyclical fluctuations had a profound impact on the London economy. We must therefore pick our way carefully, distinguishing between the economic life of the nation as a whole, and that of London in particular. The starting point is that with which we began this chapter, namely, the structure of employment in the capital.

London's broad economic mix imparted a degree of stability that was absent from regions dependent on only one or a small range of trades. This was supported both by the relative importance of the finishing trades themselves, which were more stable over the economic cycle than those concerned with manufacturing producer goods, and by the fast-growing range of service occupations. It was true, of course, that circumstances varied between trades and in some instances, such as watchmaking, silk weaving and shipbuilding, the forces of decline ultimately outweighed those promoting growth. It was equally true that for many traditional London trades, including clothing, furniture making and shoemaking, cheaper competition resulted in the restructuring of production, as we discuss later. Whilst the localization of trades inevitably meant that individual districts were vulnerable to the decline of specific trades, nevertheless, the broad industrial mix ensured that the metropolitan economy as a whole was not dependent on the fortunes of any single industry. Moreover, the significance of the commercial and financial sector meant that London was well placed to take advantage of the substantial growth in overseas trade.[68] Rubinstein has shown just how profitable this commerce was and consequently how the fortunes of London's bourgeoisie increased over the period.[69] Taken together, both the share of service employment coupled with the range of industries imparted a degree of stability and self-generated dynamism to the metropolitan economy missing from regions with a narrower economic base.

Occupational diversity and the rapid growth of the service sector, however, masked a second and less well-recognized set of economic forces. Overseas trade was a risky venture at the best of times, always liable to disruption by war, political turmoil or adverse weather. Although the volume of trade increased, the path was by no means smooth. In 1825, for example, when South American mining ventures failed, and again in 1837, when the USA suspended specie payments, investors found themselves with worthless bonds that no amount of gunboat diplomacy could remedy. 'Panic reigned supreme alike in finance and business', Henry Hyndman wrote of the financial crisis in 1825, 'The first great international crisis of the nineteenth century had begun.'[70] Whenever commerce was disrupted or the bubble of speculation was burst, difficulties arose and when this happened the entire metropolitan economy felt the chill. When trading activities functioned in the context of a close set of interlinked institutions, as was the case with commerce and banking in London, depending on the extent of that interdependency, the collapse of one firm or a set of firms was always liable to set up a chain effect that threatened the viability of others. The most spectacular example of this was when the international finance house of Overend and Gurney suspended payment in 1866. According to Jenks, the firm had stood next to the Bank of England as the mainstay of British credit and when it defaulted on its payments 'the whole brood of finance and contracting companies were swept into the court of chancery'.[71] Shock waves from the collapse not only coursed through the London economy but ran the length of the entire country, hastening the demise of Thames shipbuilding and dragging hundreds into the mire of bankruptcy.[72] Diversity alone, therefore, and a share in the rapidly growing service sector, were by no means a guarantee of stability.

Regional trends and cycles

A considerable amount of research exists on the performance of the British economy during the Industrial Revolution. Though questions remain concerning the precise rates of growth and timing of change, there is broad agreement that economic growth was particularly rapid between about 1780 and 1830.[73] However, in terms of growth and the timing of cyclical fluctuations, important regional variations occurred as a result of the specific mix of employment and the balance between growing, stable and declining industries.[74] For the period prior to the development of a rail and telegraph network, several authors have pointed to the existence of regional variations in rates of employment, the level of wages and the prices of some goods .[75] Not until the spread of the railways and telegraph from mid-century onwards smoothed the flow of people, goods and information did such differentials begin to diminish. Generalizations about national trends, therefore, need to pay close attention to the regional context of economic change.

Establishing the regional dimensions of economic change, however, presents several difficulties. Irrespective of the problems in defining geographical boundaries, economic data rarely exist at a regional scale. For the purposes here, three sets of indicators can be used to shed light on the pattern of economic activity in the capital, referring respectively to the pattern of house building shown in the Middlesex deeds registers, the flow of trade entering and leaving the Port of London, and the number of bankruptcies recorded for London in comparison with the rest of the country. These indicators reflect well the broad economic structure of the capital. As we have already seen, the building trades were immensely important in terms of the numbers employed. In 1861 more than one in ten adult male workers in London were directly employed in building, and many more depended indirectly on the construction of houses. The long turnover time of capital investment in building, however, means that construction tends to lag behind more sensitive indicators of change, and care must be taken when examining the precise chronology of cyclical change. Nevertheless, the fortunes of many other manufacturing trades were closely linked with the pattern of house building and construction can thus be taken as a general measure of industrial activity in the capital.

Other indicators are also useful in pointing to different dimensions of economic activity. Imports and exports through London's docks give a broad indication of the state of trade. Of course, much of this traffic merely concerned the city's role as an entrepôt, rather than bearing any direct relationship to its manufacturing base. However, in the context of the casual labour market this role was a significant one. In riverside districts, large numbers of publicans, chandlers, lodgings keepers, prostitutes and others derived much of their income from servicing the needs of seamen. Thousands of casual labourers depended for their livelihood on the loading and unloading of ships. In 1800 Patrick Colquhoun estimated that over and above the 10,250 employers involved in port activities, a further 120,000 persons were employed in various capacities in the docks or shipping, including over 40,000 dock labourers and a further 8000 lightermen and watermen.[76] Later in the century Mayhew estimated that at peak periods of employment, as many as 9000 labourers were employed in the London Dock, St Katharine's Dock and the East and West India Docks alone, although he added that when easterly winds prevented ships from docking, between 25,000 and 30,000 labourers were thrown out of work.[77] Thus, for the purposes of gauging the ebb and flow of the local economy, particularly in relation to eastern and riverside districts, the volume of seaborne trade can usefully serve as an indication of the state of the casual labour market.

Bankruptcies comprise the third, and in some ways most problematic, regional economic indicator. Whilst some authors have questioned the precise relationship between insolvency and economic fluctuations, others have emphasized their importance as an indicator of business activity. For the eighteenth century, Hoppitt has demonstrated that the rate of insolvency rose during upturns, as the number of businesses increased, and fell during economic downturns.[78] For the nineteenth century, Lester has suggested that random factors, rather than any systematic relationship with cyclical patterns of activity, were responsible for fluctuations in levels of bankruptcy. However, others have been keen to point out a relationship between the rate of bankruptcy and the state of the economy. Silberling, Gayer *et al.* and more recently, Duffy, have argued that bankruptcies were a sensitive barometer of business activity.[79] In particular, the hazardous nature of overseas investment and the inherent problems of long-term credit arrangements meant that the rate of insolvency was closely related to fluctuations in foreign trade. Given the importance of the commercial sector in London, as well as the size of its economy, it is no surprise that the capital accounted for over 40 per cent of the nation's bankrupts during the eighteenth century and about a third for the period from 1800 to 1870.[80] Although some reservations persist concerning the interpretation of such figures, nevertheless, the number of bankruptcies provides a useful indicator of the ebb and flow of business activity not just in London but in the country as a whole.[81]

Construction

In view of the importance of construction in the metropolitan economy, secular and cyclical fluctuations in building had a significant impact on levels of employment in the capital. According to the number of house deeds registered in Middlesex, for the first half of the century building progressed gradually but from the 1850s the trend was sharply upwards.[82] However, as Figure 2.11 illustrates, this broad pattern was interrupted by a series of long cycles with a duration of between 17 and 20 years and it is this aspect which is of main interest here. The peak in house building was halted by the outbreak of the Napoleonic Wars in 1793 and the corresponding tightening of credit. But as the ratio of government revenue to borrowing improved and interest rates fell, so construction began to rise once more and from 1799 to 1811 it grew steadily.[83] High government expenditure and tighter credit thereafter brought an end to the building boom and the difficult conditions persisted until the war ended. In 1817 easier credit, together with growing demographic pressure, fuelled a sharp upturn that culminated in 1825 in the last great Georgian building boom.

Strong as the upturn was, the financial crisis of 1825 brought the boom to a sudden halt. From that date, according to Cairncross and

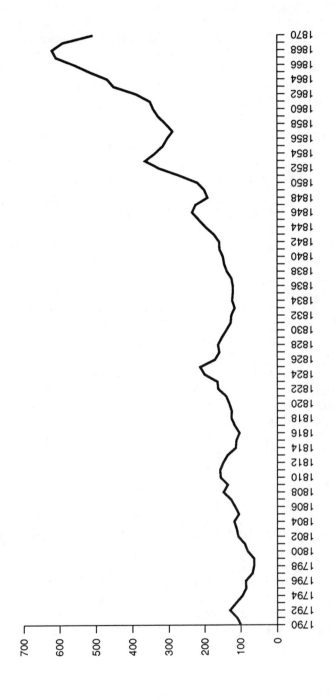

Source: Sheppard, Belcher and Cottrell, 1979

Figure 2.11 Middlesex building deeds (1790=100).

Weber, 'The decline in London over the years 1825–32 amounts almost to a secular drop to a new and lower level of activity', an opinion confirmed by the falls in brick production and the number of deeds registered.[84] Figure 2.12 clearly demonstrates the strength of the construction boom leading up to 1825, and the dramatic fall thereafter. In 1831, an estimated 12,000 carpenters were unemployed in London, and although workers blamed the spread of machinery and the growing use of cast iron for the lack of employment, the collapse of construction was of greater importance.[85] Throughout the 1830s and early 1840s, house building was sluggish and unemployment remained high.[86] To some extent this collapse simply represented a readjustment in the supply of housing, which had moved out of balance with demand during the boom years prior to 1825. Figure 2.13 shows that from 1801 to 1821 demographic growth exceeded the increase in house building but that from 1821 to 1831 the situation was reversed. For the next two decades the rate of increase in the rate of house building fell behind the growth of population. Not until the 1850s was the balance between supply and demand re-established.

The mid-century upturn in building, which began in 1849 and continued until the late 1860s, was interrupted only briefly between 1854 and 1857, and marked a new secular increase in the rate of construction. Falls in interest rates, brought about by the discovery of gold in California and Australia, coupled with investment in transport, provided the impetus for this building boom. Street clearances and railway construction gathered pace, as did the spread of omnibus services, and pressure mounted for the provision of suburban housing.[87] From the 1850s large numbers of houses were put up in Kensington, Notting Hill and Bayswater not to mention other outlying parts of London.[88] During these years Camberwell began to 'congeal into a new suburban continent', linked to the centre by a rapidly expanding network of omnibus routes.[89] Elsewhere fingers of development shot with equal rapidity along transport routes leading from the centre. In their eagerness to encourage commuter traffic, managers of the Eastern Counties Railway offered builders free season tickets in return for erecting houses along their route. They dutifully responded by building up Hackney.[90] Viewed from the workers' perspective, this frenzied pace of activity not only meant steadier employment and higher wages but also provided them with a stronger basis for trade union organization and a sound platform for workplace militancy, a position which they seized with considerable enthusiasm.[91]

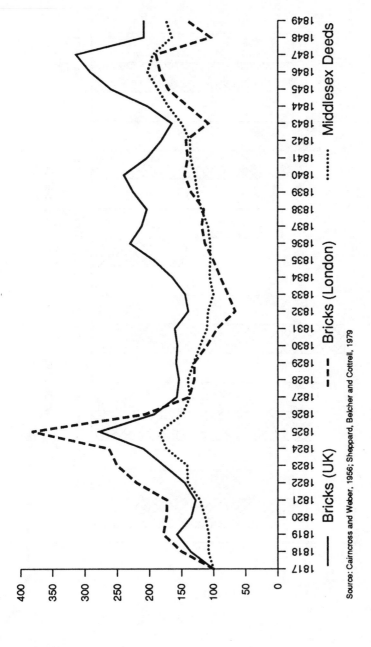

Source: Cairncross and Weber, 1956; Sheppard, Belcher and Cottrell, 1979

Figure 2.12 Brick production and building deeds (1817=100).

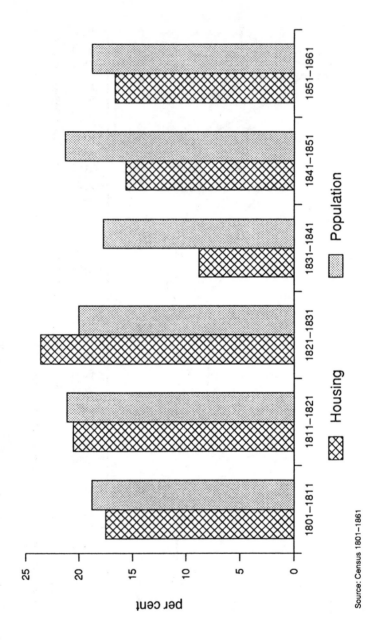

Source: Census 1801–1861

Figure 2.13   Housing and population change, 1801–1861.

Trade

Dock construction in London followed a similar pattern to housing. A vast amount of building had taken place in the first quarter of the century, commencing with the West India Dock in 1802, followed by the London Docks in 1805, the East India Dock in 1808, the South West India Dock and Regent's Basin in 1820 and finally St Katharine's Dock in 1828. From then until the opening of the Royal Victoria Dock in 1855, no further building took place. By then, Liverpool matched London in terms of tonnage and by 1860 it had usurped the capital's position as the country's leading port.

Several reasons were responsible for the lengthy lull in construction during the 1830s and 1840s. The dock companies themselves feared that potentially ruinous competition could have arisen if new docks were built and they therefore refrained from further construction, despite the congested state of the river and the fact that larger vessels were unable to unload in some of the older docks.[92] A contributory factor was the relatively slow rate of growth in the volume of trade passing through the Port of London, particularly after the downturn of 1825. The pattern of trade passing through London compared with the combined totals of Liverpool, Hull and Newcastle, its three closest rivals, is charted in Figure 2.14. Over the period as a whole, the tonnage entering and leaving London rose from 1,247,873 tons in 1816 to 6,273,951 by 1865, compared with 988,167 and 9,487,475 for the three other ports. The figures show three distinct periods during which London's trade grew at a much slower rate than that of other ports. The first, albeit brief, recession, took place between 1819 and 1822, reflecting a downturn in exports, particularly to the United States.[93] The subsequent expansion of trade was cut short by the financial crisis of 1825, and from then until 1835 the figures suggest that there was no increase in the overall volume of trade passing through the Port, in contrast to the situation elsewhere. Although trade increased between 1836 and 1839, it dipped again during the early 1840s and not until the latter years of the decade was there any sign of a strong recovery in London. After that time the volume of trade rose strongly, punctuated by downturns in 1847 to 1848 and from 1855 to 1857, the latter years mirroring the recession in house building noted above. Thus, for almost twenty years, from 1826 to 1846, the volume of trade passing through London's docks grew relatively slowly, and in some instances not at all. This lengthy period of sluggish growth coincided with the secular downswing in building discussed earlier, suggesting that these years witnessed a general slowing-down of growth within the metropolitan economy. We now turn to the bankruptcy series to shed further light on this state of affairs.

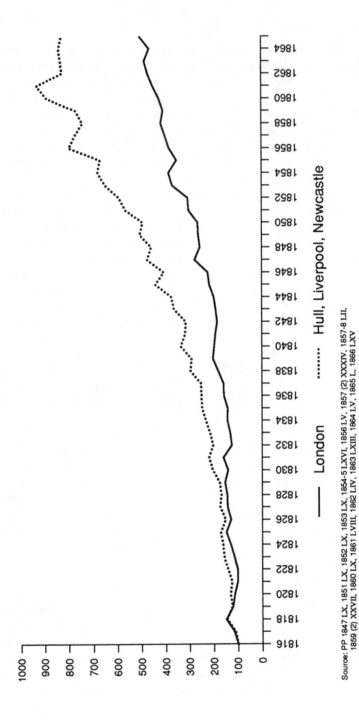

Source: PP 1847 LX, 1851 LX, 1852 LX, 1853 LX, 1854-5 LXVI, 1856 LV, 1857 (2) XXXIV, 1857-8 LII,
1859 (2) XXXVII, 1860 LX, 1861 LVIII, 1862 LIV, 1863 LXIII, 1864 LV, 1865 L, 1866 LXV

Figure 2.14 Imports and exports from London, Hull, Liverpool and Newcastle, 1816–1865 (1816=100).

Bankruptcies

Recent work by Julian Hoppitt has shown that during the eighteenth century the number of bankruptcies in England and Wales more than tripled, with the rise being particularly steep from the 1780s onwards.[94] Based on the number of bankruptcies recorded in the *London Gazette*, the series plotted in Figure 2.15 shows that this increase was maintained in the first two decades of the nineteenth century before flattening out from 1818.[95] Even allowing for the impact of legal changes in the framework governing insolvency, the fall in the number of bankruptcies after that date suggests that levels of risk in the economy were being reduced and that as a result insolvency was becoming less common. It is not our purpose to speculate on the reasons for this, although the growing integration of the economy arising from improved means of transport and communications, together with the development of joint stock companies and a sounder financial system brought about by the Bank Acts of 1826, 1833 and 1844, were factors that encouraged greater stability. What is of interest, however, is the extent to which changes in the level of bankruptcy were felt with equal force in London compared with the rest of the country.

An answer to this question comes from considering the totals in Table 2.3 and the detrended bankruptcy series shown in Figure 2.16. Between 1790 and 1859 London accounted for about a third of the total number of bankruptcies, a figure considerably lower than for the eighteenth century but which nevertheless was far in excess of the size of the city in relation to the rest of the country. Although more research on the sectoral breakdown of insolvency in the capital needs to be carried out for the nineteenth century, the explanation offered by Hoppitt for London's dominance during the eighteenth probably still held true.[96] Economic factors were probably of greatest importance. The large number of wholesalers – mostly merchants – who went bankrupt in the eighteenth century was witness to the high risks involved in commerce and overseas trade and this, probably more than any other factor, accounted for the significance of London in the overall figures. Similarly, the involvement of many metropolitan financiers in the provision of credit also meant that pressures arising elsewhere in the country often had an impact in the capital. More specifically, for those engaged in the bespoke consumer trades, the follies and frequent changes of fashion heightened the risks involved in conducting business. Legal factors also had a part to play in explaining London's dominance. The ease with which proceedings could be started in London no doubt encouraged creditors in the capital to sue for bankruptcy more often than those elsewhere. During the nineteenth century these factors may have changed

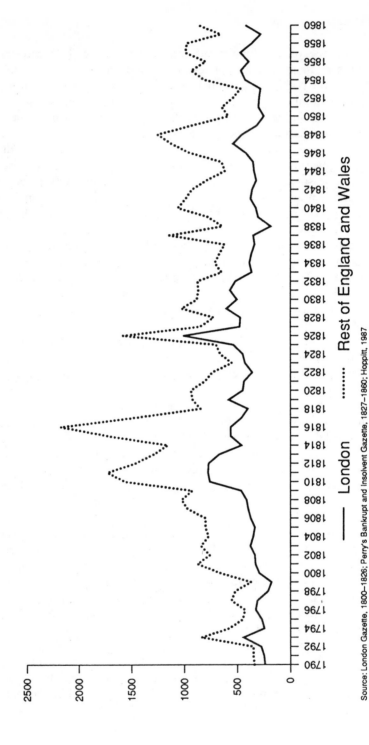

Source: London Gazette, 1800–1826; Perry's Bankrupt and Insolvent Gazette, 1827–1860; Hoppitt, 1987

Figure 2.15   Bankruptcies, 1790–1860.

in degree but probably altered little in terms of overall structure, as the relative stability of London's share of national bankruptcies would seem to confirm.

This stability, however, masks the fact that there was considerable annual variation in the totals for the capital and the rest of the country. Table 2.3. shows that from 1790 to 1819, the relative share of metropolitan bankruptcies fell. That pattern was reversed in the following decade as a result of the large number of failures arising from the financial panic of 1825. Over 70 provincial banks failed within six weeks, leading to a run on London banks which was only halted with difficulty by the intervention of the Bank of England. Thereafter, the number of failures remained high for several years as the impact of the crisis continued to reverberate through the metropolitan economy and although a more stable pattern resumed in the 1830s, it took several more years for London's share of bankruptcies to return to the average for the period as a whole.

A better picture of the variations in bankruptcies emerges from the detrended series plotted in Figure 2.16.[97] This shows the annual variation from the trend and provides a clearer indication of cyclical fluctuations. Three important points are worth noting. The first is that over the period as a whole the intensity of the bankruptcy cycle declined. During the Napoleonic Wars the costs and uncertainty of overseas trade increased, and consequently the risks of bankruptcy were greater. This set of factors accounts for the particularly high totals between 1808 and 1814. After that date more stable trading conditions returned, with the exception of the panic of 1825, and in the rest of the country deviations from the

Table 2.3   Bankruptcies, 1790–1859

	London	Rest of England and Wales	Total	London (per cent)
1790–99	2,731	4,753	7,484	36.49
1800–09	3,645	8,401	12,046	30.26
1810–19	5,987	14,306	20,293	29.50
1820–29	5,192	8,549	13,741	37.78
1830–39	3,874	7,818	11,692	33.13
1840–49	3,805	9,272	13,077	29.10
1850–59	3,528	7,407	10,935	32.26
Total	28,762	60,506	89,268	32.22

Source: see Appendix 2.1

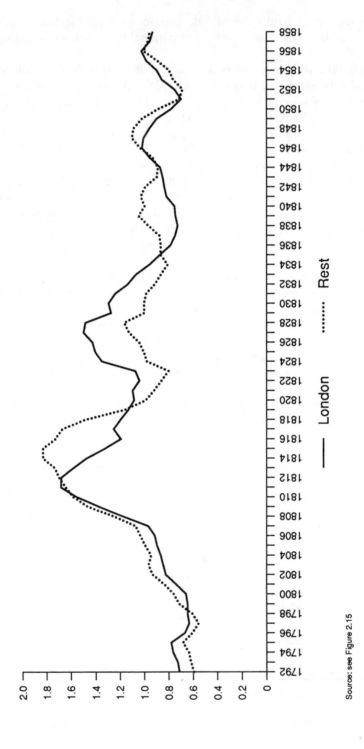

Source: see Figure 2.15

Figure 2.16 Detrended bankruptcy totals (five-year moving average), 1792–1858.

trend were reduced. In London, the severity of the financial crisis was more clearly marked and a return to stable levels of bankruptcy was delayed until the mid-1830s. From then on, fluctuations from the trend of bankruptcies in London and the rest of the country moved in broadly similar ways.

That similarity, however, did not necessarily mean that the incidence of bankruptcy was the same. Comparison of Figures 2.15 and 2.16 shows that differences occurred in the timing of bankruptcies between London and the rest of the country, particularly in the period from about 1812 to 1844. During the War years, bankruptcies peaked at similar times in both places. However, whilst the post-War depression had a major impact on the rest of the country, it seemed to pass almost without notice in the capital. During the 1820s, however, and most notably from 1824 to 1828, the situation was reversed. Figure 2.16 shows that the rate of London bankruptcies increased sharply during those years, far more so than elsewhere, suggesting that the crisis of 1825 was to some extent a peculiarly metropolitan phenomenon. The downturn in building and the sluggish pattern of trade, discussed earlier, would lend weight to this suggestion. Not until the mid-1830s did the fluctuation in London bankruptcies return to a level comparable with the rest of the country. But even then, the London series was at odds with experiences elsewhere, showing relatively little response to the suspension of specie payments in the United States in 1837 and hardly varying at all during the depression of the early 1840s. Not until the mid-1840s did metropolitan bankruptcies turn strongly upwards in conjunction with the national series. Thereafter, the London total conforms more closely to the national trend, reaffirming the closer integration of the national economy.

Conclusion

What lessons can be drawn from this analysis of the metropolitan economy? Perhaps the most important is that the regional context is evidently of crucial importance in understanding the course of economic change. Although further work needs to be done to establish more accurately regional variations in economic performance, nevertheless both the building and bankruptcy series, and to a lesser extent the trade figures, suggest that significant differences in the timing and intensity of cyclical fluctuations existed between the capital and elsewhere. Secondly, although London's broad economic mix provided a degree of stability that was absent from regions more heavily dependent on one or a handful of industries, nevertheless the metropolitan economy was still subject to marked cyclical booms and slumps in activity. Given the pivotal role of commerce and overseas trade in generating demand for consumer goods, this should come as little surprise. The reliance of manufacturing on the local market meant that interruptions to the normal flow of trade and finance were transmitted rapidly to other sectors of the local economy. When the winds of trade blew cold, the chill settled broadly over the capital's workforce. This became most clear in the second quarter of the century, a period during which years of recession outnumbered those of boom. In London, the slowing of construction and trade, coupled with relatively high levels of insolvency, also suggest a prolonged period of moderate growth. If this evidence is to be believed, then the second quarter of the nineteenth century was a particularly difficult period for London.

This suggestion must be set in the context of the city's changing relationship with the rest of the country. In terms of finance and commerce, its dominant position was enhanced by the banking reforms after 1826 and by the tentacles of transport that spread from there to encompass the rest of the nation. But for manufacturing the reverse was true. As a high-cost centre of production, London was always vulnerable to cheaper competition from foreign and provincial manufacturers. As long as high transport costs insulated local industries from competition, London's manufacturing base was protected. But the spread of turnpikes from the 1750s had already undermined some metropolitan trades and further improvements in road travel, coupled with the expansion of canals and more importantly the spread of the railway network from the 1830s and 1840s, eroded London's viability as a manufacturing centre. Added to these growing pressures was the fact that in the second quarter of the century the system of protective tariffs was dismantled and foreign goods were able to compete on a more equal footing with domestic manufacturing. This growing competition, combined with the impact of cyclical downturns and sluggish growth, imposed severe pressures on London employers to reduce costs of production. How these savings were achieved, and the conflicts that the process of industrial restructuring generated, are the subject of the next two chapters.

Notes

1. Fisher, 1948, pp.37–50.
2. Defoe, 1766, p.206.
3. See Berg and Hudson, 1992, pp.30–2; Bythell, 1978; Sabel and Zeitlin, 1985; Samuel, 1977.
4. Lee, 1984, pp.149–53; *idem.*, 1986, pp.138–40; Rubinstein, 1981, pp.106–10; *idem.*, 1994, pp.25–31.

5. Jenks, 1971, pp.10–16, 188–92.
6. Schwarz, 1992, pp.23–30.
7. Rubinstein, 1977a, pp.616–19; *idem*, 1992, pp.85–6; *idem*, 1994, p. 31.
8. Evans, 1845, p.191.
9. The census distinguished between handicraft production and manufacture, the former based on the use of hand tools and the latter on machines and referring primarily to the newly mechanized factory trades. In London the only major trade classified as manufacturing was silkweaving.
10. Thompson, 1968, p.284.
11. The geographical area refers to the City of London and the metropolitan parishes of Middlesex, Surrey and Kent. See Appendix 1.1 for a full listing of registration districts.
12. In London 11,991 males were employed in manufacture compared with 130,937 in handicraft production.
13. Hall, 1962b, pp.26–7; see also Jones, 1971, pp.21–9.
14. PP 1831–32 XIX *SC on the silk trade*, q. 10012, 10030.
15. Price, 1980, p.304.
16. See in particular Jones, 1971, pp.67–98.
17. Rubinstein, 1981, p.109; *idem*, 1992, p.77, 86.
18. Schwarz, 1992, pp.24–30.
19. Rubinstein, 1977a, pp.609–12, 616–18.
20. See Alexander, 1983, pp.20–2.
21. *Operative*, 25 November 1838.
22. Jones, 1971, p.29.
23. *Northern Star (NS)*, 17 January 1852.
24. Hall, 1962b, p.119.
25. Mayhew, 1980, vol. 1, p.115, 119; *NS*, 14 September 1844.
26. Mayhew, 1982, vol. 5, pp.194, 200.
27. *ibid*. vol. 5, pp.192–3.
28. *NS*, 2 November 1850.
29. PP 1843 XIV *RC on children's employment*, pp.834, 838.
30. Dodd, 1843, includes descriptions of visits to 22 establishments in different trades which 'were conducted on a scale sufficiently large to involve something like "factory" arrangements.'
31. Mayhew, 1968, vol. 3, pp.303, 310.
32. *NS*, 17 January 1852.
33. Alford, 1964, p.107.
34. In Camberwell between 1850 and 1852 over 90 per cent of builders constructed fewer than twelve houses. See Dyos, 1977, p.125.
35. *Reynolds Newspaper (RN)*, 14 August 1859.
36. Shaw Lefevre and Bennett, 1860, p.52.
37. *Gorgon*, 17 October, 1818; *London Mercury*, 26 March, 18 June 1837.
38. Matthias, 1979, p.220.
39. *Trades Newspaper and Mechanics Weekly Journal*, 4 March 1827.
40. Howe, 1943, p.4.
41. *RN*, 2 October 1853, 2 December 1856.
42. *Reply of the Journeymen Bookbinders*, 1831, p.6; Dodd, 1843, pp.363–7.
43. *Memorial of the machinists and engineers*, 1813, (PRO HO42/133); *To the manufacturers and tradesmen of the United Kingdom*, 1813 (ULMC); *Meeting of the committee of master manufacturers*, 1813 (ULMC); The origin, objectives and operation of the apprentice laws, 1814.

44. PP 1825 IV SC on the combination laws, pp.189–91.
45. *NS* 2, 30 September, 30 December 1843, 24 August 1850; Place Coll., vol. 53, pp.62, 77.
46. *London Mercury*, 26 March, 18 June 1837.
47. Jones, 1971, pp.33–51.
48. Schwarz, 1992, pp.106–116.
49. During downturns manufacturers were less likely to produce in anticipation of demand, thereby accentuating seasonal patterns of production. For a discussion of cyclical fluctuations see below, pp.44–57.
50. Beveridge, 1909, pp.34–5.
51. Atkins, 1990, p.46.
52. Mayhew, 1968, vol. 2, p.299; Weld, 1843, p.18.
53. Webb and Freeman, 1912, pp. 336–41.
54. PP 1843 XIII *RC on children's employment*, pp.438–9.
55. Atkins, 1990, pp.39–47.
56. Summerson, 1945, pp.146–59, 174–80; Olsen, 1979, pp.129–89.
57. Evans, 1845, p.190.
58. Ashton, 1959, pp.10–11; Northcote Parkinson, 1948, p.154, 188, 195, 199.
59. Beveridge, 1909, pp.87–8.
60. Skyring, 1831; see also PP 1833 VI *SC on manufactures, commerce and shipping*, q.1680; PP 1840 XXII *RC on the handloom weavers*, pp.119–20.
61. Green and Parton, 1990, pp.73–4.
62. Landers, 1993, pp.211–13, 228.
63. Drummond, 1943, p.23; see also Brooks and Hunt, 1933, pp.383–4.
64. Mayhew, 1968, vol. 3, p.312. A figure of 20,000 is given in *idem*, 1968, vol. 2, p.298.
65. Society for the Suppression of Mendicity (SSM), 1830, p.21.
66. SSM, 1838, *idem*, 1841.
67. Webb and Freeman, 1912, p.46.
68. Lee, 1981, pp.448–51; *idem*, 1984, pp.149–51.
69. Rubinstein, 1981, pp.106–9.
70. Hyndman, 1892, p.33.
71. Jenks, 1971, p.261.
72. Hyndman, 1892, pp.95–7; Pollard, 1950, p.79.
73. For recent summaries see Crafts, 1985; Crafts and Harley, 1992; Crafts, Leybourne and Mills, 1989; Jackson, 1992.
74. Few authors have examined the regional context of economic fluctuations prior to 1841. For later decades see Marshall, 1987, pp.103–36; Southall, 1988a, pp.239–56. Regional economic diversity during the first half of the nineteenth century has been discussed by Berg and Hudson, 1992, pp.38–9; Hudson, 1992, pp.101–32; Hunt, E.H., 1986; Langton, 1984.
75. Crafts, 1982, p.68 has suggested that in terms of prices there was relatively little regional diversity. The major exception to this was coal and rents. In 1843 the price of coal was three times higher in the Home Counties that in Northern districts. Hunt, 1973, pp.102–4 has also argued that the major cause of regional differentials in the cost of living was the levels of rent. For regional variations in the price of shares see Michie, 1985, pp.65–71.
76. Colquhoun, 1800, pp.xxx–xxxii.
77. Mayhew, 1968, vol. 3, pp.300–12.
78. Hoppitt, 1987, pp.106–20.

79. Silberling, 1923, pp.236–9; Gayer, Rostow and Schwarz, 1953, vol. 2, pp.885–7; Duffy, 1973, pp.165–76.
80. Hoppitt, 1987, p.63; see Appendix 2.1
81. A fuller discussion of the bankrupcty series is provided in Appendix 2.1
82. The figures are drawn from the published series in Sheppard, Belcher and Cottrell, 1979, pp.212–14.
83. Silberling, 1924, p.217; Mitchell and Deane, 1962, p.455.
84. Cairncross and Weber, 1956, p.292.
85. *Poor Mans Guardian*, 13 August 1831.
86. Place Coll. vol. 56, fol. 11.
87. Parry Lewis, 1965, pp.88–101.
88. Olsen, 1979, pp.166–88.
89. Dyos, 1977, pp.66–9, 180.
90. Olsen, 1979, pp.298–322.
91. Bowley, 1901, pp.107–9. See below, Chapter 5, pp.132–4.
92. See PP 1836 XIV *SC on the Port of London*, p.185.
93. Gayer, Rostow and Schwarz, 1953, vol. 1, p.145–6.
94. Hoppitt, 1987, p.183.
95. See Appendix 2.1 for a fuller discussion of the data.
96. Hoppitt, 1987, pp.59–74.
97. The detrended series is based on the deviations over time from the secular trend as calculated by a linear regression equation. In this instance the trend line is represented as 1.0.

CHAPTER THREE

The structure of economic change

Henry Mayhew and the London working class

In October 1849 Henry Mayhew started work as the Metropolitan Correspondent of the *Morning Chronicle* newspaper. 'To me has been confided the office of examining into the condition of the poor of London', he wrote. At the time, interest in the 'condition of England' question was at its height. Economic conditions in the preceding years had been difficult with high rates of unemployment and widespread distress amongst the working class. The Chartist demonstrations were still fresh in the memory, and the fearful death toll arising from the cholera epidemic of 1848–49, which claimed the lives of 15,000 Londoners, was only just subsiding. Mayhew was kept fully occupied for over a year, pouring out articles at the rate of one or two a week, answering correspondents, organizing meetings, interviewing workers and visiting their homes. His output was impressive, his grasp of the complexities of the London labour market second to none. Reviewing the series in 1850, John Ludlow remarked 'Never before, certainly, on so great a scale was this great and vital branch of the Condition-of-England question exhibited to us with such completeness and in such relief.'[1] Years after the series had ended workers still recalled the meetings arranged by Mayhew and the articles which had ensued.[2] In Edward Thompson's measured judgement, he was 'incomparably the greatest social investigator in the mid-century'.[3] It is with Henry Mayhew, then, that we start to navigate our own way along the channels of economic change in the capital.

According to Mayhew, the poor could be divided into two categories: the honest poor, consisting of the striving and the disabled, and the dishonest poor who subsisted on public charity or crime. He clarified his position further: ' ... I shall consider the whole of the metropolitan poor under three separate phases, according as they *will* work, they *can't* work, and they *won't* work.'[4] Despite his original intention, however, Mayhew initially focused on the first category, justifying this on the grounds of numbers: 'The people that cannot or will not work, are neither a very various, nor, compared with the artisans and labourers, are they a very numerous class.'[5] Fully three-quarters of the *Morning Chronicle* letters, therefore, dealt with the labouring poor, starting with the Spitalfields silk weavers before considering the dock labourers, coalheavers, shoemakers, clothing workers and woodworkers with briefer discussions of coopers, shipbuilders, seamen, tanners, hat makers and a variety of others involved with transport and distribution.[6] Only later, in his four-volume series, *London Labour and the London Poor*, did Mayhew extend his analysis to cover the other categories of the metropolitan poor.[7]

A reading of Mayhew's output would have convinced most that conditions for the London working class had worsened considerably within living memory. In part, this reflected the purposes underlying his concern with the London poor which led him to consider those activities in which economic decline was most obvious. His intention from the start had been 'to devote myself to the consideration of that class of poor whose privations seemed to be due to the insufficiency of their wages'.[8] For this reason, he ignored several important trades: domestic service, the largest female occupation, received no mention, nor did newer trades, such as engineering, or the better-paid trades, such as printing. Despite these omissions, the trades examined comprised a sizeable proportion of the metropolitan workforce and provide us with a unique opportunity to examine the course and impact of economic change in the years leading up to mid-century.

Standards of living

For many workers interviewed by Mayhew the history of economic decline was still fresh in the memory. Most could recall a time when conditions had been better: when wages were higher, hours of work were shorter and competition was less severe. In some cases the start of the downward slide could be pinpointed with accuracy. For example, sawyers blamed the fall in wages and rising unemployment on the spread of steam machinery from 1826. For tailors it was the disastrous strike of 1834 and subsequent dismantling of their trade union. In other trades the timing was less specific but the trend was nevertheless the same. Carpenters complained about the increasing use of apprentices and the intrusion of 'strapping' masters and 'scamp' work; cabinet makers also condemned large firms for employing excessive numbers of apprentices. Chair makers blamed middlemen and wholesalers, 'slaughterers' as they were known, for screwing down prices. Shoemakers saw growing competition with factory-made shoes in Northampton as a major cause of their distress. Specific circumstances may have differed in each trade but the experiences of decline within living memory were common to all.

These experiences sit uneasily with current knowledge of standards of living in the first half of the nineteenth century. Recent studies broadly agree that real wages rose for much of the period, particularly after 1815 when prices fell faster than money wages.[9] Though some disagreement persists concerning the timing and full extent of the rise, most research concurs that living standards broadly improved for the majority of workers. Yet, if Mayhew's findings are to be believed, many London workers failed to benefit from this general improvement. Paraphrasing the experiences of many, one female waistcoat maker remarked, 'Prices have come down very much indeed since I first worked for the warehouse – *very much* ... The work has not riz, no! never since I worked at it. It's lower'd but it's not riz.'[10] Whether it had 'riz' or not for others is a question that needs to be addressed.

The cost of living

Two recent cost-of-living indices, by Crafts and Mills (CM) and by Phelps Brown and Hopkins (PBH), cover the period in its entirety and provide us with a means of gauging the movement of prices insofar as they affected a bundle of commodities. Both indices are plotted in Figure 3.1.[11] Differences in the weighting of individual items account for the fact that the CM index is consistently lower than the PBH index. Whilst the PBH index gives cereals a weighting of 20 per cent, meat 25 per cent and butter 12.5 per cent, the comparable weights for the CM index are 44 per cent, 11.2 per cent and 4.4 per cent respectively. The CM index also takes account of falls in the cost of clothing brought about by cheaper supplies of cotton and woollen textiles. The PBH index is therefore best regarded as an index for artisans, whilst the CM index is more indicative of the budgets of poorer workers.[12]

Despite these differences both series follow a similar pattern. The cost of living increased sharply during the early years of the Napoleonic Wars, with exceptionally steep rises in 1799–1800 and from 1808 to 1812. Poor harvests in 1811 and again in 1812 forced the price of wheat to rise steeply, reaching a record level of £7 12s. a quarter in August 1812.[13] Thereafter, with the exception of 1816 and 1817, when poor harvests again briefly forced the cost of living to rise, prices fell precipitously and by the early 1820s had returned to their pre-War level. In the second quarter of the century, the cost of living followed a shallow downward course, interrupted briefly by periods of sharply rising prices in the mid-1820s, the late 1830s and the latter 1840s. From mid-century prices again began to rise, reflecting an upturn in economic activity during the years which have come to be known as the 'Great Victorian Boom'.[14]

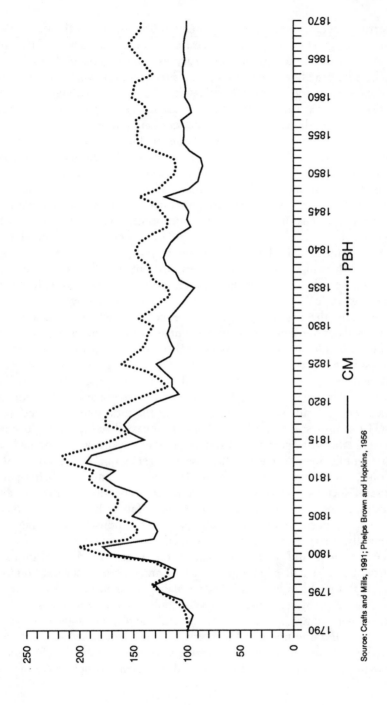

Source: Crafts and Mills, 1991; Phelps Brown and Hopkins, 1956

CM ——— PBH ·········

Figure 3.1 Cost of living, 1790–1870 (1790=100).

Money wages

Charting the course of earnings presents more difficulties than does the cost of living. There is, first, the question of non-monetary additions to the wage. During the eighteenth century, as Peter Linebaugh has shown, workers habitually appropriated perquisites from the workplace as part of their customary income. 'Bugging' for the hatters, 'cabbage' for the tailors, servant's 'vails', 'sweepings' in the docks, carpenters' 'chips' or 'tapping the admiral' amongst the coopers all formed important supplements to money wages. According to Linebaugh, such practices came under sustained attack towards the end of the century resulting in a greater emphasis being placed on the money wage itself as a primary measure of earnings.[15] The fact that industrial disputes during the nineteenth century focused mainly on monetary wages suggests that the importance of customary forms of appropriation had indeed declined. Disputes over quasi-legal forms of pilferage periodically ruffled the surface of industrial relations but these were the exceptions rather than the rule.[16] It is unlikely that perquisites died out completely but without further research we can say little more about the extent to which they continued to form a significant addition to the money wage.

Secondly, there is the question of the extent to which the income of male heads of household was supplemented by the earnings of wives and children. In shoemaking, it was normal for women to work as binders alongside husbands and fathers and the earnings of married men reflected that practice.[17] During the 1840s in St George-in-the-East, the Statistical Society of London discovered that the average weekly earnings of household heads was 19s. 11d. but that the total family income was 23s. 1d. Amongst the poorest paid and most casualized workers, such as carmen, labourers, porters and watermen, the proportion contributed by other family members generally rose to over a quarter of household income, compared with less than 10 per cent amongst better-paid artisans, such as engineers and gun makers.[18] Depending on the trade in question, therefore, the money wages of male family heads alone should be seen as a partial, albeit important, segment of household earnings.

Finally, there is the difficult problem of assessing the impact of unemployment and underemployment on wages. In the notoriously seasonal and casualized labour markets characteristic of several London trades, this problem may have been a major factor influencing workers' earnings. Equally, employment levels could vary considerably within trades, depending on the nature of skill and the balance between unionized and non-unionized workers. Amongst less skilled workers and in the poorly organized sector of trade, where the winds of competition blew most strongly, unemployment and underemployment were higher compared with more skilled workers or those in the better-organized sector of production. In several trades, such as tailoring, shoemaking and furniture making, the problems of unemployment and underemployment worsened as the proportion of skilled and unionized workers declined. Unemployment, and thus by implication the level of earnings, thus depended not only on the state of the economy but also on the changing relationships between skill and trade-union strength.

Setting these problems aside for the time being, information on money wages exists for several London trades. Data for building workers, based on research by Leonard Schwarz, are plotted in Figure 3.2, together with those for compositors and a 'blue collar' index recently produced by Crafts and Mills.[19] Rates of pay for carpenters and bricklayers followed each other closely, primarily because workers from each of these trades laboured side by side and therefore changes in rates of pay in one branch were quickly transmitted to the others. 'If the carpenters were advanced', Thomas Martin told the Select Committee investigating the repeal of the Combination Acts in 1824, 'the bricklayers and plasterers advanced also.'[20] The carpenters also compared themselves with other artisans, including tailors and shoemakers, and their wages were therefore indicative of levels and trends amongst a wider group of skilled workers.[21] Comparison with compositors' wages shown in Figure 3.2 confirms this fact. Moreover, the movement of artisan wages also had implications for those of less skilled workers. The wages of labourers who worked alongside artisans bore a close relationship to those of more skilled workers, generally being about two-thirds their level.[22] In 1845, for example, the daily summer rate for bricklayers and plasterers was 5s.9d. whilst that for labourers was 3s.9d.[23] Movements in the one rate would normally be matched by a similar movement in the other.

The data on money wages plotted in Figure 3.2 reveal three distinct periods of change. First, money wages rose sharply during the tight labour market and inflationary years of the Napoleonic Wars. Writing about London tailors, Francis Place noted at the time:

> From 1777 to 1793 there were few strikes and very little advance in wages. During this period the price of food rose somewhat, but the price of most other necessaries fell and wages were nearly stationary. Soon after the commencement of the war against the French Republic prices rose enormously – and in one of these trades a very numerous trade, a strike took place in 1795 when the weekly wages were raised from twenty two shillings to twenty five shillings. In 1802 another strike raised the wages to twenty seven shillings. In 1807 another strike raised the wages to thirty shillings. In 1810 another strike raised the wages to thirty three shillings, and in 1813 another strike raised the wages to thirty six shillings at which sum they have remained ever since. The journeymen in the other trades

by their strikes raised their wages in similar portion, though not
exactly in the same periods. [24]

After the War money wages fell for several years before stabilizing in the
second quarter of the century. Carpenters' wages, for example, went
from 30s. a week in 1816 to 27s. during the 1820s, only returning to
their former level in the early 1830s at which point they remained for
nearly two decades.[25] Wages were particularly sticky where rates of pay
were regulated by price books, changes in which often involved detailed
and sometimes costly alterations and thus tended to occur at irregular
intervals. In 1837, for example, cabinet makers petitioned for a change
to their price book of 1811, the first time they had done so since it was
first published.[26] Finally, Figure 3.2 shows that all changed from the
1850s. According to Crafts and Mills, the steep wage rises that occurred
in the mid-1850s and late 1860s took money wages for the first time
above levels reached during the Napoleonic Wars. Given that prices over
the same period had fallen by as much as 30 per cent, it appeared that,
from this time on, workers in general were in a position to benefit from
improvements in their standard of living.

Real wages

Current work on real wages in the first half of the nineteenth century
broadly agrees that the trend was unmistakeably upwards, although
debate continues regarding the precise level and timing of the rate of
growth.[27] Inter- and intra-sectoral variations in wage levels complicated
the situation, and regional wage differentials and variations in costs
added a further set of qualifications, but the overall trend is no longer in
serious doubt.[28] As far as London is concerned, data for building workers
and for blue-collar workers in general, as compiled by Crafts and Mills,
provide a basis for plotting real wages as shown in Figure 3.3.[29] Three
main phases stand out. First, during the Napoleonic Wars price rises
more than kept up with any increases in money wages. Indeed, during
the very steep rises of 1799–1801 and 1811–12, real wages fell
appreciably. From 1814 prices fell faster than money wages and real
wages rose accordingly, although any gains that were made have to be
weighed against higher levels of unemployment arising from the
demobilization of large numbers of men and the post-War depression.
Once this had passed, however, the overall trend is gently but firmly
upwards. From about 1850, although prices were starting to increase,
money wages rose faster, thereby laying the basis for real gains in
earnings. Depending on the precise base year chosen, between about
1814 and 1850 artisans' real wages may have risen by at least 50 or 60

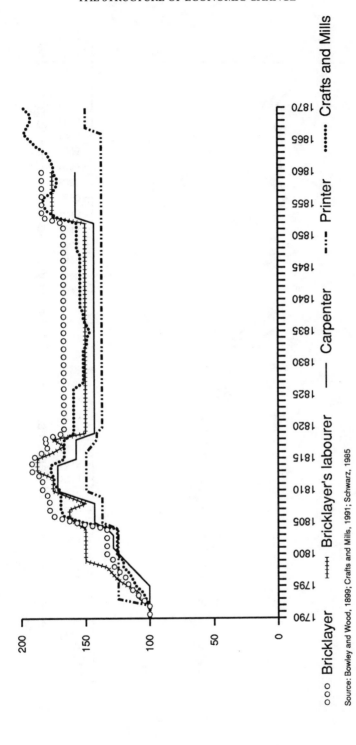

Source: Bowley and Wood, 1899; Crafts and Mills, 1991; Schwarz, 1985

Figure 3.2   Money wages, 1790–1870 (1790=100).

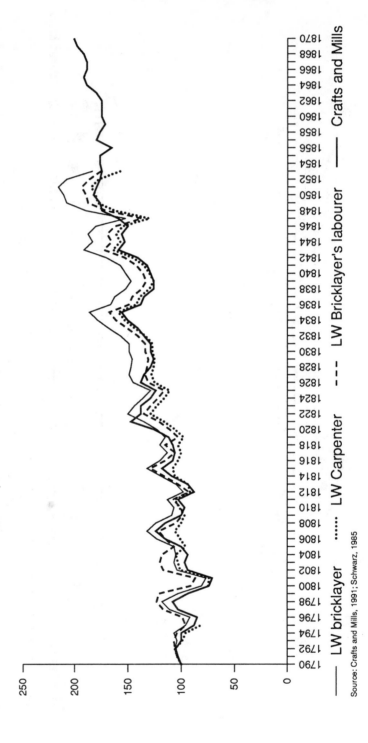

Source: Crafts and Mills, 1991; Schwarz, 1985

Figure 3.3   Real wages, 1790–1870 (1790=100).

per cent.[30] Real wages rose in 33 of the 52 years between 1818 and 1870 and between 1848 and 1870 they rose in all but six.[31] Thus, from the end of the Napoleonic Wars, and particularly after 1850, there are strong grounds for optimism.

Patterns of employment

The trend in real wages sits uneasily with the collective experiences of workers interviewed by Henry Mayhew. In part, this was the inevitable outcome of his focus on the London poor – 'those persons whose incomings are insufficient for the satisfaction of their wants', as he defined them.[32] In part, it was also a function of the timing of his research which, as we discuss below, took place at a period of exceptionally high unemployment. But more significantly it reflected the fact that in the second quarter of the century the labour process in many trades was being restructured in response to falling prices, relatively slow demand and increasing competition. This process of restructuring took various forms but the most common thrust was the replacement of skilled labour by less skilled, primarily through an intensification of the division of labour and the subsequent simplification of tasks. Coloured by these experiences, workers provided Mayhew with a vision of change that was anything but optimistic.

Echoing the views initially expressed by London Chartists in 1848, Mayhew wrote 'In the generality of trades the calculation is that one-third of the hands are fully employed, one-third partially, and one-third unemployed throughout the year.'[33] That such a surplus existed is witnessed by the pattern of unemployment shown in Figure 3.4, based on evidence from the Friendly Society of Bookbinders, the London Cabinet Makers Society and the Friendly Society of Ironfounders.[34] The figures are based on the number of society members in each trade who drew unemployment benefit during a given year. In addition, figures for the cabinet makers also show the proportion of members claiming benefit for at least ten weeks. The data show clearly the severe problems brought about by the 1847–48 depression when unemployment rose to over 30 per cent in each trade. Thus, although unemployment was falling at the time of Mayhew's survey in 1849, the experience of the preceding years was the opposite, with rates mostly higher than they had been during the 1830s and rising sharply for much of the 1840s. Real wages may indeed have been rising, but only for those in work. For the remainder, the situation was less promising.

For this reason, although Mayhew recognized the importance of low wages as a cause of poverty, his focus was elsewhere, notably on the

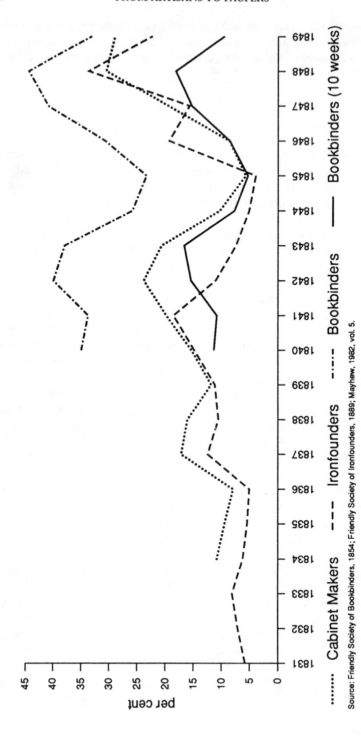

Source: Friendly Society of Bookbinders, 1854; Friendly Society of Ironfounders, 1889; Mayhew, 1982, vol. 5.

Figure 3.4   Unemployment amongst bookbinders, cabinet makers and ironfounders, 1831–1849.

irregularity of work and the 'vast national evil' of casual employment:

> In almost all occupations there is in this country a *superfluity of labourers*, and this alone would tend to render the employment of a vast number of the hands of a casual rather than a regular character ... Hence we see that a surplusage of hands in a trade tends to change the employment of the great majority from a state of constancy and regularity into one of casualty and precariousness.[35]

He blamed this situation on three sets of causes: alterations in the hours, rate of pay or mode of working; an absolute increase in the size of the workforce; and a decrease of work resulting from changes in fashion, seasonal and cyclical fluctuations.[36] Of these main causes, Mayhew argued that the latter was of relatively minor importance and that it was the first two that rendered employment less certain and thus forced down wages. Workers were caught in a vicious spiral of decline. They could only compensate for lower rates of pay by working longer hours but by so doing they merely increased the overall level of competition for employment:

> We find that, as the wages of a trade descend, so do the labourers extend their hours of work to the utmost possible limits ... Not only therefore, does any stimulus to extra production make over-work, and over-work makes under-pay; but under-pay, by becoming an additional provocative to increased industry, again gives rise in its turn to over-work. Hence we arrive at a plain unerring law – *over-work makes under-pay and under-pay makes over-work*.[37]

Once started, the inexorable pressures resulted in a surplus of labour, leading in turn to lower wages and longer hours of work. 'This system of over-work', Mayhew remarked 'is the principal means by which the cheap trade is maintained.'[38]

Competition: the engine of change

Mayhew was not alone in blaming this state of affairs on the growth of competition. Marx also noted how 'The battle of competition is fought by the cheapening of commodities.'[39] It was a battle in which London workers and small masters were, however reluctantly, forced to participate. From Mayhew's first visit to the Spitalfields silk weavers, he noted the regular complaints voiced about the effects of competition. The weavers 'all agreed in referring their misery to the spirit of competition on the part of the masters, the same desire to "cut under"'.[40] One shoemaker told Mayhew, 'Gentlemen run to the lower priced shops', but the same was true in all trades.[41] In bespoke tailoring, honourable West End shops were being crowded out by cheap 'show shops' and 'slop shops', whose owners either had orders made up by outworkers, or who stocked ready-made items produced by sweated tailors and seamstresses in eastern districts. At the start of the century Francis Place boasted that his was the first shop to show goods for sale in the window but by mid-century his example had been copied by many others.[42] By 1844 journeymen tailors in the West End claimed that less than a sixth of employers were 'honourable', or had their work done entirely on the premises, and whilst their number fell in subsequent years, the numbers employed in the 'dishonourable' sector continued to rise.[43] 'Even the first rate houses', Mayhew noted, 'are gradually subsiding into cheap advertising slop tailors.'[44]

Circumstances may have differed between trades but the pressures of competition everywhere were similar. Journeymen shoemakers complained that 'a greater evil than all is the competition among the masters; almost every one, excepting the most respectable of them, is trying to force a trade by underselling the others'.[45] Cabinet makers blamed competition between wholesale 'slaughterhouses' for screwing down rates of pay and increasing the numbers of small garret masters in the trade, particularly in the eastern districts.[46] Although the sawyers complained bitterly about the spread of steam driven sawmills, they too recognized that 'Machinery's very powerful, sir, but competition is much stronger.'[47] In 1831 the carpenters similarly pointed to competitive tendering as the source of their troubles.

> The greatest evil the carpenters have to encounter arises from the baneful system of competition in contracting for buildings, compelling the contractor to estimate at the lowest possible price, and generally his only source of profit is what he can screw out of the labour of his workmen; hence the various attempts at the reduction of wages, and the seeming opposite interests of masters and men.[48]

Those engaged on contracts for public buildings faced the strongest competition and workers in that branch argued that 'competition puts all honourable trade out of the field; high character, and good material, and the best workmanship are of no avail'.[49]

What lay behind the seemingly relentless competitive pressures on manufacturers to lower costs? Undoubtedly, a belief in the iron hand of the market as the arbiter of price was in part responsible. However, we must also be aware of the specificities of time and place and for this we need to cast our minds back briefly to the previous chapters, to the changing relationship between London and the rest of the country brought about by improved communications, to the cyclical fluctuations in prices, and to the nature of production itself.

Throughout the period, improved road and canal transport, and later the spread of the railways, brought London manufacturers into closer competition with cheaper, provincial production. This was particularly true of the finishing trades in which products had a relatively high value in relation to bulk and could therefore absorb the additional costs of transport. Once the corrosive effect of cheaper competition had begun to spread in a trade, all but a small number of honourable masters were forced to concede. Such was the case with silk, watches, and to a lesser extent, shoes and clothing. In each of these trades, cheaper provincial competition was felt with increasing urgency from the early decades of the century. Indeed, provincial competition in the first half of the century was instrumental in hastening the collapse of London silk weaving and watch making. As far as clothing and shoemaking was concerned, the main source of competition came from other London manufacturers. The decline in government orders after the Napoleonic Wars, forced wholesale clothiers and shoemakers in the capital to seek alternative outlets. Attention thus turned to the domestic market and from that time competitive pressures increased. As Mill remarked, '... it is generally found a better speculation to attract a large business by underselling others than merely to divide the field of employment with them'.[50] In London, the primary means of doing so was through savings in labour costs and from this tendency stemmed the growing pressures to restructure production by deskilling the labour process and employing cheaper labour

The restructuring of production

Outside London, savings could be made by restructuring the technological framework of production through what Marx termed the 'deepening' of capital. Although it is now recognized that handicraft work persisted in many branches of production, and mechanization itself spawned new skills, nevertheless the thrust of the factory system, according to Andrew Ure, was to facilitate the division of labour by substituting 'mechanical science for hand skill'. In so doing, 'skilled labour gets progressively superseded, and will, eventually, be replaced by mere overlookers of machines'.[51] In London, however, the handicraft basis of the finishing trades, coupled with the difficulties of establishing factories, militated against such technological restructuring of production. Instead, the main strategy depended on intensifying the division of labour within a relatively static technological framework of production. From this flowed various forms of cost savings and improvements in productivity, including lengthening the hours of work, the introduction of piece work, the spread of subcontracting, the consequent rise of small masters and the growth of sweated labour.

Employers could adopt two general strategies to increase the amount of labour extracted from their workforce. As Marx noted, they could increase the length of the working day without any changes to the labour process itself.[52] Physical and social constraints, however, imposed limitations on the extent to which this strategy could be adopted. At the best of times, hours of work were extremely long. In the first half of the century, most artisans worked about ten hours a day, six days a week. Until the reduction of hours in the 1860s, for example, society carpenters normally worked between 58 and 60 hours a week. Engineers also worked for a similar length of time.[53] In the sweated trades hours of work were even longer. In silk weaving it was not uncommon for workers to remain at their looms from morning to dark, often labouring 14 or 16 hours.[54] Where demand was seasonal, as in clothing, the rush of orders frequently entailed working throughout the night.[55] Under these circumstances, the extent to which any further lengthening of hours was possible was severely restricted, both by the existing intensity of labour, as well as by workers' struggles to control working time.[56]

More productive methods existed of raising the productivity of workers than merely an extension of the hours of labour. Where large workshops or concentrations of workers existed, employers could raise the pace and intensity of work through closer control and supervision. Amongst building firms in which day work was the norm, 'strapping' shops emerged in which workers were encouraged to emulate the efforts of the fastest hands and where talking to fellow workmates was punishable by fines or dismissals.[57] In bookbinding and furniture making workshops, learners or 'improvers' who failed to keep up with the fastest workers were dismissed.[58] The stonemasons complained about the 'chasing system' and showed strong antipathy towards foremen with reputations for strictness.[59] Such strategies, however, could bear fruit in large workshops but elsewhere and in other circumstances different methods were required to improve productivity, most notably, as Smith, Ure and Marx appreciated, an intensification of the division of labour.

The division of labour

In *The Wealth of Nations* Adam Smith begins by stating 'The greatest improvement in the productive powers of labour ... seems to have been the effects of the division of labour.'[60] But whilst the subdivision of tasks increased the dexterity of the worker, and in some cases may even have produced bottlenecks that allowed certain groups of workers to exert greater control over production, it was also a prime means of reducing the overall level of skill. The result, as Marx noted, was a clearer separation between skilled and unskilled work:

> Manufacture begets in every handicraft that it seizes upon, a class of so-called unskilled labourers, a class which handicraft industry strictly excluded. If it develops a one-sided speciality into a perfection, at the expense of the whole of a man's working capacity, it also begins to make a speciality of the absence of all development. Alongside of the hierarchic gradation there steps the simple separation of the labourers into skilled and unskilled. For the latter, the cost of apprenticeship vanishes, for the former it diminishes, in consequence of the functions being simplified. In both cases the value of labour power falls.[61]

In fact, two distinct but related outcomes flowed from the division of labour. Most obviously, subdivision allowed the simplification of tasks and this in turn encouraged the employment of less skilled, and hence cheaper, forms of labour. As Thomas Dunning, the bookbinders' leader, put it in 1856, 'No power on earth can keep wages high when the labour requires but little skill.'[62] Less obviously, however, by subdividing work into component and fairly uniform tasks, piece rates could be introduced and from this originated the pressures on sweated labour. Although by no means new, the spread of piece work was everywhere given fresh impetus by the expanding division of labour and in whichever trade it took hold, opportunities for the exploitation of labour increased accordingly.

Piece work and sweating

'Superintend them as you will', Mayhew wrote, 'day labourers are so much inferior to those who work by the piece, that ... the latter system is practised in all industrial occupations where the work admits of being put out in definite portions.'[63] When the quantity of work determined the level of earnings it was clearly in individual workers' interests to complete as much in as short a time as possible. Consequently piece work encouraged an intensity of effort that was unlikely to occur under hourly or daily rates of pay. For example, after the introduction of piece work in tailoring, Mayhew was told 'Men have more work to do now to get the same amount of money; and the consequence is, fewer hands are employed, and the surplus workmen offer their labour at a lower price.'[64] In turn, any increase in output only served to increase competition within the labour market and so resulted in further downward pressures on wages. By such means, as Mayhew recognized, over-work and under-pay were but two faces of the same coin.

Piece work also provided employers with other opportunities for implementing savings. Since earnings were directly proportional to output, it was no longer necessary to supervise workers. Fines and

deductions for poor quality work or late delivery added further
incentives to complete tasks in a satisfactory manner. In addition,
because piece workers themselves bore the cost of any additional labour,
employers were able to substitute cheaper, inferior materials that were
often harder to work up. In hat making, for example, poor quality
'stuff', to which glue had been added, slowed the pace of work.[65] Tailors
working on piece rates in the slop trade voiced similar complaints in
relation to 'Yorkshire shoddy' or 'devil's dust'. Made from old rags and
thickened with flour, this material was notoriously difficult to work with
and invariably meant longer hours and thus lower earnings.[66] Given this
range of savings to be made by piece work, it was little wonder that
Marx deemed it to be 'the form of wages most in harmony with the
capitalist mode of production'.[67]

Over and above these direct forms of cost cutting, piece work also
encouraged the spread of middlemen and subcontractors whose main
source of profit came from the employment of the cheap forms of labour,
notably widows and the wives and children of casual workers. In 1843
the Royal Commission on children's employment noted 'It is when work
passes through several hands, each of which is to take a share of profits,
while only the last does the work, that the pay which reaches the
workwoman is miserably disproportioned.'[68] This opinion was one that
Mayhew's experiences confirmed: 'Whether he goes by the name of
"sweater", "chamber-master", "lumper", or contractor, it is this *trading
operative* who is the great means of reducing the wages of his fellow
working-men.'[69] Ultimately, of course, the heaviest burden of low pay
and exploitation fell on the shoulders of the cheapest, least skilled and
most vulnerable group of workers, the most ubiquitous of which were
women and children. Needlework was the clearest example of this trend,
but wherever the middleman system occurred it rested on a basis of
sweated, domestic labour. 'Since the increase of the puffing and sweating
system', a tailor noted, 'masters and sweaters have sought everywhere
for such hands as would do the work below the regular ones. Hence the
wife has been made to compete with the husband, and the daughter with
the wife.'[70]

Where small masters undertook production themselves, as opposed to
employing others, levels of self-exploitation were high and lengthy hours
of work the norm. 'If the labourer at piece work is made to produce a
greater quantity than at day-work, and this solely by connecting his
interest with that of his employer', Mayhew noted, 'how much more
largely must the productiveness of workmen be increased when
labouring wholly on their own account!'[71] In many trades, barriers of
skill or the need for capital were low and consequently the opportunities
for becoming a small master were numerous. However, if the promise of

making good turned workers' attention to becoming a small master, many more were pushed into that situation through lack of employment. 'Whenever there's a decrease in wages', Mayhew was told, 'there's always an increase of small masters.'[72] Indeed, the two went hand-in-hand, for as much as low pay encouraged workers to set up for themselves, so the proliferation of small masters increased overall competition for work and was thus instrumental in forcing down general rates of pay.

Unskilled labour

Throughout the *Morning Chronicle* investigation, the contrasts between skilled artisans and unskilled labourers exercised Mayhew's imagination. In seeking to classify labour, he wrote, 'The first great division that naturally presents itself is, according to the skill of the operative, into *artisans* and *labourers* – an artisan being a skilled workman and a labourer an unskilled one.'[73] As strong as the distinction was, skilled handicraft work was everywhere under threat. By the 1840s the 'march of the slop shop capitalists' in tailoring had reduced the number of workers in the bespoke sector by half and increased the proportion of women and children employed.[74] From the 1830s women in large bookbinding workshops were beginning to replace male artisans, and in printing, journeymen were threatened by the employment of excessive numbers of apprentices. In building work, 'green' improvers from the country were supplanting older, London workers. Wherever Mayhew turned less skilled and unskilled labourers were overtopping the barriers, confining artisans to ever shrinking islands of honourable production.

Whilst the pressures to employ unskilled labour were felt in most artisan trades, the nature of cheap labour varied according to specific circumstances. Table 3.1, which outlines the age and sex structure of several of the largest manufacturing trades together with construction, is an attempt to analyse these various experiences. There are numerous problems in using the census in this manner, notably the under-enumeration of women, but in the absence of other forms of evidence we are forced to rely on the figures. Broadly speaking, trades can be divided into those characterized by a relatively high proportion of female workers and those in which male workers predominated, including printing, engineering and the building trades. The former set of trades can be further divided into those in which outwork was common, such as clothing, shoemaking and furniture making, and those workshop trades, including bookbinding and hat making, in which women worked in particular branches of production. In tailoring, male artisans claimed

Table 3.1　Age structure of the labour force, 1851–1871 (per cent)

TRADE	1851				1861				1871			
	M >20	M<20	F>20	F <20	M >20	M<20	F>20	F <20	M >20	M<20	F>20	F <20
Bookbinder	41.2	8.9	32.8	17.2	38.0	9.6	32.5	19.9	36.2	10.5	32.5	20.8
Tailor	65.8	7.2	21.5	5.5	58.5	5.8	28.8	6.9	55.4	6.0	32.1	6.5
Hat maker	63.9	9.1	20.4	6.6	67.2	8.0	19.9	4.9	57.9	8.0	26.1	8.1
Boot and shoemaker	70.1	11.1	14.9	3.9	67.7	10.8	17.3	4.2	77.8	9.1	10.0	3.2
inc. shoemakers wife	52.6	8.3	35.9	3.2	51.6	8.2	36.7	3.5	NA	NA	NA	NA
Cabinet maker/upholsterer	75.4	11.4	12.0	1.2	73.5	12.1	13.6	0.8	73.3	12.1	12.5	2.1
Printer	77.9	22.1	0.0	0.0	71.3	27.7	0.7	0.3	69.6	29.3	0.8	0.4
Engineer	85.7	14.1	0.1	0.0	82.9	17.1	0.0	0.0	86.0	13.8	0.2	0.0
Bricklayer	90.5	9.3	0.2	0.0	90.4	9.6	0.0	0.0	90.7	9.3	0.0	0.0
Carpenter	90.1	9.7	0.2	0.0	90.0	10.0	0.0	0.0	90.3	9.5	0.1	0.0
Painter, lumber, glazier	89.7	10.1	0.2	0.0	89.1	10.5	0.3	0.0	89.2	10.4	0.3	0.1

Source: Census, 1851, 1861, 1871

that large numbers of women and children had entered the trade from the 1830s and 1840s after the introduction of piece work.[75] Table 3.1 shows that by 1851 women accounted for over a quarter of the workforce, but by 1871 this proportion had risen to nearly 39 per cent. Shoemakers voiced similar concerns. One worker interviewed by Mayhew expressed it thus: 'A man's own children will soon be the means of driving him from the market altogether, or compelling him to come down to their rate of wages.'[76] Even in the honourable sectors of shoemaking, it was so common for wives to be employed alongside their husbands that in 1851 and 1861 the census recorded their occupation as 'shoemaker's wife', a practice which the 1871 census unfortunately discontinued and which therefore makes comparison impossible.

In hat making women were used in two distinct branches of manufacture. Where fur was used – initially beaver but by mid-century more commonly rabbit or hare – women performed the dirty task of cleaning the skins.[77] In silk hat making, they sewed the lining and bound the body of the hat to the rim, tasks which again were associated with women's domestic role.[78] Since both tasks were traditionally considered to be 'women's work', male artisans had few objections to their employment. Of more concern amongst society hat makers was the employment of 'foul' men, those who had not served a correct term of apprenticeship and who were thus refused admission to the union, and disputes over this issue were not uncommon. In bookbinding, the production process itself demanded little strength and certain tasks, such as collating and sewing the pages, again linked well with the domestic roles of women.[79] From the 1830s, in conjunction with the spread of machinery, large numbers of women as well as girl 'learners' and young male apprentices began to supplant adult male artisans. The figures for bookbinding shown in Table 3.1 confirm the rapidity of this process. In 1851 women comprised over half the workforce, of which more than one in four was aged below 20 years. By 1871 the age structure had shifted still further in favour of learners and apprentices and nearly one in three of those employed were juveniles aged below 20 years. There was perhaps no clearer example of the feminization of work than this.

By contrast, in the male-dominated workshop trades, the threat from cheap labour came not from women but from the excessive number of boy apprentices. The situation was most pronounced in printing, where frequent disputes occurred over the employment of apprentices.[80] Despite repeated efforts by journeymen to restrict the numbers employed, the census evidence in Table 3.1 shows that over the period the proportion of workers aged below 20 rose and by 1871 accounted for nearly one in three of those employed in printing. In engineering the situation was less pronounced and until self-acting machinery lowered required levels of skill, the position of journeymen engineers was relatively secure.[81]

The final group of trades examined in Table 3.1 refers to the building trades and here again the pattern was different. Building required physical strength as well as a certain degree of skill, and although lads and apprentices had become more common by the 1840s, adult improvers from the country provided the main source of cheap labour. After having served their apprenticeship, it had been common for carpenters from rural areas to visit London for one or two years to improve their skills. By the late 1840s, however, Mayhew was told that 'not one in twelve who come to town from the country ever return'.[82] Such 'improvers' were frequently used to replace older London workers. especially in strapping shops where it was said that the 'masters best like strong hearty fellows from the country as improvers'.[83] For this reason the census figures fail to distinguish any significant shifts in either the age or sex structure of the workforce compared with those of the other trades discussed above. The picture of stability, however, was illusory, as workers' experiences testified.

Conclusion

In recent years, we have witnessed significant revisions to our interpretation of the Industrial Revolution. We can no longer accept that the process of industrialization was a simple case of the transition from handicraft production to a highly capitalized factory system.[84] The fact that during the nineteenth century relatively few workers were fully proletarianized factory employees, and the continued existence, even expansion, of simpler, handicraft processes alongside the more technologically advanced factory system, has forced historians to reconsider the classical interpretation of British industrialization.[85] As a means of raising output, mechanization is now seen as only one of a number of means of redeploying capital and labour. Other, less technologically-based strategies existed, notably the subdivision of work and the intensification of the division of labour, and it is these with which we are most concerned.

The fragmentation of work and the development of small-scale manufacturing reached its utmost limits in nineteenth-century London. Whilst this has been interpreted in the past as indicating the backwardness of metropolitan manufacturing, the very opposite may have been closer to the truth.[86] Instead of factory-based industrialization, the pattern in the capital was for a significant intensification of the division of labour accompanied by the proliferation of small masters. To some extent this was the result of the inherent difficulties associated with fixed capital investment in the city. This was not to say that large employers were absent. Indeed, as we saw in Chapter 2, in several trades large firms were extremely important both in terms of production *per se* as well as the organization of extensive webs of subcontracting. The main trend in the redeployment of capital and labour in London, however, was towards a profound transformation in the relations of production within the existing technological framework of manufacturing, focusing on changes in the division of labour, levels of skill, the nature of the wage and the organization of production.

We should certainly not underestimate either the extent to which improvements in productivity or savings in the costs of manufacture could derive from these seemingly small changes to the labour process. As Mayhew perceptively observed:

> Whenever the operative unites in himself the double function of capitalist and labourer, making up his own raw materials or working on his own property, his productiveness single-handed is considerably greater than can be attained under the large system of production, where all the arts and appliances of which extensive capital can avail itself are brought into operation.[87]

Nor should we assume that this system somehow represented a pre-industrial pattern of production. On the contrary, as well as being immensely productive, small-scale units of employment were inherently flexible, and those involved were able to respond quickly to sudden shifts in demand. In an exceptionally fluid market, in which the foibles of fashion and novelty were of paramount importance, it was essential to avoid the rigidities inherent in large-scale factory production and London's consumer trades exhibited this tendency *par excellence*.

Such changes were driven forward by the relentless pressure of competition that pitted London masters against cheaper provincial and foreign producers, and West End manufacturers against sweated East End wholesalers. In a world of cheap goods, the availability of equally cheap labour was essential and nowhere was this more so than in London where labour costs were high. The importance of competition was not lost on contemporaries and certainly not on those artisans who found themselves threatened by the flood of unskilled workers drawn into employment by virtue of the growing division of labour and consequent simplification of the labour process. From the 1820s, the chill blast of competition blew through the metropolitan trades with greater frequency and rising ferocity. Though Mayhew could argue at mid-century that custom still guided the fortunes of society men whilst competition dictated the earnings of the rest, in reality the balance had shifted decisively in favour of the latter. Writing in 1848, John Stuart Mill was surely closer to the truth in arguing 'Competition ... must be regarded, in the present state of society, as the principal regulator of wages, and custom or individual character only as a modifying circumstance, and that in comparatively slight degree.'[88] The conflicts that this shift entailed are the subject of the next chapter.

Notes

1. Ludlow, 1850, p.1.
2. See PP 1856 XIII *SC on masters and operatives*, q. 972.
3. Thompson, 1968, p.276; see Himmelfarb, 1984, pp.312–23; Humphreys, 1977; Thompson, 1967b; *idem.*, 1973, pp.9–55; Yeo, 1973, pp.56–109.
4. Mayhew, 1980, vol. 1, p.40.
5. Mayhew, 1982, vol. 5, p.188.
6. For a full listing see Thompson and Yeo, 1973, pp.581–3.
7. The first two volumes were mainly reprints of a weekly series published in 1851–52 under the title *London Labour and the London Poor*. Volumes 1 and 2 dealt mainly with street traders whilst volume 3 included material from the *Morning Chronicle* letters together with sections on street entertainers and those involved in transport. The final volume was written in collaboration with Rev. William Tuckniss, Bracebridge Hemyng, John Binny and Andrew Halliday and concentrated on charitable agencies and those who refused to work. The four volumes of *London Labour and the London Poor* finally appeared in 1861–62.
8. Mayhew, 1980, vol. 1, p.51.
9. For a summary of recent research see Scholliers, 1989; Crafts and Mills, 1991.
10. Mayhew, 1980, vol. 1, pp.121–2.
11. The CM index is a composite series consisting of the revised Lindert and Williamson cost of living index for the period 1790 to 1850, together with Bowley's figures for 1851 to 1870. See Crafts and Mills, 1991, p.7; Lindert and Williamson, 1983, pp.8–11; *idem.*, 1985, pp.148–50; Phelps Brown and Hopkins, 1981, p.14; Williamson, 1985, p.210.
12. Schwarz, 1992, p.172.
13. Gayer, Rostow and Schwarz, 1953, vol. 1, p.115.
14. See Church, 1975.
15. Linebaugh, 1993, pp.330, 404–41.
16. In 1813, for example, 46 tailors employed by an army clothier were accused of robbing cloth by using various illicit methods to increase its weight, including soaking in urine, thereby allowing them to retain a portion of it for their own use. Evidently, the practice was widespread. See *St James Chronicle*, 16–19, 19–21 October 1813.
17. *Operative*, 25 November 1838.
18. Statistical Society, 1848a, pp.200–1.
19. The figures are taken from Bowley and Wood, 1899; Schwarz, 1985; Crafts and Mills, 1991.
20. PP 1824 V *SC on artizans and machinery*, p.166.
21. *ibid.*, p.180.
22. Hobsbawm, 1960, p.116.
23. Skyring, 1845.

24. Place Coll. Add. Ms. 27834, fol. 108. The pattern of strikes most closely fits tailoring, a trade with which Place was very familiar, having himself been a leather breeches maker and small master in his own right.
25. Place Coll. Add. Ms. 27799, fol. 124; PP 1833 VI *SC on manufactures, commerce and shipping*, q.1665–67; PP 1840 XXII *RC on the handloom weavers: report from the assistant handloom commissioners*, part 2, p.119; Jones, 1851–52, vol. 2, p.542; Webb Coll. E, ser. A, vol. X, fol. 126; *idem.,* vol. XI, fol. 110.
26. *London Mercury*, 5 February 1837.
27. See Flinn, 1974; Tunzelman, 1979; Crafts, 1985; Lindert and Williamson, 1983; *idem.,* 1985.
28. See Crafts, 1982; Hunt, E.H., 1986; see also Scholliers, 1989.
29. Crafts and Mills, 1991.
30. The debate about real wages during the Industrial Revolution continues. For recent estimates of gains during th period see Crafts, 1985, p.143; Crafts and Mills, 1991, pp.27–8; Lindert and Williamson, 1983, pp.11–13; *idem.,* 1985; Scholliers, 1989.
31. These figures are based on the series in Crafts and Mills, 1991.
32. Mayhew, 1980, vol. 1, p.40.
33. Mayhew, 1968, vol. 2, pp.300–30. See *Northern Star (NS)* 29 April 1848.
34. *Bookbinders' Trade Circular*, September 1854, pp.198–9; Mayhew, 1982, vol. 5, p.138; *Friendly Society of Ironfounders*, 1889, p.4. The latter figures refer to national rates of unemployment whilst the former two are based on London alone. In 1865 London had a total of 350 members belonging to the ironfounders union, the largest single membership but still only three per cent of total membership.
35. Mayhew, 1968, vol. 2, pp.300–1.
36. *ibid.,* p.301.
37. *ibid.,* pp.303–4.
38. *ibid.,* p.302.
39. Marx, 1954, vol. 1, p. 586
40. Mayhew, 1980, vol. 1, p.59.
41. *ibid.,* 1981, vol. 3, p.142.
42. Place, 1972, p.201.
43. Mayhew, 1981, vol. 2, p.123.
44. *ibid.,* p.86.
45. *ibid.,* 1981, vol. 3, pp.127, 130.
46. *ibid.,* 1982, vol. 5, pp.164, 174–5
47. *ibid.,* vol. 5, p.81
48. *Poor Man's Guardian*, 17 September 1831; see Cooney, 1955.
49. Mayhew, 1981, vol. 5, p.107.
50. Mill, 1976, p.246.
51. Ure, 1835, p.20.
52. Marx, 1954, vol. 1, pp.476–85.
53. Jones, 1851–52, vol. 2, p.541; Webb Coll. E, series A, vol. 10, fol. 126; PP 1840 XXIII *Reports from the assistant handloom commissioners*, part 2, p.124; Jeffereys, M. and J.B., 1947, p.32
54. PP 1843 XIV *RC on children's employment*, pp.831–2; *General Convention of the Industrious Classes*, 1839, fol. 3–18, British Library Additional Manuscript 34245.
55. See *Pioneer*, 10 May 1834.

56. See Chapter 5, pp.125–7.
57. Mayhew, 1982, vol. 5, p.103.
58. *Appeal of the Journeymen Bookbinders*, 1849, p.3; Marx, 1954, vol. 1, p.518.
59. *NS*, 23, 30 October 1841; Place Coll. vol. 53, p.7.
60. Smith, 1974, p.109.
61. Marx, 1954, vol. 1, p.331.
62. PP 1856 XIII *SC on masters and operatives*, q. 2179.
63. Mayhew, 1968, vol. 2, p.303.
64. Mayhew, 1981, vol. 2, p.79.
65. PP 1824 V *SC on artizans and machinery*, p.96.
66. *NS*, 9 December 1843.
67. Marx, 1954, vol. 1, p.520.
68. Quoted in Marx, 1954, vol. 1, p.519.
69. Mayhew, 1968, vol. 2, p.329.
70. Mayhew, 1981, vol. 2, p.8.
71. Mayhew, 1968, vol. 2, p.303.
72. Mayhew, 1982, vol. 5, p.192.
73. *ibid.*, 1981, vol. 3, p.189.
74. *ibid.*, 1968, vol. 2, pp.74–5.
75. *ibid.*, 1968, vol. 2, pp.79–80, 98–9.
76. *ibid.*, 1981, vol. 3, p.128.
77. Dodd, 1843, pp.141–3.
78. Mayhew, 1982, vol. 6, pp.156–7.
79. Hunt, 1986, pp.73–5.
80. Howe, 1947, pp.298–303.
81. Crossick, 1978, p.78. The spread of machine tools from the 1830s also resulted in significant changes in the utilization of labour. See Burgess, 1969, pp.225–30.
82. Mayhew, 1982, vol. 5, p.84.
83. *ibid.*, vol. 5, pp.84–5, 102, 112 .
84. See Berg, 1985, pp.69–91; *idem.*, 1993, pp.17–20; Sabel and Zeitlin, 1985; Tilly, 1983.
85. Samuel, 1977, pp.17–21.
86. This is the view expressed by Jones, 1971, p.26.
87. Mayhew, 1968, vol. 3, p.227.
88. Mill, 1976, p.343.

CHAPTER FOUR

Association and solidarity: structures of artisan resistance

Artisans and labourers

In comparison with other cities, London's working-class population was extraordinarily diverse. The heterogeneity of its population, the immense variety of trades, the fragmentation of occupations and geographical differences between localities collectively ensured that a complex pattern of social stratification existed within the metropolitan working class. As John Parker noted in 1853, 'The working classes are composed of strata, differing in appearance and density, yet imperceptibly gliding into and blending with each other.'[1] However, a fundamental distinction also existed between skilled artisans, and less skilled and unskilled labourers. For Mayhew the distinction was based on education and skill: 'An artisan is an educated handicraftsmen, following a calling that requires an apprenticeship of greater or lesser duration ... whereas a labourer's occupation needs no education whatever.'[2] The distinction, however, was more than just a question of education and manual dexterity, for the possession of skill provided artisans with a degree of control over the labour process, and hence power at the workplace, that was absent or at best relatively weak amongst labourers. In turn, such control provided the basis upon which to establish structures of solidarity that buttressed artisans' position, including associations linked to the workplace, community, house of call, friendly society and trade union. It is with these forms of association we are concerned together with the ideological framework within which they operated.

For those groups without a strong basis of skill, notably women, domestic workers and the huge army of casual labourers, control at the workplace was more difficult, though not impossible, to achieve. Workers were more isolated, employment was less secure and earnings lower and less certain. Accordingly, the ability to erect associational structures of resistance was more limited. Suspicion on the part of artisans also meant that for much of the period such workers were excluded from craft unions. Only from the late 1860s did artisans recognize that their interests were best served by incorporating less skilled workers into a more general union of the trade, and not until the

1880s did unionization of the unskilled attain any significant proportions. Until that time, unskilled workers remained largely outside the formal structures of unionism and trade association and as such were in a far weaker position to protect themselves against the competitive pressures of industrial capitalism.

Our focus, then, is on the nature of association and solidarity amongst London artisans. This is not to deny the significance of labourers in the metropolitan economy; indeed, the reverse holds true. It is, however, to recognize the centrality of skilled workers in erecting formal structures of resistance to cushion the impact of industrial capitalism. It is also to appreciate both the quantitative and qualitative importance of artisans within the metropolitan working class. Dorothy George's estimate of 100,000 in the early 1800s is near enough to the 1831 census total of over 130,000 handicraft workers to suggest that both figures are close to the truth.[3] By 1848, if the estimate of the Chartist convention held in London was correct, the number of artisans and mechanics, 'that is persons working at trades', had risen to 200,000, comprising a sizeable proportion of the male workforce.[4] Though not all would have necessarily been involved in houses of call, trade unions and friendly societies, they nevertheless shared an identity of interests based on the preservation of skilled status at the workplace. Furthermore, the level of artisan wages also had implications for the earnings of the labourers with whom they worked and their success of the struggles thus acted as a barometer for the fortunes of a far wider set of workers in the capital.

Artisan ideology

Two broad strands of artisan resistance to the impact of industrial capitalism can be discerned. The most immediate concerned those struggles over wages and conditions of employment that periodically disrupted relations between capital and labour. We should not assume, however, that because such resistance focused on the workplace the issues were confined to there alone. To do would be to denude artisan consciousness of any wider role than just a concern for the bread-and-butter questions of wages and working conditions. Those who have studied working-class radicalism have pointed out that artisan ideology embraced a far wider conception of the role and status in society of skilled workers that sought to establish links between workplace issues and the wider political sphere.[5] As Mayhew pointed out, 'The artisans are almost to a man red-hot politicians ... They are sufficiently educated and thoughtful to have a sense of their importance in the State.'[6] Thus, trade union leaders, such as John Gast of the shipwrights and William

Lovett of the cabinet makers, were also active in wider forms of working-class radicalism, and thoughts of political representation or the legitimacy of existing political structures were rarely far from their minds. Many of the Chartist leaders in London were similarly involved in trade unions.[7] To divorce workplace disputes from the wider social and political contexts in which they occurred, therefore, is to run the risk of simplifying the nature of the industrial conflicts. Such disputes were not purely about wages and conditions of employment but were also imbued with a sense of artisan custom and legitimacy that elevates them to a more central role in understanding the relationships between the working class and wider society.[8]

The question of wages and unemployment provides a good example of the ways in which links between the workplace and the wider political sphere were forged. According to the wage fund theory of bourgeois political economy, wages were paid directly from capital and thus higher wages meant lower profits and greater unemployment. The underconsumptionist argument favoured by artisans was entirely the opposite, namely that broader economic prosperity depended directly on the payment of higher wages since only that would encourage higher levels of consumption. Low wages, on the other hand, were blamed for underconsumption and this in turn was seen as the explanation for cyclical crises of overproduction that were ultimately responsible for higher unemployment. Therefore, anything that lowered real wages, such as inflation or high taxation, or indeed competition with cheaper workers brought about by *laissez faire* policies, was viewed not merely as a threat to living standards but also as factors responsible for general economic downturns and unemployment.[9]

From that perspective it was but a short step for artisans to lay the blame for downturns on unrepresentative government as well as undercutting masters; the former for the imposition of high taxes, and the latter for reducing wages and thus fostering underconsumption. In terms of wages and employment, two aspects with which we are especially concerned, this ideological framework provided artisans with a clear means of identifying the links between their own standard of living and the lack of working-class political representation. To divorce struggles over wages and conditions from the fight over political representation is thus to draw a false separation between labour disputes and working-class radicalism.

In addition to this shared ideological framework, artisans also participated in a common lifestyle that encompassed the workplace, community and the home. First, earnings had to be sufficient for skilled workers and their families to remain independent from charity and the poor law. Money was also needed for membership of friendly societies, trade unions, savings clubs and burial societies, all of which to some extent cushioned workers from the vagaries of the market and the impact of unemployment, illness or death. Secondly, wages had to be sufficient to allow male artisans to support their families without the need for their wives to work. Over and above any considerations of patriarchal family relations, this was important because artisans recognized the threat women posed to male employment, particularly in trades such as tailoring and shoemaking.[10] For this reason, male earnings had to be sufficient to make it unnecessary for wives and children to work.

For similar reasons, artisans placed great emphasis on customary rates of pay as opposed to those dictated by market forces. In terms of payment, Mayhew remarked 'The wages of "society men" are regulated by custom; those of non-society men, however, are determined by competition. It is the competitive men who are invariably the cheap workers, and the prey of the slop seller of every trade.'[11] Whilst we may question, along with Mill, the proportion of the workforce at mid-century that still derived their income according to notions of custom, nevertheless the concept was important by virtue of the emphasis it placed on independence and the continued ability to participate in the associational structures of artisan life.

Finally, artisans had to be able to demonstrate their independence from employers, both within and beyond the workplace. Traditions of conviviality were normally lubricated by drink and any who wished to participate in the inner life of a workshop had to be in a position to foot the bill for beer.[12] Similarly, artisans demonstrated their independence from the pressing need to work through keeping trade holidays and the preservation of 'St Monday'.[13]

Artisans consistently sought to protect themselves by a variety of means against unbridled competition and free-wage bargaining. By the early 1800s paternalist regulation of wages had virtually ceased, a situation formally confirmed in 1813 by the repeal of earlier wage-fixing legislation. But even before that time groups of workers had negotiated wages directly with employers and agreed price lists operated in several trades, including building, cabinet making, clothing, coopering, printing, shoemaking, shipbuilding, and tin plating.[14] In several cases these price books were complex and expensive to produce. The tailors' log of 1810, for example, covered over 150 items whilst the cabinet makers' price book ran to over 600 pages and took between two and three years to produce.[15] Newspaper compositors had a pay scale that took account of different groups of workers and provided 'full hands' a weekly minimum level of earnings based on a stipulated amount of work. When book publishing and newspaper printing became specialized trades in their own right in the early 1800s, the scales were renegotiated to take account of the changing circumstances.[16] Unless forced to change by sharp fluctuations in prices, technological transformation of production, or by the introduction of new items – always a problem in the fashion trades – the difficulties and expense of amending such complex lists meant that the rates agreed with employers often persisted for lengthy periods and thus took on the mantle of a customary agreement.[17]

Custom, however, extended beyond the immediate context of wages to embrace a wider set of workplace issues. Thus, entry to the trade, including the regulation of apprentices and enforcement of the closed shop, together with the regulation of hours of work, materials and privileges, were also part of a set of accepted practices, the alteration of any one of which was grounds for complaint. Each issue had implications both for the level of wages and the status of artisans. Apprenticeship, for example, was essential for controlling entry to a trade and thus was patently important in influencing the level of wages. In addition, however, it was also the period during which boys learned the customs of a trade. Thus, attacks on apprenticeship not only reflected employers' attempts to widen their choice of workers but also represented a distinct threat to the continuity of trade customs. Custom, therefore, had wider implications than just that relating to wages and was of broader significance for the nature of artisan society as a whole.

The structures of artisan resistance

Whilst the ideological framework constructed by artisans was important in legitimating their social status in society and at the workplace, the associational structures they erected to protect themselves against the impact of industrial capitalism were of equal significance. These structures operated at varying scales, spreading outwards from the workplace and community to embrace wider regional and national spheres of activity. Participation in these wider spheres rested on membership of various forms of working-class institutions, ranging from the house of call to friendly societies, trade unions and political associations. Here our analysis is concerned with those institutions directly concerned with protecting wages and conditions of employment, focusing on the roles of community and workplace, the house of call, friendly societies and trade unions.

Workplace and community

For artisans, the workshop was the main focus of economic and social life and the primary point of resistance to industrial capitalism. In

London, workshops often employed no more than five or ten persons, and even where the size of employment units was larger, as amongst general builders for instance, the workgroup itself was often relatively small.[18] Whilst such fragmentation of workplaces and workgroups may have created difficulties in relation to forging a wider class consciousness, at a local level it meant that close-knit relations between workers were able to develop and adherence to artisan norms was therefore easier to implement. Where the closed shop was enforced, such as amongst the hatters in the early 1800s, none but 'fair' men could be employed, and those who had not served an apprenticeship or who refused to join a union were shunned. Kinship often added to the cohesiveness of such groups, especially where boys were apprenticed to their fathers. The range of informal borrowing and lending, coupled with the comradeship of the workgroup, also helped reinforce the social ties of those who worked in close proximity for lengthy periods of time. Each link bound members of the workgroup closer together and helped to forge a strong, cohesive social unit based closely around the workplace.[19]

Ultimately, of course, the norms of artisan society could be enforced by coercion and those who offended stood the risk of being ostracized from the community or else suffer physical attack. In 1804, for example, hat makers at Wall's factory in Southwark, struck against the employment of a man called Kiernan, whom they accused of breaking the rules of the trade. The ringleaders were arrested and at their trial it was revealed that:

> The journeymen hat-makers had established a system of bye-laws, and to compel observance of which they had contrived a sort of practical 'Round Robin' or 'Garrat Match' ... If an individual in a manufactory disobeyed them, the Master was either obliged to turn him off, or they would all forsake their engagement. Any man changing his Master must have a certificate from this fraternity; if a Master received him without a certificate 'of his cleanliness', all the other men were to forsake this new Master, until he had got rid of this 'foul man'.[20]

William Lovett faced similar problems when he was employed at a cabinet maker's without having served a formal apprenticeship. Fellow workers talked of 'setting Mother Shorney' at him, a cant term for being such a nuisance as to drive the offending person from the workshop.[21] Others were less fortunate, especially during disputes when feelings were running high, and 'scabs' or 'knobsticks' were often the subject of threats or attack. In 1867, during a lengthy and bitter dispute amongst West End tailors, journeymen picketed their own workshops to ensure that no one entered without their knowledge. Those who did were followed home by strikers, remonstrated with and on occasions they were attacked.[22]

Intimidation and assault, frequently of those within the same community, were thus not uncommon means of enforcing compliance with acceptable codes of behaviour.

In many ways the organizational structures of artisan life meshed imperceptibly with working-class residential communities. The pub, house of call, friendly society and trade unions were primarily local institutions that reinforced the close spatial links between workplace and home. Not until later in the century, when cheap public transport and shorter hours allowed workers to live at a distance from their place of work, were those links broken.[23] The close confines of working-class communities are well illustrated by the spatial world inhabited by Francis Place, mapped out in Figure 4.1. From the time of his marriage in 1791, until 1801, Place and his family moved eight times, eventually taking a shop at 16 Charing Cross, where they remained until their final move in 1833 to Brompton. At no point until this last move did the family live more than about a kilometre from St Clement Danes church, the place from which they started.

Nor was Place's pattern of residential mobility in any way unusual.

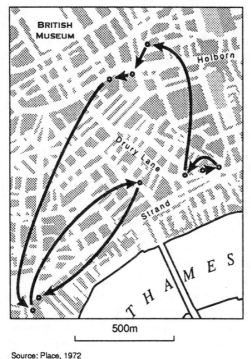

Source: Place, 1972

Figure 4.1   The spatial world of Francis Place, 1791–1833.

Even amongst the very poor, long-term stability in an area was more common than contemporaries appreciated. For example, over half the paupers who applied for poor relief to St Giles between 1832 and 1862 had resided in the union for longer than five years, and nearly 40 per cent had been there over ten years.[24] For these unskilled and casual workers, localized social networks were of even greater importance. The provision of credit by local shopkeepers, links with kin and a host of other formal and informal ties tied the urban poor, no less than skilled artisans, to specific localities. Amongst casual labourers being known was a prerequisite for getting work, and being near to hand when the opportunity arose was essential. News of work was shared in pubs, on street corners and in courtyards. Drink often lubricated the channels of information. In the docks, for example, publicans doubled as recruiting agents, gaining custom in return for providing employment. Being known by the contractor or sweater was similarly important for outworkers in the slop sector of clothing and local shopkeepers often put up the security needed by workers before they were entrusted with cloth. More formal ties concerning poor relief also existed. Until 1846, in order to receive poor relief other than an overnight stay in a casual ward, the poor had to have a settlement in a union or face the possibility of being removed. Even after this threat was lifted, non-settled poor had to have resided for five continuous years in a union in order to be eligible for relief.[25] Thus, although the length of residence at any one address may have been relatively short, it was not common for the working-class to reside in a locality for lengthy periods of time.[26] In this manner, structures of information and assistance were highly localized and reinforced the role of the neighbourhood in working-class life.

The significance of these patterns of residential mobility and persistence was that the working-class community overlapped closely with that of the workplace. For example, between 1855 and 1877 more than a quarter of the permanent workforce employed by Henry Poole of Savile Row, the foremost bespoke tailor in London, lived within one kilometre of the workshop. Not until the 1890s was this close link between work and home broken.[27] The marked localization of trades further acted to reinforce the close links between work and residence. Propinquity thus provided a local setting for the construction of dense, social networks in which neighbours and fellow workers were one and the same. Those who offended against the trade, by refusing to join the union, for example, or acting as a blackleg, ran the risk of alienating both workmates and neighbours alike. This pattern of residential propinquity had much to do with the solidarity of working-class communities, and specifically with the close associational life of artisans.

Houses of call

Whilst the workplace and community functioned at the scale of a neighbourhood, the trade house of call operated at a slightly different spatial level. Within a given locality, groups of workers meeting in a house of call coordinated the activities of artisans from several workshops and acted as the point of contact within the system of tramping that developed amongst the artisan trades. In terms of the immediate locality, the house of call, which usually met in a public house, had several functions: it operated as an informal labour exchange, a place to debate matters relating to the trade and to seek support beyond the immediate confines of the workplace, and most significantly, it functioned as a node within the wider framework of trade unionism.[28] It was in such places that subscriptions would be collected for the support of the sick and infirm, or more informally workers would pass round a hat for colleagues in distress. But equally, it was there that strikes were coordinated or sanctions decided upon against recalcitrant masters or blackleg workers.

As an informal labour exchange, the house of call was a central feature of the day-to-day running of the trade. It was common amongst the tailors' houses of call to hold one, two or sometimes three books containing the names of those who were seeking work, often in order of seniority or length of residence in London. When sent for by an employer, workers were obliged to attend within a specified time on pain of a fine and hence had to live in close proximity.[29] Meanwhile, masters who tried to circumvent this system by employing non-society workers stood the risk of provoking a strike. The bookbinders had two houses of call and operated a similar system. In each, a book was kept with the names of employers in need of workmen and this was open for inspection to any member either authorized by the trade committee or who could produce a working ticket to prove his membership of the union. If a landlord permitted others to see the book, he risked losing the custom of the society.[30]

The rules of the house of call also sought to regulate the quality of workmanship. Amongst the tailors, for example, the committee directed the nature and amount of work members should do, each man being obliged to do a quantity in a 'workmanlike manner' as measured by the amount that could be performed by an ordinary hand in a 12-hour day. Should a journeyman's work fall below an acceptable standard on three occasions, membership of the house of call could be revoked.[31] Whilst this stipulation ensured that the relationship between employers and the house of call was reciprocal, it also ensured that none but skilled workers could become members, thereby offering further protection for artisans against the threat posed by those with less skill.

The extent to which the trades maintained a network of houses of call varied but in several cases it was extensive. In 1818, the tailors had upwards of 30 'flint' houses, frequented by journeymen paid day wages, and a further nine or ten 'dung' houses, for those paid by the piece.[32] The shoemakers probably had a similar number: in 1824 there were at least five meeting houses for the 600 or so 'society' men in the City and at least the same number, if not more, in the West End.[33] In 1861, when the *First Trades' Union Directory* was published under the auspices of the London Trades Council, 36 shoemakers' meeting houses were recorded, most of which met on Mondays.[34] The carpenters had an even more extensive network with 45 meeting houses scattered across the city, again mostly meeting on a Monday. In total, the *Directory* listed 233 public houses in which trades met on a regular basis, with many hosting meetings of different trades on various days of the week.[35]

Houses of call were pivotal in the wider organization of trade unionism both in London and elsewhere. Amongst the tailors, whose system Francis Place considered to have been 'the most perfect of any', delegates from each house were elected to a committee of the trade, often 'by a kind of tacit consent frequently without its being known to a very large majority who is chosen'.[36] This committee, known as the 'Town', was responsible for negotiating prices with employers and organizing disputes and its decisions were passed speedily through the delegates to their respective houses of call. The hatters had a similar arrangement, though their meeting was known as the 'Congress'.[37] In calling upon magistrates to refuse licenses to publicans who permitted combinations of workmen or political debating clubs to meet on their premises, Patrick Colquhoun made clear his understanding of the role that houses of call played in the wider sphere of working-class radicalism and trade unionism.[38] His views were shared by others. In 1800, exasperated by a dispute with their journeymen, master tailors demanded that magistrates revoke the licences of publicans who allowed houses of call to operate:

> That these houses of call are the very basis and foundation of such combinations is unquestionably the fact ... so long as these Societies or rather houses of call are kept up, it will be impossible for the masters ever to be secure from the combinations of their men.[39]

During the shoemakers' dispute of 1804, George Hoby, chairman of the masters' committee in the City, similarly called for magistrates to close public houses in which strikers met.[40] Not surprisingly, when the tailors' strike of 1834 was defeated, one of the first actions taken by employers was to replace the house of call system with one controlled by the employers and shorn of all trade union connections.[41] Perhaps this was the reason why none appeared in the *First Trades' Union Directory* of 1861.

Friendly societies and trade unions

Sickness, death, old age and unemployment were common experiences in working-class communities and it was to mitigate the impact of these critical life situations that benefit or friendly societies initially developed. Membership was drawn largely from those whose earnings were sufficient to afford the fees and regular dues required at meetings of the society. In many cases, it was convenient to organize friendly societies on the basis of a shared trade and where this occurred the distinction between the functions of a benefit society and those of a trade union were blurred. In London, where trade and locality were inextricably linked, this situation was common. Francis Place, who was active in organizing benefit societies amongst several trades, had no illusions about the functions of his own, the Breeches Makers Benefit Society: 'The club, though actually a benefit club, was intended for the purpose of supporting the members in a strike for wages.'[42] Without funds, workers were clearly in no position to strike. So, when approached by fellow leather breech makers in 1794, Place organized a tontine to continue for three years, it being 'well understood that the real purpose was to raise money for another strike'.[43] The Friendly Society of Cordwainers also recognized the importance of a strike fund, stating that such a fund was 'the joint property of every individual member of the Society, and will be employed (if occasion requires) to shield him from injustice and oppression'.[44]

In terms of friendly societies as a whole, the number that existed in England and Wales, and more specifically in London, bears witness to their importance within working-class communities. When societies were first required to register their existence with local magistrates in 1793, they may have had as many as 648,000 members, rising to 704,350 in 1803 and over 925,000 by 1815. But even these figures are likely to have been gross underestimates since it was claimed in 1800 that only half the societies had bothered to register their rules.[45] Despite this level of under-registration, by 1800 a total of 654 societies had lodged their rules with the Middlesex magistrates and a further 255 had done so with the City of London authorities.[46] These totals represented as much as a third of all friendly societies in the country, a proportion that persisted throughout the century.[47] Judging from these numbers, the 4000 members from 54 friendly societies in the capital that turned out with flags, banners and full trade regalia to support Queen Caroline in 1820, were clearly the tip of the iceberg as far as London membership was concerned.[48]

The quantitative importance of trade-based friendly societies in the capital can be gauged with reference to the number that lodged their rules with the Registrar of Friendly Societies.[49] For the period from 1790 to 1870, a total of 926 trade-based societies were registered, representing a wide variety of occupations in the capital. The building trades were the largest single group, accounting for 108, followed by a more general category of tradesmen with 66, engineering and metal workers with 45 and domestic servants with 43. The remainder covered the spectrum of metropolitan trades, including several organized by less skilled or unskilled workers, such as labourers, dockers and coal whippers, as well as those belonging to the traditional manufacturing trades, such as clothing and shoemaking.

Some idea of the size of membership emerged in 1824 during the investigation by the Parliamentary Select Committee on artisans. Judging from the working-class officials who appeared as witnesses, many such societies were extremely large. The hat makers' society had approximately 600 members. City shoemakers also claimed a membership of 600 with between 700 and 800 members in the equivalent West End society. Even this number was exceeded by the carpenters who claimed that their five societies in London had a collective membership of 2500.[50] Robert Raven, secretary to the Friends of Humanity Society of Coopers claimed a membership of 700, covering about half the total number employed in the trade. Most impressive of all was the Shipwrights Provident Union, organized by John Gast, which boasted a membership of between 1300 and 1400 men within a year of its foundation.[51] Even allowing for some exaggeration, the evidence presented is consistent with the impression gained elsewhere that trade-based friendly societies, which were trade unions in everything but name, had continued to function despite the operation of the Combination Acts.[52]

Although it is difficult to establish the longevity of friendly societies, and it is therefore impossible to determine with any accuracy the total number of societies in existence at any one time, nevertheless the timing of the foundation of trade-based friendly societies, shown in Figure 4.2, provides an insight into the organization of the London trades. Three main periods of growth seem to have occurred. The first took place during the Napoleonic Wars when repression of trade unions under the Combination Acts was at its height. Because journeymen could meet with relative impunity as members of friendly societies, they were able to evade the restrictions on combination and thus friendly societies offered an alternative and legitimate means of organizing the trade. Certainly, many of those who appeared before the Select Committee on artisans in

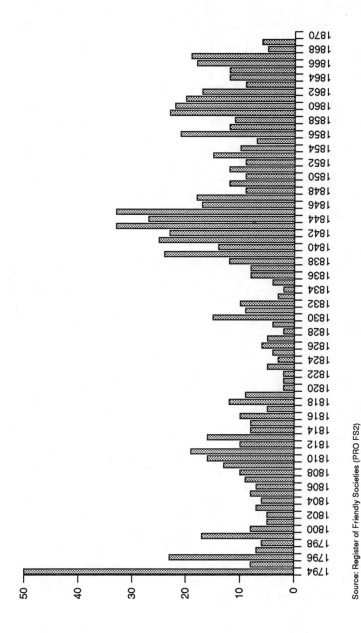

Source: Register of Friendly Societies (PRO FS2)

Figure 4.2 Friendly societies in London, 1794–1870.

1824 recalled the role of such societies in maintaining wages during the Napoleonic Wars.[53] Similarly, the frustration felt at the time by large engineering employers over their inability to control their workforce was evident by their antipathy towards friendly societies which they condemned as 'institutions which have created, cherished and given effect to the most dangerous combinations among several journeymen of our district'.[54] The next phase of growth came during the late 1830s and early 1840s, and was linked to the collectivist impetus that Chartism generated amongst London artisans. The final period of growth came in the late 1850s and early 1860s, paralleling the widespread agitation amongst artisans for shorter hours and the general upsurge in trade unionism. By that time, however, not only had middle-class attitudes towards unions themselves softened but more permanent amalgamated unions had begun to appear which made the trade function of friendly societies appear less important. From that time on, friendly societies lost their obvious connections to specific trades and more general ones, such as the Ancient Order of Foresters or the Hearts of Oak, assumed greater importance.

The manner in which these trade-based friendly societies operated, particularly in relation to membership, the conduct of meetings and participation in the life of the society, provides a good insight to their importance for artisans in particular and working-class communities in general. First and foremost, the costs of joining meant that membership was drawn largely from regularly employed male artisans.[55] The Friends of Humanity Coopers Society, for example, had a monthly contribution of 2s., in return for which members were insured against sickness, old age, death and loss of tools by fire. Though the rates of membership may have varied, such a range of benefits were typical of most friendly societies.[56]

Membership was normally restricted to those who had served an apprenticeship. In 1792 the rules of the Friendly and United Society of Cordwainers specifically excluded 'unqualified intruders', namely those who had not served an apprenticeship, and scabs, who 'first sells the journeymen, and is himself afterwards sold in his turn by the masters'. Although it was claimed that these restrictions would help to raise the trade 'to a more respectable rank among mechanical professions', the underlying reason was to limit competition from cheap labour.[57] Similar rules were a common feature of other trade societies. Rules for the Friendly Society of Journeymen Bookbinders stipulated that only those who had been fully apprenticed or worked in the trade for seven years, or the eldest son of a bookbinder upon reaching the age of 21, were eligible to join.[58] The Shipwrights Provident Union had similar requirements.[59] William Lovett himself ran foul of such rules when he was initially refused membership to the cabinet makers' society on the grounds of not having served an apprenticeship.[60] In hat making, regularly apprenticed 'fair' men could be denied membership to the hat makers' society if they persisted in working with 'foul' men who had not served out their full time.[61] In many cases the objections to such foul men extended beyond mere exclusion from the society. The bookbinders' rules, for example, required members to leave work if non-society men were employed in a workshop, though they were not to inform their employers that they had been ordered to do so by the committee.[62]

Of equal importance to the size and nature of the membership was the way in which societies themselves functioned. As long as the authorities and employers remained hostile to combinations and suspicious of friendly societies, there were sound reasons for preventing disharmony amongst members, maintaining secrecy about their operations and sharing widely the responsibilities of office. Behaviour at meetings was thus strictly conducted so as to minimize internal dissension. At meetings of the Cordwainers Society, members who were abusive, advanced any political views or acted in 'a riotous or indecorous manner' were subject to a 6d. fine.[63] Members of the Shipwrights Provident Union who behaved in a drunk or disorderly fashion were similarly fined.[64] Those belonging to the Cabinet-makers' Society were required to abstain from all political conversation on pain of a 1s. fine.[65] Upon the preservation of harmony rested the cloak of secrecy that afforded some protection to those involved in running the society. Article 14 of the Friendly and United Society of Cordwainers made this policy clear:

> That for the security of the committee it is unanimously resolved that no member of this Society shall mention the business of the committee but in the Club-room. That no member shall mention the name of the clerk, or Stewards, or the place of meeting, to any person unconnected with this Society in forfeiture of 10s. 6d. for each offence.[66]

Whilst internal harmony and secrecy were important to the successful operation of such societies, so too was the nature of members' involvement in what Clive Behagg has termed the 'participatory democracy' of such institutions.[67] Complicated rules governed members' responsibilities over attendance at meetings and their duty to serve as an official. The rules of the Society of Journeymen Boot and Shoemakers stipulated that members failing to attend meetings would be fined on a sliding scale of 2d. the first night, 6d. the second and 1s. the third, at which point the recalcitrant member would receive a visit from the clerk of the shop's meeting.[68] In a period when paid permanent officials were rare, sharing the burdens of office was important and therefore it was essential that members participated in the running of the society.

Moreover, by sharing responsibilities widely, those who were active in organizing a trade were afforded some degree of protection against victimization. Thus, at each quarterly meeting of the brass founders' society the most senior committee member was required to retire and another elected to take his place. Any member refusing to fill a position or failing to attend the meeting was subject to a fine.[69] For similar reasons, committee men who held the keys to the box for the Shipwrights Provident Union were elected each month.[70] Although such participatory democracy was no guarantee of protection, none the less it made the victimization of individuals less likely and the responsibilities of office easier to bear.

Conclusion

In distinguishing between the eighteenth-century mob and the nineteenth-century working class, Edward Thompson placed great emphasis on the 'collective self-consciousness, with its corresponding theory, institutions, discipline, and community values' of artisan society.[71] Here we have merely outlined the ways in which that collective self-consciousness was articulated and organized around the workplace and community, the house of call, friendly society and trade union, each of which provided a focus for resistance to and measure of protection against the full impact of industrial capitalism and the implementation of *laissez faire* policies. Such institutions were crucial to the functioning of what Thompson called the 'ethos of mutuality' within working-class communities. Each acted in various ways to protect workers against the uncertainties of life: sickness, old age and death as well as victimization, unemployment and the hardships that inevitably accompanied strikes. Each also acted as a pivot for flows of information concerning wages, conditions of work and opportunities for employment within and between particular trades and localities. Without these protective barriers, artisans and less skilled workers alike struggled to resist the uncertainties unleashed by market forces and spread of industrial capitalism. In the next chapter we examine how those barriers were breached and chart the lines of industrial conflict that were drawn across the map of mid-nineteenth century London.

Notes

1. Parker, 1853, p.193.
2. Mayhew, 1981, vol. 3, p.189. It is not the purpose here to discuss the

nature of skill. However, it should be noted that skill was more than just a question of manual dexterity and definitions often rested on social criteria that had little to do with the nature of production itself. See Rule, 1986, pp.99–118.

3. George, 1966, p.xxx. The 1831 census figure refers to males aged 20 years and above. The total represented over 32 per cent of the enumerated workforce.
4. *Northern Star*, 28 April 1848.
5. This is surely the strongest message that comes across in Edward Thompson's *The Making of the English Working Class* (1968). For others who have explored similar themes, see Behagg, 1990, esp. pp.71–155; Foster, 1977; Hobsbawm, 1984, pp.252–72; McLelland, 1987, pp.180–209; Prothero, 1981, pp.328–40.
6. Mayhew, 1968, vol. 3, p.233.
7. For a discussion of the relationships between the trades and Chartism see Goodway, 1982, pp.41–9, 153–218; Prothero, 1971.
8. For a more detailed discussion of this point see Price, 1983, p.58
9. See Prothero, 1981, pp.69, 218–20, 330. For a discussion of contemporary business cycle theories see Schumpeter, 1982, pp.738–50.
10. Alexander, 1983, pp.28–33; Humphries, 1977, pp.247–50; Taylor, 1983, pp.101–16.
11. Mayhew, 1968, vol. 3, p.233.
12. See Lovett, 1876, p.31; Wright, 1867, pp.83–107.
13. Wright, 1868, pp.94–7, 108–30; Burn, 1868, p.40; Read, 1976, p.79. When the question of early closing on Saturday was being discussed in the 1850s, one of the arguments in favour was that it would reduce the likelihood that workers would regularly absent themselves on Mondays. See Taylor, 1855, p.30.
14. See PP 1825 IV *SC on the combination laws*, pp.33, 44, 57; *Artizans London and Provincial Chronicle*, 10 July 1825; Howe, 1947, pp.394–400; London Cabinet-Makers' Union, 1811; Skyring, 1831; *The humble petition of John Walker ...*, 1805, (GLRO); *Wages for the making of various sorts of tinwares*, 1805.
15. Place Coll. Add. Ms., 27799, fol. 12–14.
16. Howe, 1947, pp.374–400.
17. An example of this occurred in shoemaking in 1798 when the new fashion of having a separate right and left shoe was introduced, disrupting existing price agreements. Similar disruption occurred in hatmaking in 1820 when a larger hat, the 'Inch Yeoman' became fashionable. Difficulties of incorporating it into the price list resulted in a four-month strike. See *True Briton*, 28 February 1799; Place Coll. Add. Ms. 27799, fol. 77, 81, 85. The importance of custom helps to account for the stickiness of artisan wages compared with the movement of prices.
18. Price, 1980, pp.58–63.
19. See Wright, 1867, pp.83–107.
20. *St James Chronicle*, 1–3 May 1804.
21. Lovett, 1876, p.31.
22. *Reynolds Newspaper*, 28 April, 19 May, 2, 9, 16, 23 June, 28 July 1867.
23. Green, 1988, pp.187–91.
24. Green and Parton, 1990, p.77.
25. In 1861 the period was reduced to three years and in 1865 to one. See

Chapter 8, pp.223–6.

26. For contemporaries, the possibility that stable working-class communities existed in cities appeared to be precluded by the existence of high rates of residential mobility. In their investigations during the 1840s the Statistical Society of London discovered that 62 per cent of working-class families in Westminster and 50 per cent in St George-in-the-East had been in their homes for less than one year. Statistical Society of London, 1840, p.24 ; *idem.*, 1848a, p.219.

27. Green, 1988, p.190. At the time Poole's permanent workforce numbered about 80 men, although at the height of the season as many as 500 indoor and outdoor workers were employed.

28. Leeson, 1980, pp.94, 112, 132–47.

29. *St James Chronicle*, 27–29 January 1801. Leeson cites other examples of how tramping artisans were directed to houses of call and then shown around workshops. Leeson, 1980, pp.126–7.

30. *Articles of the Friendly Society of Journeymen Bookbinders, ... agreed March 24, 1820*.

31. *Gorgon*, 3 October 1818.

32. *ibid*. This figure, which came from Francis Place, appeared to represent the height of the tailors' network. By 1824 Place thought there were about 20 flint houses of call. By Mayhew's time, although the system still functioned, it had shrunk along with the number of society tailors and by 1861 none was recorded in the *First Annual Trade Union Directory*. See PP 1824 V *SC on artizans and machinery*, p.45; Burn, 1861; Leeson, 1980, p.245.

33. PP 1824 V *SC on artizans and machinery*, p.134.

34. See Burn, 1861; Cole and Filson, 1951, p.489.

35. For a discussion of the geography of such meeting houses see Chapter 6, pp.148–50.

36. *Gorgon*, 3 October 1818; see also PP 1824 V *SC on artizans and machinery*, p.45.

37. *ibid.*, p.15.

38. Colquhoun, 1794, p.31; see Linebaugh, 1993, pp.426–30.

39. *To his Grace the Duke of Portland ... Memorial of the Committee of Master Tailors*, 1800, quoted in Aspinall, 1949, p.34.

40. *St James Chronicle*, 1–3 November 1804; Aspinall, 1949, p.76.

41. PP 1867–68 XXIX *RC on trade unions*, tenth report, q. 1889–90, 18217 .

42. Place, 1972, p.112.

43. *ibid.*, p.125.

44. *Articles of the Friendly and United Society of Cordwainers*, quoted in Aspinall, 1949, p.82.

45. Gosden, 1961, p.5; Prothero, 1981, p.39.

46. PP 1831–32 XXVI *Return of the number of friendly societies ... since 1st January 1793*, p.291.

47. Southall, 1988b, p.469.

48. Prothero, 1981, p.142.

49. I am most grateful to Dr Humphrey Southall for allowing me access to the data he has compiled from this source. A fuller discussion of the data can be found in Southall, 1988b.

50. See PP 1824 V *SC on artizans and machinery*, pp.91, 134, 176–7; PP 1825 IV *SC on the combination laws*, p.42.

51. *ibid.*, pp.42–3, 251.

52. The Combination Act of 1799 (39 Geo. 3, c. 81) and that of 1800 (39 & 40 Geo. 3, c. 106) prohibited combinations for the purposes of raising wages, lessening or altering the hours of work, decreasing the quantity of work, preventing or hindering masters from employing workers of their choice and controlling or affecting the carrying-on of manufacturing, trade or business. In practice the Acts were widely evaded and other legal means of redress against trade unions were adopted. See Orth, 1991, pp.45–55.

53. See PP 1824 V *SC on artizans and machinery*, pp.91, 133, 143, 166, 175–6. Witnesses included Francis Place, John Lang and John Watkins (hatters), John Alexander and William Ablett (shoemakers), Isaac Seabrook and George Crowhurst (carpenter and joiner) The same was true of other parts of the country. See Rev. W. R. Hay, J. P. to Viscount Sidmouth, 4 February 1813, in   Aspinall, 1949, pp.156–8.

54. *Memorial of Machinists and Engineers Resident in London respecting combinations and benefit societies ... 27 May 1813*, quoted in Aspinall, 1949, p.162.

55. In a few instances specific societies for women were formed but these were in a small minority.

56. PP 1825 IV *SC on the combination laws*, p.42.

57. *Articles of the Friendly and United Society of Cordwainers, instituted at Westminster on 4 June 1792*, quoted in Aspinall, 1949, p.83.

58. *Articles of the Friendly Society of Journeymen Bookbinders ... March 24 1820*.

59. PP 1825 IV *SC on the combination laws*, pp.42–7.

60. Lovett, 1876, p.30.

61. PP 1824 V *SC on artizans and machinery*, p.82

62. *Articles of the Friendly Society of Journeymen Bookbinders*, 1820.

63. Aspinall, 1949, p.80; see also *Rules and Orders of the United Benevolent Sawyers, instituted 18 December 1825*.

64. PP 1825 IV *SC on the combination laws*, p.47.

65. *Rules and Orders of the Cabinet Makers Society*, 1830.

66. *Articles of the Friendly and United Society of Cordwainers, instituted at Westminster on 4 June 1792*, second edition 1794, quoted in Aspinall, 1949, p.87.

67. This term is discussed more fully in Behagg, 1990.

68. *Rules of the Society of Journeymen Boot and Shoemakers*, quoted in Aspinall, 1949, p.80.

69. *Brassfounders, Braziers and Coppersmiths manual*, 1829.

70. PP 1825 IV *SC on the combination laws*, p.47.

71. Thompson, 1968, p.463.

CHAPTER FIVE

Lines of conflict: labour disputes in London, 1790–1870

Introduction

Few of those involved in the historiography of the English working class would now accept that the history of labour protest can be written simply in terms of a linear progression running from ephemeral, spontaneous and localized outbreaks of rioting and machine breaking, to more organized strikes and permanent, formally constituted trade unions.[1] Although the development of such structured forms of protest may have become more common in the nineteenth century, workers in earlier periods nevertheless developed a range of forms of workplace resistance, depending on the particular circumstances of the trade and the issues in question.[2] It is now commonly appreciated that apparently modern forms of labour protest and organization, such as strikes and trade unions, had a long ancestry stretching back in many cases at least to the early eighteenth century.[3] This was certainly true for London, where artisans and labourers were at the forefront of labour protest and political radicalism throughout the eighteenth century.[4] It was equally true for the early decades of the nineteenth century, when the growth of radical associations amongst the artisan trades was well marked. Our prime concern, however, is not to trace this history of working-class radicalism in nineteenth-century London, for to recount the class struggles of working men and women in the capital is to go over ground already well laid out by others.[5] Instead, our focus is somewhat narrower, concentrating on the outbreak of labour disputes as a means of understanding the impact of economic change and the manner in which it came into conflict with workers' expectations and aspirations.

The course of economic change in the early decades of the nineteenth century was a stormy passage in the history of the London trades and the structures of resistance outlined in the previous chapter were frequently needed to defend working-class interests. The labour disputes that occurred provide a window through which to view the relationships between economic change and working-class fortunes. Disputes took many forms, ranging from subtle forms of workplace resistance, such as absenteeism and high labour turnover, to large-scale strikes and outbursts of machine breaking or rioting. All were immensely disruptive to working-class communities and thus hint at major points of conflict between capital and labour. 'Workmen dread a strike', Francis Place told the Select Committee discussing the Combination Acts in 1824, 'I know well from experience that a strike is always a matter for serious consideration and never can be effectual unless it be really necessary.'[6] As well as causing immense hardship to those involved, strikes could open deep rifts within working-class communities, often involving violent confrontations between strikers and those who remained at work. In these communities, the 'scab', 'blackleg', or 'knobstick' was a figure of universal disapprobation, and always liable to be subjected to the rough justice of the striking crowd. The significance of strikes, therefore, should not be underestimated. Indeed, the record of such disputes provides a crucial insight to the ways in which economic change clashed with workers' expectations and as such provides a lens through which to examine the varying fortunes of the London trades.

Labour disputes and strikes

In the context of industrial relations, the point at which routine negotiations between workers and employers shaded into a labour dispute is poorly defined. What was the normal course of events was rarely recorded and instead we are left with the residues of rancorous disputes, recorded precisely because they represented ruptures in the normal functioning of labour relations. For this reason it is vital to recognize what precisely distinguished labour disputes, and particularly strikes, from more routine forms of workplace bargaining.

The term 'labour dispute' itself covers a variety of forms of industrial protest, ranging from disagreements between groups of workers and their masters to machine breaking, riots and strikes. Each form, however, involves a degree of contestation focused on workplace issues and it is this characteristic that distinguishes these from other forms of working-class protest. As a subset of such disputes, strikes can be defined with reference to four main criteria.[7] First, a strike is a collective activity by a group of workers rather than an isolated act by one individual. This differentiates them from personal grievances that surface from time to time between workers and their employers and which do not necessarily have any wider significance for understanding the relations between capital and labour. Secondly, a strike involves a cessation of work, thereby distinguishing it from other forms of protest such as go slows or overtime bans. Thirdly, in order to differentiate them from mass resignations of the workforce, strikes are temporary phenomena and workers fully expect to return to their jobs subject to a satisfactory conclusion being reached with their employer. Finally, a strike is calculative in the sense that it expresses a grievance or attempts to force a claim on the part of workers against their employers. Causation is therefore an essential element although it must be recognized that amidst the accusations and counter-accusations it is often difficult to establish the precise points of disagreement.

In a paper on labour disputes presented to the Royal Statistical Society in 1880, George Bevan noted 'Strikes, numerous as they are, have been so imperfectly chronicled ... that the labour of getting at the simple fact of their occurrence has been very considerable.'[8] Since then, several historians have tackled the problem and our knowledge is no longer as imperfect as it once was.[9] However, gaps still exist at a local level and more generally in relation to the nineteenth century prior to the publication of strike statistics from 1888 by the Board of Trade. Thus, whilst we can attempt to reconstruct the geography and chronology of disputes for the eighteenth century, using the newspaper evidence provided by C. R. Dobson, no comparable set of data currently exists for the nineteenth century. Here we can do little more than sketch the broad outlines of disputes in London.

Evidence of labour protest comes from a variety of sources but mainly from a systematic investigation of the working-class press, augmented by *The Times* and other contemporary newspapers and documents.[10] In several cases the circulation of such papers, measured albeit imperfectly by the amount of stamp duty paid, was impressive. In 1839 the *Northern Star* had a circulation of 1.8 million copies although this had declined to little more than 150,000 by 1851. The circulation of *Reynolds Newspaper*, which was particularly active in reporting London trade disputes, rose from 275,250 in 1850 to over 1.5 million by 1853. Even the unstamped press of the 1830s, such as the *Poor Man's Guardian*, the *Pioneer* and the *Radical*, had circulations of between 10,000 and 20,000 copies, most of which were distributed in London.[11] Given that working-class readership was many times larger than the number of papers printed, these totals are impressive and suggest that news referring to the trades and labour disputes would have been widely disseminated amongst London workers. The fact that the papers were themselves printed and sold in the capital also meant that information on metropolitan disputes was more readily available than that for more distant parts of the country. Inevitably, in a city the size of London and where workplaces were often small and widely dispersed, many minor disputes would have escaped notice. However, where disputes involved large numbers of workers, or where ringleaders were dealt with harshly by the courts, interest was high and reports appeared frequently in the press. Thus, although we must be cautious about reaching firm conclusions concerning the absolute number of disputes gathered from the press, it is nevertheless likely that the evidence collected here is broadly representative of the general pattern of industrial conflict.

Labour disputes in London

Whilst political radicalism and public disorder has often been the focus of attention on the eighteenth-century London working class, the capital's role in industrial unrest has sometimes been overlooked. In this respect, the fact that between 1717 and 1800 Dobson has calculated that nearly a third of the total number of strikes recorded in Britain occurred in London is significant.[12] In addition to the tailors, who themselves struck thirteen times between those dates, seamen struck on nine occasions, silk weavers on seven, carpenters and shoemakers on six, cabinet makers, coal heavers and hatters on five. In all, there were disputes in no less than 43 London trades during the period, confirming the view that industrial relations were anything but smooth.[13]

As the eighteenth century came to a close, however, breaks in the continuity of workers' experiences and disruption of customary patterns of industrial relations began to appear. The inflationary pressures of the Napoleonic Wars eroded price lists and wage agreements. At the same time, traditional methods of settling wages based on the regulatory role of justices at the Quarter Sessions fell into disuse, both as a result of the disruptive effects of inflation as well as the growing belief in the iron hand of the market as the ultimate arbiter of prices and wages.[14] If the experiences of Francis Place are anything to go by, then the number of strikes began to mount from this time.[15]

The record of labour disputes gleaned from reports in the contemporary press confirm this to have been the case. Indeed, the handful of strikes that Place noted were some 294 labour disputes recorded in London between 1790 and 1870. Of this number, at least 227, comprising over 77 per cent of the total, were strikes or prosecutions of workers for combining during the course of a strike. Of the remainder, 42 were court actions over specific issues, nearly half of which occurred during the apprenticeship campaign of 1810–13, nine were lockouts by employers, and the rest were a miscellaneous collection of various forms of protest, including deputations to employers, petitions and isolated instances of machine breaking. Clearly, workers in London were not backward in arguing their case, even if stoppages entailed severe and sometimes prolonged hardship.

All of these disputes took place at a time when the attitudes of government and the authorities to strikes varied from distrust and dislike to open hostility. As the sad history of the Tolpuddle labourers testifies, a range of legislation could be invoked against workers who joined trade unions or participated in disputes. Between 1799 and 1824 the Combination Acts could have been used as a means of punishing strikers.[16] These outlawed collective agreements or combinations concerning wages, hours of work, the hiring of labour and the carrying-on of trade. Violations of the Acts were dealt with summarily and were punishable by sentences of up to three months' gaol. In practice, however, employers were reluctant to invoke the Combination Acts, preferring instead other legislation with which to discipline strikers and those who belonged to a union.[17] The laws against common conspiracy, though more cumbersome and slower than the Combination Acts, carried harsher penalties and were frequently used to prosecute the ringleaders of strikes. In 1810, for example, the striking *Times* printers were indicted for conspiracy and received gaol sentences varying from nine months to two years.[18] Even after the repeal of the Combination Act in 1824, and despite the hastily drawn-up legislation that replaced it in the following year, workers who went on strike still risked prosecution for conspiracy, breach of contract, unlawful oaths or the use of threats, violence or intimidation in the course of a strike.[19] Given the range of legislation, and the general suspicion of trade unions and hostility towards strikes on the part of the courts, the fact that so many were not only ready to endure the privations of a strike but also to run the risk of imprisonment bears witness to the importance of such disputes in the lives of the London working class.

Labour disputes and the trades

In 1812, at the height of the Napoleonic Wars and when the Combination Act was in force, Thomas Large, a Leicester stocking weaver, visited London to lobby Parliament on behalf of workers in the hosiery industry. Despite the laws against trade unions, he discovered that combinations existed in a variety of trades. Somewhat sarcastically he reported that when delegates from the carpenters' union heard that the weavers had no strike fund of their own, 'Their noses underwent a Mechanical turn upwards.' Incredulity soon turned into a lecture on the benefits of combination:

> What would our trade be if we did not combine together? ... Look at other Trades! they all Combine (the Spitalfields weavers excepted, and what a Miserable Condition are they in). See the Tailors, Shoemakers, Bookbinders, Gold beaters, Printers, Bricklayers, Coatmakers, Hatters, Curriers, Masons, Whitesmiths, none of these

trades Receive Less than 30/- a week, and from that to five guineas this is all done by Combination without it their trades would be as bad as yours ...[20]

That London artisans were at the centre of much trade-union activity in the eighteenth and early nineteenth centuries is not in question, and from the experiences of Thomas Large it appeared that the list of trades involved was wide. Later in the century, the trade-union leader George Howell, concurred with this view, noting 'In the struggle for increased wages the artisans and mechanics of London were always in the forefront of battle.'[21] The list of trades involved in labour disputes between 1790 and 1870, shown in Table 5.1, reveals that whilst artisans were indeed the focus of many disputes, more proletarian occupations, notably dock work, were also important. Skill alone, though important as a basis for organization, was not the sole factor underlying labour militancy amongst the trades, and other circumstances need to be taken into account.

In general, the frequency of disputes reflected the size of the workforce in question, although in some cases, such as the coopers, shipbuilders and silk weavers, the number of disputes was dispro-

Table 5.1   Labour disputes by trade, 1790–1870

Trade	Number of disputes		
Building	65		
Clothing	58	(shoemaking	34)
		(tailoring	15)
		(hat making	9)
Dock work	20		
Engineering and metal work	20		
Transport	20		
Printing and bookbinding	18		
Coopering	12		
Shipbuilding	12		
Furniture	10		
Food	8		
Silk weaving	7		
Leather	7		
Others	37		
Total	294		

Source: See Appendix 5.1

portionately high in relation to employment. Building and clothing, the two largest manufacturing trades, accounted for nearly half the disputes that occurred, a fact that can be explained partly by the structure of employment in each trade and partly by the state of demand. The nature of building itself, and the scale of operations particularly on large construction projects, meant that different groups of workers were required to cooperate and this made it more likely that a dispute in one branch would spread to others. Similarly, since bricklayers, carpenters, painters, plumbers and glaziers sought to maintain a rough parity in wages and conditions, changes amongst one group of workers would rapidly be transmitted to the rest. Grievances were therefore likely to spread from one branch to the other in quick succession.

Disputes amongst clothing workers, led by boot- and shoemakers, formed the next largest category. Shoemakers were noted for their political radicalism and evidently this was translated into a tradition of workplace militancy.[22] The tailors, and to a lesser extent the hat makers, had similar if less extreme reputations and in the first half of the century each trade was actively involved in wider labour movements in London. These trades shared certain structural similarities. Firstly, they depended on the London market and were therefore subject to changes in fashion and marked seasonal fluctuations in demand. Secondly, separate bespoke and wholesale sectors existed in each, catering for distinct markets and involving different methods of production. In the high-quality, bespoke sector, most work was carried out on masters' premises, whilst in the cheaper, slop-branch catering for the ready-made, wholesale trade, sweated domestic labour was of greater importance. Finally, in shoemaking, clothing and to a smaller degree in hat making, the division of labour, the spread of piece work and competition from various forms of cheap labour threatened the status of artisans. These structural similarities meant that each trade, although ostensibly separate, waged parallel struggles at the workplace.

Next in terms of frequency came several groups of skilled artisan trades, all of which, with the exception of the furniture making, tended to involve relatively large units of employment. London engineering workers were well known for their militancy. The Combination Act of 1799 had been promoted specifically to deal with the London millwrights and the campaign to repeal the apprenticeship laws in 1814 had similarly been organized by large engineering employers as a means of weakening combinations in the trade. Compositors and pressmen also had a similar reputation and the celebrated prosecution of workers from *The Times* in 1810 was the catalyst that had persuaded Francis Place of the need to repeal the Combination Acts. In both trades there existed a firm basis of skilled work, and this, coupled with increasing demand, helped to foster the development of strong unions.[23] The preservation of skill also helps to explain the frequency of disputes amongst coopers, who although relatively few in number nevertheless maintained a strong tradition of artisan independence.[24] Shipwrights also relied on their skilled status, as well as the pressure of work, to pursue their claims. In the first quarter of the century, when demand for London ships was at its height, the Thames shipwrights were amongst the best organized and most militant groups of workers in the capital. By contrast, as the fortunes of the industry waned, so the power of the shipwrights declined and after 1825 they embarked on few strikes.[25]

Almost alone of the skilled artisans, furniture workers appeared reluctant to strike. This, however, may partly reflect the nature of the data. Disputes were often confined to a single workshop and were therefore more difficult to detect in the historical record.[26] Industrial relations may have been smoothed by the continued use of an agreed book of prices, which persisted longer in cabinet making than in many other trades.[27] Also, the fact that relatively little capital was needed to set up in the trade meant that rather than face a strike, journeymen could themselves become small masters. Little more than £3 or £4 was required to set up as a 'garret master' in cabinet making.[28] Perhaps for this reason the cabinet makers' unions never reached sizeable proportions, especially in the poorly paid East End sector.[29] Without a well-supported union, it was extremely difficult to undertake, let alone sustain, strikes.

Whilst the preservation of skill provided a basis for labour militancy, other factors were involved in relation to dock labourers and coal heavers. The frequency with which they struck, especially coal heavers, acts as a reminder that disputes were by no means confined to the artisan trades alone. In their cases, over and above being available for work, the main requirement for employment was physical strength and consequently the dock labour market was notoriously overstocked, Nowhere was the daily struggle for work more fierce: 'Presently you know, by the stream pouring through the gates and the rush towards particular spots, that the "calling foremen" have made their appearance. Then begins the scuffling and scrambling forth of countless hands high in the air, to catch the eye of him whose voice may give them work', observed Mayhew.[30]

Despite this desperate struggle for work, dock labourers were not without some power to influence the course of wages. In the age of sail, when the pattern of arrivals in port was dictated by the winds, seasonal pressure to unload ships provided both dockers and coal heavers with a window of opportunity through which to press their claims. In terms of the coal heavers, employment was much more highly regulated than amongst dock labourers and nominally, at any rate, they had to be registered to be eligible for work. These restrictions on employment temporarily provided them with a basis upon which to organize, and they were thus in a better position to sustain strikes. Thus, on several occasions from the 1840s, when the numbers of unregistered men began to increase and downward pressures on wages mounted, coal heavers went on strike.[31]

Transport workers comprised a broad category of trades, including seamen, cabmen, omnibus drivers and railway engine drivers. Circumstances of employment differed considerably between these trades and it is difficult to generalize about the course of industrial conflicts. However, most of the disputes occurred after 1850 reflecting both the growing importance of transport in the metropolitan economy as well as the need to establish rules of work in newly formed trades. Engine drivers and firemen were completely new trades and many of the early disputes in that branch reflected the initial sorting-out of rules between the railway companies and the drivers.[32] The amalgamation of omnibus companies in mid-century also created problems of integration and when customary practices came under attack by the London General Omnibus Company in 1857 a third of the workforce struck.[33] New rules over lighting on cabs and plying for trade at railway stations also met with stiff resistance from the London cabmen in 1867 and 1868.[34] Although questions of pay were often linked to such disputes, working practices and rules for the job were the main catalysts for conflicts in each of these trades.

By contrast, desperation, rather than the erosion of skill, the settling of rules or mere opportunism, drove the silk weavers to strike. No group of workers suffered more from structural decline during the period than did the Spitalfields weavers. Their willingness to strike, which on rare occasions extended to machine breaking and the cutting of silk on the looms, reflected the forlorn efforts to halt the inexorable slide in their fortunes. Four of the seven strikes occurred between 1819 and 1829, reflecting precisely the depth of depression during those years and the struggles in 1824 over the repeal of the protective mantle afforded by the Spitalfields Act.[35] Disputes after that time were miserable affairs undertaken reluctantly by the weavers against a small number of 'unprincipled' masters and in the knowledge that they could expect little relief from the Poor Law in Bethnal Green.[36] In practice, little could be done to break the vicious spiral of decline and by mid-century silk weaving was synonymous with poverty and Bethnal Green, the centre of the trade, was the poorest district in London. As one weaver ruefully remarked to Henry Mayhew in 1849, 'It's been a continuation of reductions for the last twenty-six years, and a continuation of suffering for just as long.'[37] Under such adverse circumstances, the number of protests faded into insignificance.

Finally, it is worth noting the outbreak of disputes in several other traditional London trades. Given their quantitative importance, the food trades are under-represented by the figures in Table 5.1. Indeed, disputes in the food trades primarily concerned the bakers who in the 1850s and 1860s became involved in the campaign for shorter hours. In part, the limited number of disputes may have reflected a lack of opportunity: the food trades were not as seasonal as dock work nor were they as skilled as the artisan crafts. In addition, the structure of employment may also have reduced the opportunities, or indeed the necessity for disputes. With the exception of brewery workers, those involved in the preparation of food and drink tended to be self-employed or worked in small groups. The 1851 census shows that 92 per cent of butchers and 96 per cent of bakers employed less than five men each, making them amongst the most fragmented trades in the capital.[38] As a result, workers experienced few of the direct conflicts between capital and labour, or indeed the transparency of exploitation that characterized many other London trades in which larger firms were important, such as building, printing or engineering, or in which sweating predominated.

Until we have other surveys of labour disputes, we can say little more about the propensity to strike of individual trades. What emerges from this brief survey is how widespread labour disputes were throughout the London trades. Artisans led the way but when the opportunity arose, less skilled workers also flexed their industrial muscle. Skill alone, although important, was not the sole factor underlying the ability or propensity of workers to strike. Opportunity, the structure of employment and, in some case, sheer desperation, were also important considerations influencing the outbreak of disputes.

The causes of conflict and rhythms of resistance

In the heat of battle, accusations and counter-accusations between striking workers and employers flowed freely. Rarely were the causes of disputes clearly defined or widely accepted by the groups involved. Even as a strike wore on, there was no certainty that the issues at the centre of the dispute would remain the same. What began as a wage claim on the part of workers, for instance, could rapidly be transformed into an attack by employers on membership of a trade union. Therefore, we must tread cautiously when examining the causation of disputes. At the risk of oversimplification, however, we can do worse than to follow George Potter's distinction between aggressive strikes, in which workers downed tools in pursuit of improvements in wages and conditions, and defensive actions, when they resisted reductions in wages, encroachment on trade privileges, the use of cheap labour or alterations to customary modes of work.[39]

Establishing the causation of disputes demands an attention to detail and, where possible, the capacity to follow the conflict for its duration. In this respect the newspaper evidence outlined earlier is invaluable, particularly where reports can be cross-checked against papers of a differing political persuasion and with varying degrees of sympathy for trade unions and strikes. For this reason, *The Times* was consulted for the entire period, alongside the major working-class newspapers in existence. Based on this evidence, it was possible to establish the main cause of conflict for most of the 294 labour disputes recorded in London between 1790 and 1870. The data shown in Figure 5.1 confirm that wage disputes accounted for the majority of conflicts, with strikes over wage rises twice as important as more defensive actions against reductions. That questions of pay should have been at the centre of so many disputes is hardly surprising. But what is of equal note is that over 40 per cent of disputes concerned other issues, notably the employment of cheap labour and control of the labour process itself.[40] Pay alone, therefore, was not the sole reason for downing tools and we need to cast our net widely to determine the reasons why workers struck.

Differences also occurred in the periodicity of each set of disputes, depending on the state of demand and the nature of the problem. Wage-related disputes, as discussed below, were closely linked to the ebb and flow of prices and industrial output and it was these economic fluctuations that influenced the timing of such conflicts. However, disagreements over the use of cheap labour and control of the labour process danced to a slightly different rhythm, as the disputes plotted in Figure 5.2 suggest. As far as cheap labour was concerned, the battles were mainly fought over the excessive use of apprentices and the employment of non-union labourers. Whilst the latter was a constant problem throughout the period, disputes over apprenticeship were concentrated mainly during the Napoleonic Wars, particularly between 1810 and 1812 when the labour market was most stretched. In contrast, control strikes occurred primarily after 1847, reflecting a growing interest, particularly amongst the builders, in limiting hours of work as a means of reducing unemployment. The impact of prolonged unemployment during the 1840s had clearly made an impact on workers' experiences and from that time on short-term campaigns became more common. Of course, shorter hours and questions of pay were inextricably linked and it would be foolish to draw too strong a distinction between the two, both in terms of the nature of causation or the timing of disputes. However, in addition to differences in timing,

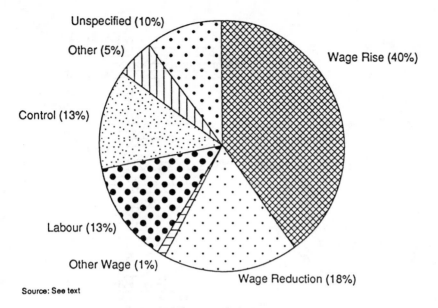

Figure 5.1   Cause of labour disputes, 1790–1870.

arguments over the hours of work had wider implications for the pattern of employment than more straightforward wage disputes and as such they deserve to be treated separately.

Wage disputes

The most common cause of disputes concerned wage rises and it is therefore appropriate to start with that category. The proportion of such disputes accords closely with Dobson's findings for the country as a whole in the eighteenth century. However, special care needs to be taken when interpreting the pattern of wage disputes and they need to be set in the context of fluctuations in the cost of living. Strikes in pursuit of wage claims that merely kept pace with prices were somewhat different to those in which an increase was being sought over and above the rise in the cost of living. The former would fall more easily under Potter's definition of a defensive strike and the latter under the aggressive category. Similarly, when prices were falling, resistance to wage cuts that were less than the reduction in prices could also be interpreted as aggressive actions. In contrast, when wages fell faster than prices, any strike against cuts in pay were clearly of a more defensive nature. These reservations need to be borne in mind if we are to make sense of the

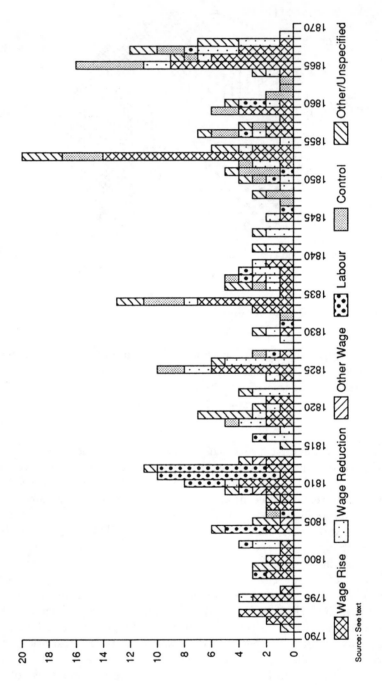

Source: See text

Figure 5.2   Labour disputes, 1790–1870.

pattern of such disputes.

Figure 5.3, which plots wage disputes against the three-year moving average in the cost of living and the Crafts, Leybourne and Mills index of industrial production, is an attempt to gauge this distinction between aggressive and defensive wage disputes. Clearly, we would need to know the exact level of wage claims in comparison with the fluctuation in prices before specific strikes can be categorized accurately. Broadly speaking, aggressive wage strikes that occurred when prices were stable or falling were relatively rare. The disputes that broke out between 1810 and 1813, and between 1818 and 1821 can probably be included in this number. The outburst of strikes in 1833–34, associated with the Grand National Consolidated Trades Union (GNCTU), also took place when prices were relatively low, although the upturn in production at the time provided workers with promising conditions for embarking on disputes. Similar conditions also prevailed in 1865–67 when, despite falling prices, workers took advantage of the upturn in production to press their claims for higher wages. Such disputes would seem to fall most easily in Potter's category of aggressive strikes.

The nature of wage rise disputes in 1825 and 1853 is less clear cut. By averaging the cost of living and production series, it appears that wage rise disputes in 1825 lagged behind the steep rise in prices. When the individual strikes are examined, however, it is clear that rises were being sought concurrently or in response to upturns in prices and production. This was certainly true of the carpenters and was also the case with the barge builders, carvers, coopers, and shoemakers, all of whom struck in the summer of 1825 before the financial bubble burst.[41] The wave of strikes in 1853 also followed steep price rises and disputes were thus similarly defensive in nature. A poor harvest in that year prompted a 20 per cent increase in the price of bread and there were even greater rises for meat and other provisions.[42] Set against these increases, wage claims were modest, asking in the most part for a 10 per cent rise. Building workers throughout the capital, for example, sought an increase of 6d. a day, together with shorter hours, which was equivalent to a rise of about 10 per cent.[43] A host of other trades also sought rises commensurate with the increase in prices, including rugmakers, shoemakers, coal porters, lamplighters, dock labourers and the normally acquiescent East End slopworkers. Even police constables petitioned the Home Office for an increase in pay.[44] In each case, the reasons were the same, as the striking dock labourers made clear: 'We only ask for what we consider ourselves justly entitled to, namely such an advance in wages as will enable us to maintain our wives and families in comfort, and fairly and honestly pay our way, as we have always endeavoured to do.'[45]

If the pattern of wage strikes described above is an indication of how

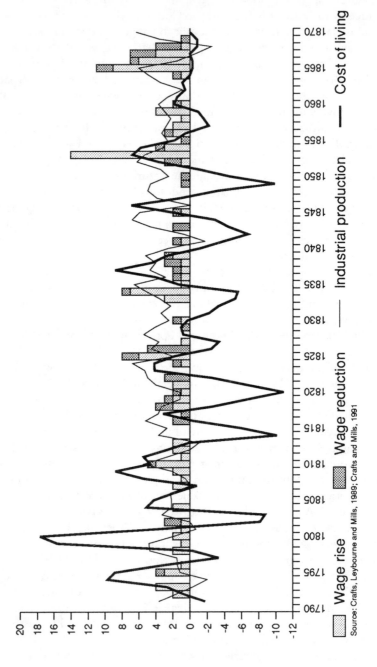

Figure 5.3   Wage disputes, economic activity and the cost of living, 1790–1870.

London workers fared in the period, it was clear that gains made during upturns were normally modest and likely to come under attack once recession set in. Before leaving the question of aggressive and defensive wage strikes, then, it is worth briefly examining disputes over wage reductions. Although smaller numbers make generalization difficult, what stands out is that such reductions normally occurred in the context of falling prices and downturns in production. Disentangling these two factors is difficult, but during downturns, the competitive pressures on manufacturers to reduce costs meant that cuts in wages were more likely, particularly in London where labour costs were such an important element of the total cost of production. Shortly after the collapse of trade in 1825, for example, ladies' shoemakers found themselves embroiled in a bitter dispute over wage reductions and attacks on the union.[46] Similarly, upholsterers and compositors found that the pay rises they had previously obtained were also under attack.[47] After the collapse of the GNCTU in 1834, employers also took advantage of the disarray of the trade unions to embark on a series of wage cuts. Poor economic conditions in the 1840s dampened much workplace militancy, but again those wage strikes that did occur were mainly concerned with resisting cuts in wages. Finally, economic downturn also prompted a wave of cuts towards the end of the period in 1867 and 1868, although these must be seen at least in part as attempts by employers to claw back some of the rises conceded in the aggressive outburst of wage strikes in the previous years.

Labour and employment issues

Falling wages, as Mayhew was at pains to point out, was but one issue amongst several that London workers had to face during the period. The employment of cheaper forms of labour was, if anything, a greater threat to the livelihoods of workers and it is therefore of little surprise that it formed an important category of labour disputes. Employment issues concerning the replacement of skilled by less skilled or unskilled labour, including apprentices, improvers, learners, women and children, and non-unionists or 'foul' men, accounted for 13 per cent of all disputes. The precise circumstances relating to the employment of unskilled labour depended on the characteristics of individual trades and generalizations are accordingly difficult to make. Where a basis of skill was retained, as in engineering and printing, the excessive use of boy apprentices was a constant source of contention. In clothing, the employment of women caused greatest concern amongst male artisans, whilst the influx of female learners and improvers in bookbinding was also the cause of several disputes.[48] Where the union itself was powerful, such as amongst the hat makers in the early 1800s, the employment of foul men was always likely to prompt a dispute. But these differences cannot hide the fact that the root problem in each instance was essentially the same, namely the replacement of skilled by less skilled or unskilled workers. As such, these disputes are best considered as comprising one and the same category.

The years from 1810 to 1813 witnessed a large number of such employment-related disputes associated mainly with the campaign to reform the Elizabethan apprenticeship laws. Although the issue has been discussed elsewhere, the disputes concerning apprenticeship are instructive for the general light they shed on the question of skill, labour control and social mobility in the capital.[49] London artisans had just cause to oppose what appeared to be the widespread evasion of the apprenticeship laws. Not only were apprentices frequently used to break strikes, as happened in printing in 1798 and 1810, but also, as labour shortages worsened during the Napoleonic Wars, non-apprenticed men and boys began to be employed in greater numbers.[50] In 1809 London artisans started a concerted campaign to force compliance with the apprenticeship regulations and from December of that year until May 1813, at least 21 employers were prosecuted for evasion of the regulations.[51] But prosecutions were expensive, magistrates proved reluctant to convict and it soon became clear that further action on the part of workers was required. In 1813 artisans and small masters presented a large number of petitions to Parliament in favour of retention or extension of the Elizabethan apprenticeship laws. One alone contained over 32,000 signatures, of which 13,000 were from London artisans and 800 from small masters.[52] Nearly half the money subscribed for that particular petition came from four London trades: shipbuilding, building, baking and engineering. In April the petitions were submitted and in the following month a Select Committee sat to consider the situation.

That the issue aroused such widespread support from London artisans and small masters alike should come as little surprise. Over and above the fact that London was, as Thompson described it, the 'Athens of the artisan' and the focus of political activity, the problems of controlling the influx of cheap labour were more acute there than elsewhere. The fragmentation of work, and the difficulties that geographical size presented for organizing widely dispersed groups of workers, made the task of control particularly difficult. In many trades there was little to choose between artisans and small masters, and over their lifetime journeymen could reasonably expect to become employers in their own right. For both groups, enforcement of the apprenticeship regulations was seen as a means of combating competition from larger firms and from employers who had themselves set up business without having served an apprenticeship. Evasion of the laws in this fashion thus posed a direct threat to the employment of artisans and encouraged unfair and ruinous competition by large firms. For both small masters and skilled workers alike, the apprenticeship issue was clearly also about the blocking of opportunity.

Large employers, meanwhile, viewed these proceedings with some alarm. Any extension of the apprenticeship laws to cover trades not originally included under the Elizabethan statute, such as engineering, and any strengthening of the sanctions against the employment of non-apprenticed labour, were viewed with deep suspicion. If the laws were strengthened, employers feared that it would add significantly to the power of combinations. Such fears were felt most keenly by engineering employers who themselves had been responsible for introducing the Combination Acts of 1799 and 1800. Faced with the prospect of an organized campaign to extend the apprenticeship statutes, large employers launched a concerted counter-attack.

In May 1813 an influential group of five of the largest engineering firms in London, led by Henry Maudslay, petitioned for the repeal of the Statute of Apprentices, arguing that apprenticeship was a restraint on trade: 'Your memorialists can affirm that the most skillful and useful journeymen ... are those who have not served any apprenticeship.'[53] It was clear, however, that Maudslay and the other employers had a broader struggle in mind than just the question of skill. They recognized that by aiding artisans' control over entry to a trade, the apprenticeship laws strengthened the power of combinations. By repealing the laws, a blow could be struck against trade unions and this was clearly uppermost in their thoughts:

> The mischief, however, the manufacturers feel they have most reason to dread, from the extension or continuation of this act (5 Eliz. c. 41), is one which strikes at the root of all our prosperity. It is that which arises from the pretensions it countenances, and the color [sic] it gives to the combination of workmen for the raising of wages, and the prevention of improvements.[54]

In November a wider committee of manufacturers was formed to press the case for repeal. Chaired by Alexander Galloway, proprietor of one of the largest engineering concerns, it included all those who had signed the May petition together with several large employers in other trades. At the time Maudslay's workforce numbered about 150, whilst the Bermondsey tannery of Samuel Bevington, one of the firms represented, employed about 85 men. Luke Hopkinson, another committee member, was one of the largest coach makers with 50 men at his Long Acre workshops.[55] For various reasons, the apprenticeship question succeeded in polarizing the interests of large capital against those of small employers and London artisans. That such a confrontation occurred at such an early point in the century should be sufficient confirmation that labour relations between capital and labour were anything but smooth.

In 1814 the matter was duly decided and the Elizabethan apprenticeship statutes were repealed: *laissez faire* arguments won the day and large capital triumphed. Despite repeal, however, struggles over apprenticeship continued not only because control of employment opportunities was the cornerstone of craft unionism but also because the issue was related to the wider question of social mobility. Journeymen and small masters rightly feared that large firms able to subdivide work and simplify tasks could employ learners and apprentices and thus had correspondingly greater opportunities to cut costs. Speaking on behalf of striking bookbinders in 1839, John Powell argued the case against large firms: 'If these monopolists wish to underwork a small master the whole of these apprentices are put upon a particular work for which an estimate is to be given and then taken at a very low rate.'[56]

Similar concerns were voiced by others. Where work was subdivided, apprentices and learners were no longer taught the complete range of skills necessary to set themselves up as small masters and therefore had little prospect of social advancement. Again the journeymen bookbinders expressed this better than most. Appearing before the Royal Commission on children's employment in 1843, William Crawford, a bookbinder with 50 years' experience, recounted the change that had taken place:

> The trade is carried on now in a different manner from what it was many years ago. Formerly, when a man was bound to the trade he was taught the whole of the business; but now the binding of a book is so subdivided into many branches, and each man does only one of them. For instance, one man puts on the boards, another man does the back, a third puts on the leather, another does the lettering, another the general finishing. Thus an apprentice now learns only an exceedingly little and is unfit to get his living setting up for himself; or to work anywhere, except in large shops, where the work is done on a large scale, and can be so subdivided.[57]

Journeymen bookbinders and small masters had good reason to fear the threats posed by large firms employing excessive numbers of apprentices. In December 1838 a dispute broke out at Bones of Blackfriars, one of the bookbinding firms that employed large numbers of apprentices and learners. The dispute rapidly spread to other employers who had adopted similar practices, including the six-storey establishment of Westley and Clark, and Remnants of Paternoster Row, who, it was claimed, had taken on 24 apprentices just prior to the strike.[58] All these employers were members of the masters' association and on the commencement of the dispute had locked out their workers unless they renounced union membership. The journeymen, supported by many smaller masters, held out for nearly nine months before a compromise was eventually reached.

The census figures suggest that their resistance was to little avail and that workers were unable to prevent the spread of cheap labour into the bookbinding trade. Between 1841 and 1851 there was a threefold increase in the number of girls under 20 years of age employed in the book trade, compared with a fall in the number of boys.[59] In the larger firms, female piece workers supplanted hourly-paid male artisans, occasioning yet further disputes.[60] Such were the pressures generated by this practice that in 1850 the bookbinders' union split between time and piece workers. By the 1861 census, when figures for bookbinding itself become available, more women than men were employed and girls outnumbered boys by two to one. By that time the artisans' struggle to limit apprentices was effectively lost. And what was true of bookbinding also held for other trades.[61] Indeed, as John Rule has argued, no account of unionism that fails to appreciate the extent to which the apprenticeship issue marked a fundamental divide between skilled unionists and employers can come close to understanding the events of the period.[62]

Control of the labour process

In terms of the number of disputes, the issues relating to control of the labour process were of similar significance to questions over entry to the trade. This category, however, was more amorphous and generalizations are correspondingly more difficult. Several issues were important: alterations to the hours of work and methods of payment, shorter hours, the introduction of machinery, and more general changes in the methods of work, such as speed-ups or encroachment on trade privileges. The form in which wages were paid was probably of most significance by virtue of the implications it had for the labour process. Unlike the situation in the eighteenth century, when non-monetary additions to the wage were often at the heart of labour disputes, by the 1800s it was the amount of money and the form of payment that was most frequently at issue.[63] In the context of control of the labour process, disputes concerning the shift from time wages to piece work, and from weekly or daily wages to payment by the hour were of greatest significance. In both cases the most important aspect, as journeymen themselves recognized, was not the fact that wage cuts might ensue as a result of the change but that changes to the methods of payment were generally accompanied by parallel transformations of the labour process. For example, when the tailors struck in 1834 as part of the GNCTU agitation, the tendency for masters to adopt piece work in place of a daily rate of pay was uppermost in their minds. This was objectionable primarily because it paved the way for the spread of subcontracting and the employment of cheap, domestic outworkers. In turn, the tailors argued that this made employment less certain since a rush of orders could be met by distributing jobs to outworkers rather than having them done on the master's premises.[64] Although the rate of pay was a consideration in this particular dispute, the real issue was, in fact, more fundamental than merely a question of money.

The other main issue included under control strikes related to the short time movement which emerged in the late 1840s in the context of mounting unemployment. In 1848 delegates at the Chartist convention heard that of the 200,000 artisans and mechanics in London, one-third were employed, another third were only half-employed and the remainder were unemployed, many of whom had been 'obliged to accept, as a last resort, the hateful badge of unwilling pauperism'.[65] Various suggestions were voiced to deal with the problem, including emigration, home colonization, cooperative production and local boards of trade to regulate prices, wages and competition.[66] However, as a means of combating the 'redundancy of labour', the issue that prompted most interest in terms of workplace disputes was the demand for shorter hours and this in turn brought workers into direct conflict with employers.

Unlike rates of pay, shorter hours was an issue around which trades in general could unite and, like the earlier apprenticeship campaign, it consequently drew together a variety of workers in a more or less coordinated movement. The builders, who were in the forefront of the campaign, had first argued for early Saturday closing in 1847. The same issue provoked a series of disputes in 1851 that culminated in a strike of over 1000 masons against Jay and Myers, two of the largest firms in the capital.[67] Although a fall in building activity in the mid-1850s temporarily dampened enthusiasm for a fight, the issue rumbled on.[68] In 1859 carpenters and masons resumed their call for a nine-hour day, thereby prompting a lock-out of 20,000 men by the Central Association of Master Builders.[69] Although the outcome on that occasion was inconclusive, the short hours movement continued to gather momentum and in the 1860s began to draw support not only from the builders but also from other workers including bakers, shoemakers, packers, brass finishers and railway signalmen.[70]

In several cases, the short time campaign proved successful in reducing the hours of work but in the process it threw up another set of problems. Once the length of the working day had been reduced, employers were faced with the question of whether to continue paying the old daily rates or to switch to hourly payment. For workers more was at issue than just a simple change in the methods of payment. In 1861 the decision by several large building firms to switch from daily to hourly payment prompted an exceedingly lengthy and bitter dispute. The workers objected on the grounds that hourly payment made employment less predictable and undermined their status as skilled artisans. Under daily wages, they had received payment even if inclement weather or stoppages in production occurred. Hourly payment threatened this state of affairs because only the time actually worked was to be counted for the purposes of wages. As George Potter, the builders' leader, remarked, 'The hour system destroys a recognized day and is pernicious in its influence; in one word the fruits of the hour system are long hours of labour, over production and less pay.'[71] Further objections were also raised on the grounds that the hour system was humiliating and would reduce artisans to 'the level of dock labourers'.[72] In a letter explaining their position, Potter listed seven objections, including the fear that hourly payment and hiring would 'lower the standard of respectability among workmen by degrading them to the level of those who earn their money by the most precarious means, and who have not received that training and education which every mechanic should receive'.[73] The reasons for disputes were rarely as clearly spelled out as this, but it nevertheless serves as cautionary reminder that the issues involved in control strikes were often closely related and thus difficult to separate.

Machinery

Finally, as a further insight into the way in which economic change affected the trades, we should also take note of issues that rarely led to strikes. In this respect it is interesting to speculate on the rarity of machine breaking. Although attacks on machinery were not unknown in London, the use of machinery itself was rarely the cause of disputes, primarily because it was of relatively little importance in most London trades and was therefore not seen as a major threat to employment. However, where machinery was introduced, such as in bookbinding in the late 1820s and 1830s, and in sewing in 1853, it often generated opposition but rarely resulted in any violence.[74] The outburst of silk cutting and loom smashing in Spitalfields in 1829 was somewhat exceptional, reflecting less a dislike of machinery than fierce opposition to undercutting masters who took advantage of the weavers' desperate situation to reduce prices.[75] Following the collapse of building activity in 1826 and 1827, sawyers also complained about the threat posed by the spread of machinery, and workers interviewed by Henry Mayhew recounted stories of isolated attacks earlier in the century on horse-driven saw mills.[76] These incidents, however, were exceptional, focusing less on machinery *per se* than on the actions of unpopular employers.

Different trades, different rhythms: disputes in clothing and building

In the general rhythm of resistance, not every trade danced to the same tune. As Edward Thompson observed in relation to the metropolitan trades, 'The pressure of the unskilled tide, beating against the doors, broke through in different ways and with different degrees of violence.'[77] Before we leave the subject of disputes, let us examine briefly how those tunes differed. Two contrasting sets of trades can suffice. Building and clothing together accounted for nearly half the total number of labour disputes in the capital but in each trade the rhythms of resistance differed: the bulk of disputes in clothing occurred before 1840 whilst in building the main period of unrest came after 1850. Each trade, therefore, danced to a different tune and workers' experiences thus encompassed much of the variety of conditions that characterized the general pattern of industrial conflicts during the period.

In the first half of the century, London clothing workers were often in the forefront of working-class radicalism. Shoemakers and tailors in particular lent strong support to the Grand National Consolidated Trades Union (GNCTU), the London Working Men's Association and Chartism. Hat makers, though fewer in number, were also keen participants in radical activity.[78] Such enthusiasm was matched by the readiness of workers in these trades to embark on strikes. This was hardly a surprise, given that the dividing line between political radicalism and trade unionism was all but invisible.

Labour unrest was at its height in the decades prior to the emergence of Chartism, as shown in Figure 5.4. Indeed, up to the mid-1830s no set of London workers was more willing to flex their industrial muscle than those involved in clothing. At the start of the century the tailors' trade unions were renowned for the strength of their organization and the almost military precision with which their house of call system operated. There was, according to Francis Place, 'a perfect and perpetual combination among them' and this allowed them the power to enter into strikes.[79] During the Napoleonic Wars tailors struck on at least five occasions in pursuit of higher wages. Thereafter, the situation changed as cheap outworkers flooded into the trade. In 1827 bespoke tailors struck against the employment of women in making waistcoats. When they struck again in 1830 over the question of double pay during periods of mourning, the masters imported provincial labourers to defeat the

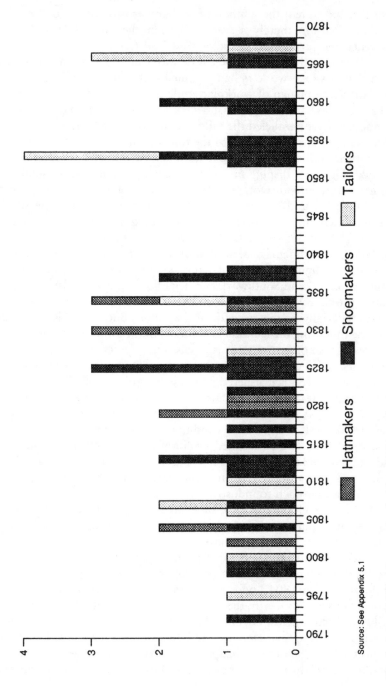

Source: See Appendix 5.1

Figure 5.4   Labour disputes in clothing, 1790–1870.

strike.[80] The strong support for the GNCTU by tailors was therefore a desperate bid to halt the dilution of skill and erosion of wages.[81] Failure on that occasion merely served to hasten the changes and further weakened the position of bespoke West End tailors. Despite efforts to revive the union during the 1840s, little was achieved and it was not until 1866 that bespoke workers had regained sufficient strength to embark on a further campaign of workplace militancy.[82]

Pressures in hat making and shoemaking were similar and the pattern of labour unrest paralleled the tailors' situation. The hatters' union had a long history stretching back to the time of Charles II and by the early 1800s their influence already extended far beyond the confines of the capital.[83] During a dispute in 1820, for example, employers found that despite advertising for workers in London and the provinces, 'so general was the strike, and so determined the workmen, than not one would return to their employ unless the masters would bind themselves to raise their wages and not keep more than two apprentices at a time'.[84] Unlike the tailors and shoemakers, who were far more numerous and widely dispersed throughout the capital, hat making was more concentrated and mainly took place in Southwark and neighbouring Bermondsey. As such, spatial proximity helped foster cohesion amongst the workforce that added materially to the strength of the union. But even this could not stem the mounting difficulties encountered in the 1820s and 1830s when changes in fashion began to disrupt customary practices and patterns of employment. When cheaper 'stuff' hats started to replace more expensive fur hats in the 1830s it ushered in a new set of less skilled workers that undermined the position of 'fair' men and eroded the power of the hatters' union. A similar situation arose in the 1840s as silk hats became more fashionable. Under these conditions, it proved difficult for hatters to sustain their long-established tradition of militancy. Strikes in 1830 and again in 1833 for advances in wages both ended in failure and from then on disputes were rare and the hatters' union adopted a more acquiescent approach to industrial relations.[85]

Of the three clothing trades, shoemakers were involved in the largest number of disputes and they alone appeared to sustain the capacity to strike. However, even this situation owes more to the fragmentation of the trade than to the strength of trade unionism.[86] At the start of the period, the shoemakers' unions were exceptionally strong in all branches of the trade.[87] In 1804 London masters complained that a combination existed throughout nearly the entire trade and that it was common for strikes to occur against anyone who refused to dismiss 'scamps', or non-society men, from their employment.[88] In 1807 shoemakers at Limebeer's of Fleet Street, one of the principal firms, struck over wages. The dispute rapidly spread throughout the city and further afield. When Limebeer himself sought replacements from Northampton, he found that the union had already been in correspondence and none could be persuaded to come.[89]

In 1812, however, a split occurred in the union when a strike succeeded in raising wages for West End shoemakers but not for those in the City. Henceforth different rates of pay prevailed between the two districts, driving a wedge between workers in different parts of the city. This split did little to foster unity within the trade and it was certainly more difficult thereafter to coordinate labour militancy.[90] The shoemakers' position was further undermined after 1815 by falling demand, lower prices and growing competition, and the strikes that occurred were mainly defensive actions to protect earnings and stem the rising tide of unskilled workers. Their participation in the GNCTU, like that of the tailors', was predicated on this basis and although shoemakers' trade unionism survived the debacle, it nevertheless remained on the defensive for the remainder of the decade. So, in 1838 a committee of employers countered a wage claim from low-paid repairers by issuing the 'document' that forced workers to renounce union membership or face dismissal. Despite lengthy resistance, shoemakers drifted back to work and by the end of the year the strike had collapsed.[91] Weak demand during the 1840s dampened even this low level of militancy, although it was evident from Mayhew's interviews with society men that trade unionism had not disappeared entirely. When conditions improved in the early 1850s, it was workers in the 'strong' trade, located mainly in the City and East End and making cheap boots and shoes for the wholesale and export markets, rather than the traditional West End artisan, who took up the mantle of labour militancy.

Though separate in the details of disputes, the similarities with respect to tailoring, hat making and shoemaking are clear. Similar pressures affected each trade: the existence of a large body of less skilled and poorly organized workers within London, coupled with growing competition from cheap provincial manufacturers, placed immense strains on customary working practices and levels of wages. Changes in fashion could also periodically disrupt labour relations. Provided that demand was high and the barriers of skill held firm, the journeymens' position was secure. Thus, the demand for uniforms, shoes and hats during the Napoleonic Wars sustained both the bespoke and slop sectors of clothing and this in turn had buttressed workers' positions in relation to that of their employers. However, the flow of contracts dwindled after the Wars and the pressures of competition mounted. Thereafter, artisans in each of the trades were forced to mount rearguard actions to defend wages and protect themselves against encroachment by cheap, unskilled labour. For them the agitation of the 1830s, primarily but not exclusively associated with the GNCTU, marked the end rather than the start of this period of labour militancy. Failure brought with it a shift in support from workplace disputes to an emphasis on working-class radicalism. Indeed, in these trades participation in political activity can be seen as much as an admission of that failure as it was a commitment to the principles of political reform.

The building trades provide a useful contrast to clothing because of their importance in relation to labour disputes and the fact that over the period workers in the trade seemed to gain rather than lose strength.[92] Unlike the clothing trades, the threats posed by cheap labour were of lesser significance than changes in the structure of the industry, and in particular the growing polarization between capital and labour. We can identify several distinct phases of unrest, as illustrated in Figure 5.5. No disputes were recorded before 1810, possibly because the relatively low level of construction during the Napoleonic Wars was not conducive to strikes, but also because traditional means of arbitration over wages still continued in the trade.[93] With the exception of a wage strike in 1810, the outbreak of disputes between then and 1813 concerned the apprenticeship campaign and as such reflected the problems faced by artisans in general rather than any specific grievances within the building trade. From that time, however, strikes began to replace arbitration by magistrates as a means of settling wage disputes and a tit-for-tat pattern emerged in which workers took advantage of peaks in the building cycle to achieve improvements and employers sought to claw back some of the concessions during downturns.

This pattern of disputes also hinted at important structural changes in the industry reflecting the rise of large general contractors and the spread of piece work and subcontracting.[94] As construction gathered pace from the late 1840s, the tide turned in favour of the workers and conflicts between capital and labour became more common. With the memory of high unemployment still fresh in the mind, building workers campaigned throughout the 1850s for shorter hours of work.[95] As we have already seen, these disputes were often large affairs focused on the major firms. Following demands for a nine-hour day in 1859, for example, 88 of the largest building firms locked out their workforce.[96] In 1861 the focus of disagreement shifted to the method of payment and a second widespread dispute erupted over the change from daily to hourly payment.[97] Although this strike was unsuccessful and the hour system was introduced, defeat was not disastrous and trade unionism continued to spread within the building trades. In the early 1860s, the newly-formed Amalgamated Society of Carpenters and Joiners drew most of its membership from London, as too did the Operative Bricklayers Society

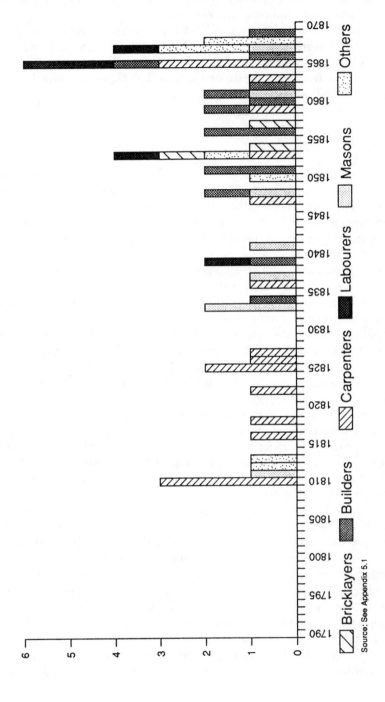

Source: See Appendix 5.1

Figure 5.5   Labour disputes in building, 1790–1870.

and the Friendly Society of Operative Stonemasons.[98] Unlike the clothing trades, therefore, building workers managed to construct a sound platform for labour militancy that was sufficiently strong to withstand occasional defeats and setbacks. That they were able to do so was the result of several factors, not least of which was the enormous boom in construction from the 1850s onwards and the correspondingly high demand for labour.

Conclusion

What lessons can we learn from this general review of the causes of labour disputes and the rhythms of workplace resistance? The first and most significant is that throughout the period both workers and employers were fully aware of the opportunities and constraints offered by fluctuations in the demand for labour. Workers well appreciated that seasonal and cyclical peaks in demand provided their best chance of gaining concessions and struck with greater frequency at such times to achieve their aims. Resources were high, alternative employment available and employers keen to settle rather than lose orders. And if successful, other trades followed suit, as happened during the Napoleonic Wars, the boom of early 1825, the GNCTU agitation of 1834, the wage strikes of 1853 and the flexing of union muscles in the mid-1860s. In contrast, heightened competition during economic downturn forced employers to seek means of reducing costs with the result that in such periods pressures to lower wages and reform customary working practices intensified. Under such circumstances, workers were naturally reluctant to become embroiled in disputes and did so primarily for defensive purposes. The collapse of labour militancy during the long downswing between 1825 and the late 1840s is particularly noteworthy in this respect and marked a low point in the strength of labour in the capital.

The second point to consider relates to the differing experiences of individual trades. As the builders and clothing workers make clear, the rhythms of conflict were to some degree determined by structural conditions in particular trades. In this context, Iorwerth Prothero's distinction between upper and lower trades, based on the extent to which they participated in wider labour movements, is a useful starting point.[99] For the period leading up to Chartism, he identified two distinct strands in London unionism. The first referred to the actions of workers in the upper trades, such as coopers, compositors and engineers, who remained relatively prosperous and to a certain extent avoided involvement in wider labour movements. The second concerned workers in the lower trades, such as carpenters, tailors, shoemakers and silk weavers, who fared less well and were more deeply involved in working-class radicalism. Whilst the position of building workers in this group from the 1850s might be questioned, the distinction in the fortunes of these individual trades still held true for most of the period, as the pattern of industrial disputes confirmed.

Finally, the chronology of disputes lends weight to the view of the metropolitan economy outlined in Chapter 2, where it was argued that London experienced a long downturn in the second quarter of the century. After 1825, housebuilding collapsed and remained depressed until mid-century whilst trade entering the port over a similar period grew relatively slowly. For those in work, the fall in prices after the Napoleonic Wars meant gains in real wages, providing that money wages could be sustained. In the immediate post-War years, and more significantly during the long downturn after 1825, this proved difficult to achieve. Not all years were ones of doom and gloom, and on several occasions brief upturns in demand provided workers with an opportunity to regain lost ground. But by and large workers struggled to protect wages in the face of growing competition in the labour market and structural changes in the pattern of production. The weakness of labour during this long downswing was reflected by a marked reluctance on the part of workers to become involved in labour disputes, especially during the depressed years of the 1840s. Desperation drove some to take direct actions, notably the silk weavers, but for most it was a case of mounting rearguard actions to stem the erosion in wages and the deterioration of conditions. That some were more successful than others is not in doubt and several trades emerged stronger at the end of the period than they had been at the start. Experiences clearly differed and we now need to examine how those differences were mapped out across London.

Notes

1. Rule, 1986, p.256.
2. See Dobson, 1980; Rule, 1981; Stevenson, 1992.
3. Even the Webbs, who argued that the creation of formal and permanent trade unions was a measure of the modernity of the labour movement, acknowledged the existence of unions from at least the start of the eighteenth century. See Webb, S. and Webb, B., 1920, pp.21–63.
4. See Rudé, 1964, pp.69–77; Stevenson, 1992, pp.69–113; Thompson, 1968, pp.22–3, 76–8.
5. See Goodway, 1982; Prothero, 1966; idem, 1981; Stevenson, 1977, pp.xiii–xxvi; Taylor, 1983, pp.101–17.
6. PP 1824 V, SC on artizans and machinery, p.47.

7. The most widely accepted definition is that of Hyman, 1984, p.17.
8. Bevan, 1880, p.36.
9. See in particular the work of Cronin, 1979; Dobson, 1980; Geary, 1984; Lees, 1982; Rule, 1981, pp. 147–93; Stearns, 1974; *idem*, 1975; Stevenson, 1992, pp.144–72, 254–62.
10. See Green, 1984, pp.422–7; for the working-class press see Berridge, 1978; *idem.*, 1986, pp.207–13; Webb, 1955, pp.32–4.
11. The number of stamps was usually an over-estimate but gives a rough guide to circulation. See Wadsworth, 1955–56, and the figures in Green, 1984, pp.428–30.
12. Dobson, 1980, p.22. Dobson suggests that 119 disputes occurred in London, although this must be taken as a minimum number.
13. *ibid.*, pp.42–4.
14. See Dobson, 1980, pp.91–2; Fox, 1985, pp.69–71; Thompson, 1968, pp.595–6.
15. Place Coll. Add. Ms. 27834, fol. 108. The pattern of strikes most closely fits tailoring, a trade with which Place was very familiar, having himself been a leather breeches cutter and small master in his own right.
16. The 1799 Combination Act lasted one year and was replaced by a similar act in 1800. For the slight differences between the two see Orth, 1991, pp.156–61.
17. George, 1936; Moher, 1988, pp.87–90; Orth, 1991, pp.45–73.
18. *The Times*, 21 July, 26 September, 9 November 1810.
19. See Haynes, 1988, pp.237–48; Simon, 1954, pp.160–6.
20. Quoted in Thompson, 1968, pp.263–4.
21. Howell, 1902, p.13.
22. Hobsbawm, 1984, pp.106, 112.
23. See Crompton, 1860, pp.77–92; Crossick, 1978; Jeffereys and Jeffereys, 1947; Howe and White, 1948; Musson, 1954, pp.3–26, 76–85; Southall, 1988b, pp.472–7.
24. See Gilding, 1971, pp.49–82.
25. See Pollard, 1950; Prothero, 1981, pp.46–9, 163–71, 217.
26. Blankenhorn, 1985, pp.29–30.
27. A dispute that took place in 1837 concerning the *London Cabinet Makers Union Book of Prices* of 1811 suggests that it was still in use. The price book ran to over 600 pages and took nearly three years to complete and consequently there was understandable reluctance to revise it. See *London Mercury*, 5 February 1837.
28. Mayhew, 1981, vol. 3, p.130.
29. Jones, 1851–52, vol. 1, p.657. In 1850 the Friendly Society of Operative Cabinet Makers had a membership of 455, rising to 528 in 1860. See Southall, Gilbert and Bryce, 1994, p.83.
30. Mayhew, 1968, vol. 3, p.304.
31. See George, 1927, pp.241–6 for a discussion of the London coal heavers.
32. See, for example, *Northern Star* (*NS*), 19, 26 August 1848, 17, 24, 31 August, 30 November, 14 December 1850, 4, 11 January 1851.
33. *The Times*, 12 May 1857; see also *The Employer and the Employed*, 1852.
34. *Reynolds Newspaper* (*RN*), 8 December 1867; *Beehive*, 25 July, 29 August, 5, 12 September 1868.
35. *Statesman*, 5 January 1820; *Trades Newspaper*, 1 April 1827; See also Clapham, 1916; George, 1966, pp.188–96; Webb and Webb, 1920, p.112.

36. PP 1856 XIII, *SC on masters and operatives*, q. 2255, 2269–70; PP 1860, vol. XXII; *SC on masters and servants*, q.421–6, 430, 447.

37. Mayhew, 1980, vol. 1, p.57.

38. See Chapter 2, p.31.

39. Potter, 1870, pp.35–7. George Potter was in a good position to know: he was the builders' leader during the exceptionally long and bitter dispute in 1859–60, and was also President of the *London Working Men's Association* and later the editor of the *Beehive* newspaper.

40. The labour process is here defined in relation both to the methods of work and the raw materials, tools and machinery used to manufacture commodities.

41. *Journeyman and Artizans London and Provincial Chronicle*, 12, 19 June 1825; *Artizans London and Provincial Chronicle*, 10, 24 July, 28 August 1825; *Trades Newspaper*, 17, 31 July 1825; Place Coll. Add. Ms. 27803, fol. 215, *idem.*, Add. Ms., 27805, fol. 365–72; Webb Coll. E, series A, vol. 10, fol. 57.

42. *RN*, 7 August 1853.

43. *ibid.*, 12, 19 June, 10, 17, 24 July, 7, 14, 21 August, 4 September 1853.

44. *ibid.*, 8, 29 May, 24 July, 7 August, 11, 18, 25 September; *The Times*, 27 July, 17 August, 9, 16, 23 Sepember 1853.

45. *The Times*, 28 July 1853.

46. *Trades Newspaper*, 6, 13, 20, 27 August 1826.

47. *ibid.*, 12, 19 November 1826; Webb Coll. E, series B, vol. 75, p.22.

48. Hunt, E.H., 1986, pp.71–93; Taylor, 1983, pp.101–17.

49. Derry, 1931–32; Prothero, 1981, pp.51–61.

50. *Gorgon*, 12 December 1818; *St James Chronicle*, 23–25 February 1804; PP 1824 V *SC on artizans and machinery*, pp.80–2, 87, 89; Place Coll. Add. Ms. 27799, fol. 97, 99; Atkinson, 1799.

51. PP 1812–13 IV *SC on the several petitions ... respecting the apprentice laws*, pp.947, 990–2. All prosecutions on behalf of the trades were undertaken by William Chippendale, suggesting that the legal campaign was coordinated by a committee of London artizans.

52. *Statesman*, 4 November 1812; *London Chronicle*, 4–5 April 1813; *Petition of the Masters and Journeymen*, 1813 (ULMC). E.P. Thompson suggested that hundreds of petitions calling for the retention or extension of the apprenticeship regulations and containing 300,000 signatures were submitted. See Thompson, 1968, p.565.

53. *Memorial of machinists and engineers*, 1813, PRO HO 42/133.

54. *The origin, object and operation of the apprentice laws*, 1814, p.21.

55. *The Times*, 19 July 1819; Spate, 1938, p.423.

56. *Operative*, 5 May 1839.

57. PP 1843 XIV *RC on children's employment*, p.806.

58. *The Times*, 10 January 1839; *Operative*, 13, 20 January, 17 February, 31 March, 14, 28, April, 5 May, 2 June 1839; *NS*, 18 May 1839; Dunning, 1860a, p.101. For a description of Westley and Clark's factory see Dodd, 1843, pp.363–7.

59. Unfortunately the census categories for 1841 and 1851 fail to distinguish bookbinders from sellers and publishers. However, in 1861, when the categories were first enumerated separately, the number of bookbinders was 7754 compared with 3118 booksellers and publishers. Therefore the figures for 1841 and 1851 probably reflect more on the state of

bookbinding than other branches of the trade.

60. *Reply to a letter from ... the Britsh and Foreign Bible society*, 1849; *An Address to the British and Foreign Bible Society ...*, 1849; *Appeal of the journeymen bookbinders*, 1849.
61. See, for example, *NS*, 14 August 1841; Howe, 1947, p.302.
62. Rule, 1986, pp.324–5.
63. Linebaugh, 1993, pp.438–41.
64. *Pioneer*, 3, 10 May 1834; Place Coll. vol. 51, pp.243–51. For a fuller account of the strike and the events leading up to it see Parssinen and Prothero, 1977.
65. *NS*, 24 April 1848.
66. *idem.*, 27 May 1848, 10 March, 7 April, 12 May, 10 November 1849, 2, 9 March, 20 July 1850.
67. *idem.*, 25 October, 15 November 1851; *Builder*, 1 November, 27 December 1851; PP 1867 XXXII *RC on the trade unions*, q. 1422.
68. *RN*, 23 November 1856.
69. *idem.*, 31 July, 7, 14 August 1859, 19 February 1860; Shaw Lefevre and Bennett, 1860, pp.60–72; Smiles, 1861, pp.166–7; Webb Coll. E, series A, vol. 11, fol. 145.
70. *RN*, 26 August, 14 October 1860; 22, 29 October 1865, 30 September 1866.
71. *idem.*, 2 June 1861.
72. *The Times*, 15 July 1861.
73. *RN*, 13 October 1861.
74. *idem.*, 2 October 1853. Although much bookbinding was still done by hand, machines were used in some of the larger binderies. See Dodd, 1843, pp.363–84; *Reply of the journeymen bookbinders*, 1831.
75. *Weekly Free Press*, 6 June 1829.
76. *Trades Newspaper and Mechanics Weekly Journal*, 23 July, 17 September 1826, 7, 28 January, 4 March 1827.
77. Thompson, 1968, p.279.
78. Prothero, 1966, pp.299–300; *idem.*, 1971, pp.207–10.
79. PP 1824 V, *SC on artizans and machinery*, p.45. See Chapter 6, pp.166–8 for more detailed discussion of these disputes.
80. *Red Republican*, 23 November 1850; Parssinen and Prothero, 1977, p.70.
81. *ibid.*
82. The two strikes that took place in 1853 both involved seamstresses in the slop trade, the first calling for higher wages and the second in protest at the introduction of sewing machines. See *Reynolds Newspaper*, 11, 25 September, 2 October 1853, *The Times*, 16, 23 September 1853.
83. *The Times*, 26 March 1804; *St James Chronicle*, 1–3 May 1804; PP 1824 V *SC on artizans and machinery*, pp.80–2, 91; Rule, 1981, pp.156–8.
84. *Statesman*, 22 July 1820; PP 1824 V *SC on artizans and machinery*, pp.74, 93; Place Coll. Add. Ms. 27799, fol. 80–3.
85. Burn, 1868, p.42. A further sympathy strike took place in 1834 at Christy's, one of the foremost hatmaking firms in London and the provinces, when provincial masters refused to employ members of the hat makers union. See *Reply of the journeymen stuff hatters of London*, 1834.
86. See Chapter 6, pp.170–2 for more detailed discussion of the shoemakers' situation.
87. The branches included mens' and ladies' shoes, together with coarser boots

made in the 'strong' trade.

88. *St James Chronicle*, 1–3 November 1804; Aspinall, 1949, pp.76–7.
89. *The Times*, 18 January 1808. Workers interviewed by Henry Mayhew in 1850 still recalled the strike. See Mayhew, 1981, vol. 3, p.145.
90. PP 1824 V *SC on artizans and machinery*, pp.137–8, 145; O'Neill, 1869, p.314; Mayhew, 1981, vol. 3, pp.146–7.
91. *Operative*, 4, 18, 25 November, 9, 23 December 1838, 20 January 1839.
92. For a detailed discussion of the building trades after 1830 see Price, 1980.
93. Place Coll. Add. Ms. 27799, fol. 120–3.
94. Cooney, 1955; Price, 1980, pp.22–7.
95. *RN*, 23 November 1856; PP 1867 XXXII *RC on trade unions*, q. 2606.
96. Shaw Lefevre and Bennett, 1860; Webb Coll. E, series A, vol. 11, fol. 145; Price, 1980, pp.50–3.
97. Webb Coll. E, series A, vol. 10, fol. 108; *idem.*, vol. 13, fol. 205–6.
98. PP 1868–69 XXXI *RC on trade unions*, appendix J, pp.659–60, 672.
99. Prothero, 1971, pp.209–10.

CHAPTER SIX

The geography of economic change: east and west London

Introduction

In London the distinction between skilled artisans and unskilled labourers was as often as not expressed in spatial terms. 'In passing from the skilled operative of the West-end to the unskilled workman of the eastern quarter of London', Henry Mayhew wrote, 'the moral and intellectual change is so great that it seems as if we were in a new land, and among another race.'[1] Few would have disagreed with this view, least of all those West End artisans whose livelihoods were being undermined by competition with cheaper labour from eastern parts of the city. Here we examine how that competition arose. We begin by considering how labour costs varied within the capital, focusing on the cost of living, the strength of trade unionism and the availability of cheap, female domestic labour. Thereafter the fortunes of several trades are discussed, focusing on those that succumbed to the pressures of competition, notably watchmaking and silk weaving, and those in which manufacturers were forced to restructure and relocate production to cheaper locations within the city as a means of ensuring survival. Clothing, shoemaking and furniture making were examples of this second group. Collectively, experiences in these trades map out, in both a geographical as well as a structural context, the path from artisans to paupers.

The geography of labour costs

'The vast populousness of London and its neighbourhood ought to lower the price of labour', Arthur Young noted during his tour around southern England in 1768. That the reverse held true, he argued in jaundiced fashion, was because of the debauched and idle habits of Londoners. 'If a low price of labour is a public benefit, sure the size of London is a public evil', he remarked.[2] The costs of labour were substantially higher in London than elsewhere. Indeed, for much of the eighteenth century wages in the capital were between a third and a half higher than in provincial towns.[3] Although rates had evened out somewhat by the late eighteenth and early nineteenth century, especially in comparison with rapidly growing northern industrial towns, marked differentials still remained. In silk weaving, for example, in the early 1800s wages in London were a third higher than in Manchester and two-thirds above those in Norwich and Kidderminster.[4] Similar differences existed in printing, engineering, shoemaking and shipbuilding.[5] Taking the artisan trades as a whole, Bowley estimated that workers in London received between 6s. and 9s. a week more than their provincial counterparts.[6] We need to understand why this situation occurred in order to explain the role of geography in the restructuring of production.

Rents and the cost of living

The main factor underlying these wage differentials was not a taste for luxurious living, as Young had claimed, nor was it the cost of food, which in the mid-nineteenth century differed only slightly between London and the provinces.[7] Instead, as Mayhew noted, 'It is the London rents which eat people up', and it was this factor that ensured that wages were higher in the capital than in other manufacturing towns.[8] But rent levels within London also varied considerably, notably between eastern and western districts, and this distinction played an important role in determining differences in the cost of labour.

Rent was an extremely important part of working-class expenditure, accounting for as much as one-sixth of weekly household incomes at mid-century, with the proportion falling as earnings rose. Between 1832 and 1862, applicants for poor relief in St Giles spent an average of 2s. 1/2d. a week on housing, representing approximately 17 per cent of total household income.[9] This proportion accords reasonably closely with the findings of Samuel Bosanquet in 1841 who showed that families with a weekly income of 30s., a figure well above that of the very poor, paid about 13 per cent of household income on rent.[10] In St George-in-the-East in 1845, as shown in Table 6.1, rent consumed on average over 15 per cent of household income, although again this varied according to the level of earnings with labourers forced to spend a higher proportion of income on housing compared with better-paid artisans.[11]

Given the importance of rent within working-class budgets, any variations in the cost of housing would clearly have had a significant impact on the levels of wages. Spatial differences in the availability of working-class housing ensured that rents varied considerably across the city. In western districts aristocratic landlords, such as the Grosvenor, Bedford and Portland estates, controlled large tracts of land.[12] In their efforts to create fashionable residential districts for the wealthy, these landlords discouraged or prevented the construction of working-class

Table 6.1   Rents and household income in St George-in-the-East, 1845

Occupation of household head	Number of families	Average household income (s.d.)	Average weekly rent (s.d.)	Rent as percentage of income
Labourer	363	19s.1d.	3s.3d	17.0
Shoemaker	101	20s.8d.	3s.6d	16.9
Carman	50	23s.7d.	3s.9d	15.9
Tailor	72	24s.6d.	3s.8d	15.0
Carpenter	76	27s.0d.	4s.2d	15.4
Cooper	64	27s.11d.	3s.8d	13.1
Gunsmith	87	45s.3d.	4s.1d	9.0
All households	1954	23s.1d.	3s.7d	15.5

Source: Statistical Society of London, 1848a

housing on their estates.[13] Cheap housing was therefore pushed to other parts of the city or confined in the West End to small pockets of back streets and alleys behind main thoroughfares, such as the St Giles rookery, in which land ownership was more fragmented.

Pressures to rid areas of slums could more easily be applied where poor housing was relatively concentrated. From the time that Regent Street was opened in 1814, street clearances in western and central districts were used as a blunt though seemingly effective means of ridding areas of their poor population.[14] In central districts, expansion of commercial and industrial premises, and from mid-century the coming of the railway added to the growing pressures on space.[15] Between 1831 and 1861, as shown in Figure 6.1, with the exception of Holborn and Clerkenwell, every district in central London lost housing. This reduction was most dramatic in the City which by the 1840s was losing its residential function and becoming primarily a commercial district.[16] Although the reductions were not as large in other central areas, they were nevertheless significant in terms of the total housing stock. Meanwhile, those areas immediately surrounding the centre to the east and south, where the fragmentation of land ownership meant that controls over working-class housing were relatively lax, received the influx of the poor.

This changing map of housing availability was reflected in the spatial pattern of rental values which can be gauged, albeit imperfectly, from the House Tax returns for 1851. This tax was levied on inhabited dwellings with an estimated annual rental value of £20 or above.[17] Although

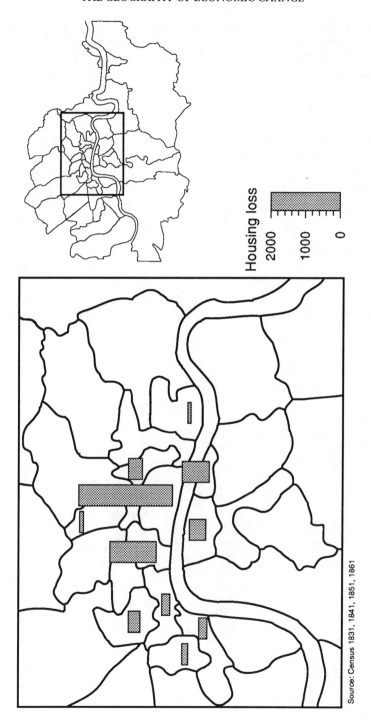

Figure 6.1   Reduction in housing in central London, 1831–1861.

Source: Census 1831, 1841, 1851, 1861

Housing loss

2000

1000

0

houses with values below this threshold were primarily those occupied by the working class, nevertheless the proportion rated in the lowest banding of £20–£30 provides a broad indication of the relative availability of cheap housing. The spatial distribution of the lowest banding of taxable dwellings, mapped in Figure 6.2, shows the broad distinction between central and western districts on the one hand, and those further to the east and south on the other. In the latter set of districts the majority of taxable housing was rated in the lowest band, compared with a much lower proportion in the West End and central parts. Indeed, in eastern districts the proportion of lower value houses was more than double that in wealthier western parishes. In both Bethnal Green and St George-in-the-East, for example, over 66 per cent of taxable houses were rated at between £20 and £30 compared with less than 30 per cent in St George Hanover Square, St Martin's and the Strand and less than 20 per cent in aristocratic St James.[18]

This geographical variation in the supply of cheap housing had important implications for the level of rents and living conditions for working-class families. In Westminster, steep rents elicited frequent complaints and were responsible for high levels of overcrowding amongst working-class families.[19] In neighbouring St George Hanover

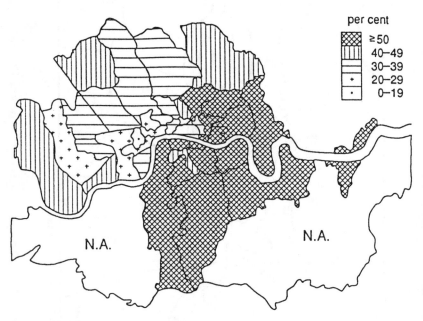

Source: PP 1852–53 XXVIII

Figure 6.2   Housing valued at £20–£30 in 1851 (14 and 15 Vict c. 36).

Square poor households in the 1840s paid an average weekly rent of 4s.3d. and nearly two-thirds lived in single rooms. By contrast, in St George-in-the-East rents were lower, averaging 3s.7d., with only about a third of working-class families forced to live in single rooms.[20] To be poor in central and western districts at mid-century clearly meant having to suffer worse overcrowding than in other parts of the city. It also meant having to pay more for the dubious privilege. Since rents were an important element in working-class budgets, and therefore were a significant consideration in determining wage levels, this fact alone imposed stricter limits on the extent to which rates of pay could be forced down in western areas compared with eastern districts.

The geography of trade unionism

For skilled workers, the barriers of trade-based associations – houses of call, friendly societies and trade unions – provided some protection against the full impact of market forces on levels of employment and standards of living. The tailors were in no doubt that without such protection their lot and that of others would have been worse. Petitioning for repeal of the Combination Acts in 1819, they stated that 'in proportion as combination among classes of workmen is more or less perfect, so is the remuneration they receive for their labour greater or less'.[21] Mayhew similarly was in no doubt over the importance of union membership:

> In almost all trades there are two broadly distinguished classes of workmen, known as 'society' and 'non-society' men; that is to say, a certain proportion (usually about one-tenth of the whole) of the operatives belong to a 'society' for upholding the standard rate of wages, as well as supporting their unemployed members. These society-men constitute what may be termed the aristocracy of the trade.[22]

However, the importance of society men, and the strength of the protective barriers of association, varied considerably between districts. Where such artisan associations remained firm, the tide of unskilled labour was held more or less at bay; where the barriers were weaker, artisans found it more difficult to resist downward pressures on wages and the erosion of status. The geography of these working-class institutions was therefore an important factor in influencing labour costs in the capital.

Evidence of the spatial variations in the number and location of trade-based friendly societies is presented in Figure 6.3.[23] Whilst it is difficult to establish the length of time that friendly societies operated, the regional breakdown indicates the relative strength of trade unionism

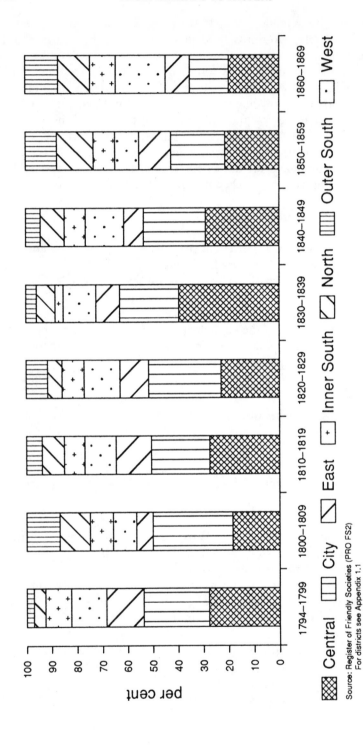

Source: Register of Friendly Societies (PRO FS2)
For districts see Appendix 1.1

Figure 6.3   Regional distribution of friendly societies, 1794–1869.

across the city. Several points are worth noting. First, although the City and central regions contained a relatively large number of friendly societies, reflecting the importance of the inner industrial perimeter for manufacturing and trade, their share declined over the period as a whole. This fall began in the 1840s and was linked to the transformation of central London from a residential to a primarily commercial core. Secondly, and related to this change the growing importance of suburban areas should be noted. Before 1800 northern and southern districts contained less than 7 per cent of the total number of friendly societies in London but by the 1850s this had risen to over a quarter. As core districts lost their industrial base, so the centre of gravity of trade-based friendly societies began to shift outwards.

The third point to note, and for our purposes the most significant, was the changing balance between eastern and western districts. This distinction is made clearer in Table 6.2. At the start of the period, each region had a similar share of friendly societies but by the end the situation had changed significantly. In western districts the proportion of friendly societies had risen sharply and indeed was over-represented in relation to population. Over the period as a whole, West End districts, such as St James, St George Hanover Square and Westminster, maintained or increased their role as the foci of trades organization. By contrast, eastern districts lost ground and by the 1860s that region was the most under-represented in the city as a whole, confirming to some extent Hobsbawm's view of the area as a trade union desert.[24] The poverty of the population, together with the problems of organizing both casual labour and domestic workers isolated in their own homes, made

Table 6.2   Population and friendly societies, 1794–1861 (per cent)

District	Friendly societies registered 1794–1799	Population 1801	Friendly societies registered 1860–1869	Population 1861
West	13.9	16.5	19.7	16.5
North	4.6	13.0	12.4	22.0
Central	27.8	16.3	19.7	9.4
City	25.9	13.4	15.3	4.0
East	14.8	18.6	9.5	20.4
Inner South	10.2	11.4	10.2	9.8
Outer South	2.8	10.8	13.1	17.7

Sources: Register of Friendly Societies (PRO FS2); Price Williams, 1885

it difficult to establish friendly societies and trade unions in this region. Under such circumstances, the mantle of protection afforded by such working-class institutions was spread more thinly here than in the west.

Further evidence of the geographical variation in the strength of trade unionism comes from the *First Annual Trade Union Directory*, compiled in 1861 by William Burn, the brick makers' leader.[25] The *Directory* contains a listing of trade-union branches together with the day of meeting and the public house in which it was held. In many cases several trades or separate branches of a union met on different days at the same public house, with Monday and Saturday being the most popular. Curriers and the cooperative tinplate workers, for example, met on alternate Mondays at the Black Jack in Lincoln's Inn Fields, whilst cooper stave sawyers, ships' riggers and the Good Intent coopers assembled on Tuesday, Wednesday and Saturday respectively at the Britannia Inn in St George-in-the-East. Another popular venue was the White Horse and Half Moon in Borough High Street, Southwark; back makers met there on Saturdays as did the carpenters (who also held their quarterly meetings there on Mondays), plasterers assembled there on alternate Tuesdays, and farriers likewise on Wednesdays. Meetings were normally held at least once a month, although they sometimes occurred more frequently. Stone masons in different parts of the city, for example, met on alternate Mondays and Tuesdays whilst the Operative Bricklayers met every Saturday. Taking into account both the number of meeting houses and the monthly frequency of meetings, the *Directory* lists 233 separate trade-union houses that collectively hosted over 730 meetings a month, an impressive total that provides a good indication of the overall strength of unionism in the capital.

When the geographical pattern of meeting houses and monthly meetings are plotted against the proportion of the manufacturing workforce in each region, as shown in Figure 6.4, three main points emerge. First, paralleling the distribution of friendly societies, the City and central districts were relatively well provided with meeting houses as well as in terms of the frequency of meetings. Despite losing population, districts in the inner industrial perimeter, including the City, and to a lesser extent surrounding districts, retained their status as centres of trade unionism by virtue of historical association and ease of access. Secondly, in western and inner southern riverside districts, the balance between manufacturing employment and the share of meeting houses was closer. Thirdly, and by way of contrast, northern and southern suburbs, together with eastern districts, were under-represented both in terms of the number of meeting houses and the frequency of meetings. However, an important distinction must be made between the suburbs, and the more built-up and industrialized districts in the east. In suburban

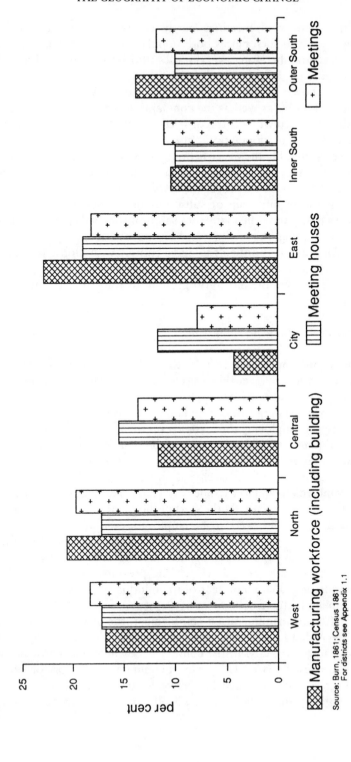

Figure 6.4 Regional distribution of trade-union meeting houses, 1861.

areas, the number of meetings partly compensated for the lack of meeting houses. In such places both population and public houses were thinly spread and therefore several trades tended to make use of the same meeting house on different days of the week.

The east, however, was already well built-up and the relative lack of trade-union houses, as well as the comparative infrequency of meetings, a trait that it shared with central districts and the City, cannot be blamed on the dispersal of population. Instead, weak organization reflected other factors, notably the overwhelming importance of casual, unskilled and domestic labour in the area. The uncertainty of such work, coupled with a hand-to-mouth existence, was hardly conducive to paying regular dues for union membership or subscriptions to friendly societies. Nor was it easy to organize the many thousands of widely dispersed domestic workers in clothing, shoemaking and furniture making, as Marx himself noted.[26] Although it is difficult to agree entirely with Hobsbawm's view that 'east London was a trade-unionist desert', nevertheless the evidence confirms that it was the most arid ground for trade organization in the capital.[27]

The geography of female employment

No labour came more cheaply in Victorian England than that of women and children and wherever they were employed in large numbers, wages were low and conditions of employment poor. Part of the blame, as Barbara Taylor has argued, can be laid at the feet of male artisans who objected to the employment of women on the grounds that it disrupted patriarchal family relations.[28] However, the economic threat that women posed was of more immediate concern and this fear, as much if not more than the preservation of patriarchy, prompted the men's efforts to restrict female employment and to exclude women from craft unions. The tailors felt the threat most keenly. At the start of the century their rules explicitly stated that no women were to be employed, even at the height of the season, and in 1806 seven of their number were imprisoned in Tothill Fields for organizing a strike against masters who employed female labour.[29] Other trades may have felt the pressure less but the tailors' concern mirrored a common fear of the dilution of skills and erosion of status implied by the employment of women.

In relation to manufacturing employment, the availability of female labour depended largely on competing opportunities and these differed markedly across the city. In the country as a whole, but particularly in London, domestic service was the most common occupation for women. At mid-century, it accounted for between 40 and 45 per cent of total female employment in the capital, with the proportion rising to over 55 per cent for those aged below thirty years.[30] However, in London as elsewhere, demand for servants depended on social status, and in this respect there were significant differences between wealthier suburban and western areas and those poorer districts to the east.[31]

By the mid-eighteenth century, significant concentrations of wealthy families already existed in western districts and in the decades that followed the association of wealth and West End residence became more pronounced.[32] By the late nineteenth century, Charles Booth's maps confirmed that the 'servant-keeping' classes were disproportionately concentrated in western and suburban districts. The location of domestic servants in 1851, mapped in Figure 6.5, suggests that this pattern also held true at mid-century. With the exception of the City, which still retained a core of high-status households and continued to generate a daytime demand for domestic services, the distribution of servants shows a marked east-west divide. The proportion of servants was more than four times higher in wealthy districts, such as Kensington and St James, than in poorer eastern and inner southern districts, such as Shoreditch, Bethnal Green and Bermondsey. Lack of a resident middle class in such districts severely restricted opportunities for female employment and women were forced to seek work in a tightly constrained and consequently grossly overstocked and poorly paid labour market. For

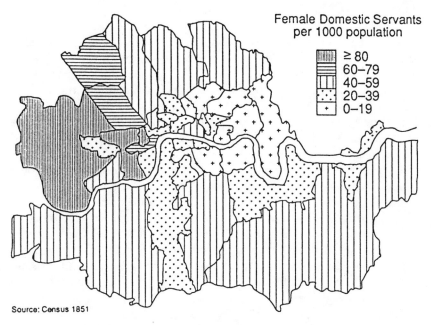

Female Domestic Servants
per 1000 population

≥ 80
60–79
40–59
20–39
0–19

Source: Census 1851

Figure 6.5 Domestic servants, 1851.

employers in search of cheaper locations, the availability of such low-paid female labour, and the impact that had on male wages within the same localities, was an important consideration in relocating production. This factor, coupled with the weakness of protective barriers outlined above, ensured that eastern districts exerted an increasingly powerful pull on manufacturing in the capital.

The geography of manufacturing

From the gallery of St Paul's Cathedral a visitor could gaze out over the workshops and warehouses of the greatest concentration of manufacturing trades in the world. In London's inner industrial perimeter, which stretched for about a mile in every direction, as many as a quarter of a million people were employed in one capacity or another in the various manufacturing trades. This total itself was more than the entire populations of most British cities of the period. A closer look would have revealed that individual trades occupied their own particular niche, tied to a locality by custom, access to markets and the advantages of agglomeration. As James Burn noted at the time, 'The geographical distribution of trades and professions are therefore as well defined in London as the natural produce of the earth in its different climes.'[33]

Broadly speaking, London consisted of several distinct economic regions. The census figures outlined in Table 6.3 indicate that the main concentrations of manufacturing were located in the City, central, inner south and eastern districts, each of which had more than 40 per cent of the adult male workforce so employed. Figure 6.6 confirms this state of affairs. The main bulk of industry was located in a belt stretching from Clerkenwell in the north to Poplar in the east and Southwark in the south. In Bethnal Green over 67 per cent of the workforce was employed in manufacturing while in neighbouring Shoreditch the figure was nearly 59 per cent. These districts were home to many of London's traditional trades including clothing, shoemaking, and furniture making, together with more highly localized trades such as hatmaking and tanning in Southwark and Bermondsey, printing in the City, watchmaking in Clerkenwell and silk weaving in Spitalfields and Bethnal Green. It was this inner set of districts, according to Joseph Fletcher, that comprised the 'great commercial, manufacturing, artisan, labourer and mariner suburbs'. More sombrely, he added 'It is the vast bodies of the labouring classes thus aggregated around the centre of town, but not absolutely in its centre, that are properly the great solicitude in a sanatory [sic] view.'[34]

Within this inner industrial perimeter, important differences in

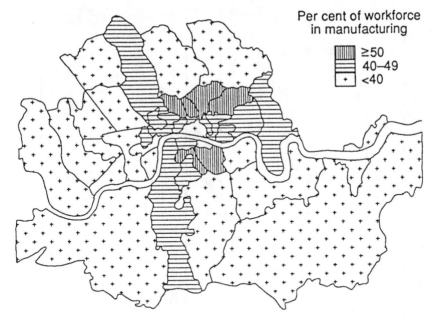

Source: Census 1851

Figure 6.6 The inner industrial perimeter, 1851.

economic structure occurred. Casual labour was of greatest significance in and around the dockside districts of the east and inner south. This was particularly true in eastern districts where the census records that over a quarter of the male workforce in 1851 was involved in transport or general labour. Not surprisingly, the irregularity of work and the uncertainties of life associated with casual labour dominated working-class life in these areas. But the census figures shown in Table 6.3 also show that it was in manufacturing that the most significant variations existed, notably in the pattern of female employment. In eastern districts women typically worked not in domestic service, as occurred in virtually every other part of the city, but in manufacturing, especially needlework and shoemaking. Lack of alternative opportunities mainly accounted for this pattern. As the proportion of middle-class residents fell in these districts, so the female labour market tightened accordingly. This pattern existed throughout the overcrowded central areas but it was particularly noticeable in eastern districts and manufacturing in that region therefore had a qualitatively different sexual division of labour to that elsewhere.

Within this broad manufacturing belt, the City itself also needs to be treated separately. By the 1840s it had already become 'one vast

Table 6.3   Employment structure, 1851

Male	WEST No.	%	NORTH No.	%	CENTRAL No.	%	CITY No.	%	EAST No.	%	INNER SOUTH No.	%	OUTER SOUTH No.	%	LONDON No.	%
Manufacture	23,596	24.4	33,543	29	31,162	44.1	13,981	40.5	51,176	41	26,019	41.3	23,531	25.2	203,008	33.9
Professional	15,161	15.7	14,886	12.9	6487	9.18	2819	8.16	6647	5.33	3743	5.94	17,824	19.1	67,567	11.3
Building	12,093	12.5	15,913	13.7	5923	8.38	1634	4.73	9663	7.74	5420	8.61	10,703	11.4	61,349	10.2
Domestic Service	11,852	12.3	7700	6.65	3063	4.34	1922	5.56	2395	1.92	1393	2.21	3478	3.72	31,803	5.31
Food Trade	8775	9.09	10,889	9.4	6933	9.81	3776	10.9	13,438	10.8	7043	11.2	8990	9.61	59,844	9.99
General Labour	8343	8.64	9634	8.32	5563	7.87	2286	6.62	15,106	12.1	6988	11.1	8328	9.98	57,248	9.56
Transport	7308	7.57	9534	8.23	5717	8.09	4532	13.1	18,499	14.8	7446	11.8	6962	7.45	59,998	10
Retail and Distribution	4728	4.9	8551	7.38	4217	5.97	2596	7.51	6110	4.9	3639	5.78	5985	6.4	35,826	5.98
Agriculture	4654	4.82	5179	4.47	1581	2.24	1006	2.91	1743	1.4	1286	2.04	6705	7.17	22,154	3.7
TOTAL	96,510	100	115,829	100	70,646	100	34,552	100	124,777	100	62,977	100	93,506	100	598,797	100

Male	WEST No.	%	NORTH No.	%	CENTRAL No.	%	CITY No.	%	EAST No.	%	INNER SOUTH No.	%	OUTER SOUTH No.	%	LONDON No.	%
Domestic Service	44,975	69.8	48,302	.63.2	14,995	43.8	10,737	52.6	18,562	31.1	11,943	42.8	27,951	60.8	177,465	53.9
Manufacture	12,817	19.9	20,032	26.2	14,296	41.7	7047	34.5	34,150	57.2	12,195	43.7	11,318	24.6	111,855	34
Food Trade	1944	3.02	2575	3.37	1934	5.64	1590	7.78	3150	5.27	1497	5.37	2129	4.63	14,819	4.5
Professional	2429	3.77	3501	4.58	1627	4.75	481	2.35	1500	2.51	907	3.25	2449	5.33	12,894	3.92
Retail and Distribution	1185	1.84	1561	2.04	973	2.84	373	1.83	1934	3.24	1012	3.63	1284	2.79	8322	2.53
Agriculture	841	1.3	58	0.08	118	0.34	56	0.27	177	0.3	128	0.46	631	1.37	2009	0.61
Transport	74	0.11	77	0.1	182	0.53	55	0.27	59	0.1	52	0.19	42	0.09	541	0.16
Building	31	0.05	21	0.03	19	0.06	9	0.04	24	0.04	10	0.04	27	0.06	141	0.04
General Labour	180	0.28	250	0.33	126	0.37	83	0.41	172	0.29	139	0.5	125	0.27	1075	0.33
TOTAL	64,476	100	76,377	100	34,270	100	20,431	100	59,728	100	27,883	100	45,956	100	329,121	100

Source: Census, 1851

counting-house', as the census breakdown of employment confirms.[35] The transformation still had a considerable way to go, and many trades clung tenaciously to the centre, but by the 1850s fashion was directing wealthy families elsewhere whilst demolitions were forcing large numbers of workers into surrounding districts. For the middle class, commuting to the City became possible once omnibus services became more common from the late 1820s and 1830s. For the working class, however, the need to be on hand dictated that they remained close to their place of employment, hence they were more tied to central locations. In turn, this meant that whilst the City retained a relatively large manufacturing workforce, it nevertheless lacked a resident middle class. Its commercial functions, though, were evident in the numbers employed in transport and retailing, which accounted for over 20 per cent of the male workforce. Similarly, servicing the large daily influx of people meant that the provision of food and services remained an important source of employment, despite the fact that the resident population was steadily falling.

The structure of employment in suburban districts differed considerably from the City and inner industrial perimeter. Whilst manufacturing was still the single largest category of male employment in the west, north and south suburbs, it was the presence of a relatively large number of professional men, and considerable numbers of both male and female domestic servants, that were the defining characteristics. In 1851, these outer districts accounted for nearly 70 per cent of the total number of female servants in London and in wealthier western and northern suburbs, the total number of domestic servants exceeded those employed in manufacturing. The economy in these 'service suburbs' was thus focused more closely on the homes of the upper and middle classes than it was on manufacturing workshops.

Whilst broad geographical differences in employment structure were important, we must not forget that economic life also functioned at a finer spatial scale. 'As London has swelled itself into its huge dimensions', Burn wrote in 1858, 'circumstances of adaptation have enabled the leading branches of trade to localize themselves in various districts.'[36] In some places, single trades dominated employment, as was the case with watchmaking in Clerkenwell and St Lukes, silk weaving in Spitalfields and Bethnal Green, and tanning in Bermondsey. In others, groups of allied trades were important, such as food processing and coopering in the docks, or ship building and rope making along the Thames. With more specialized trades and professions, individual streets were sometimes devoted entirely to particular occupations: Long Acre was noted for coach making, Savile Row for bespoke tailoring and Monmouth Street for the second-hand shoe trade. The sharing of tools and expertise and the need to coordinate different branches of manufacturing, particularly where the division of labour was most pronounced and component tasks were correspondingly fragmented, were powerful incentives to concentrate production in a specific location. In turn, the rates of pay, patterns of employment and workplace customs of specific trades meant that to a greater or lesser extent each district possessed a distinctive economic and social structure. This meant that structural change in particular trades and cyclical fluctuations in employment affected districts in highly individualistic ways.

The geography of manufacturing decline

In the first half of the nineteenth century, many of London's traditional trades battled to survive. Slack demand in the second quarter of the century, coupled with cheaper foreign and provincial competition, forced manufacturers to seek cheaper means of production with the thrust of savings falling on lowering the cost of labour. Structural decay in these trades, and the various efforts to stay that decline, thus had important implications for the welfare of the working-class population. The collapse of highly localized trades, such as watchmaking and silk weaving, was disastrous for those employed in the industry. Other, more widely dispersed trades, such as clothing, shoemaking and furniture making, survived only by cutting wages and reducing levels of skill. In both instances, the economic changes mapped out a path that led workers from the status of artisans to that of paupers.

Watchmaking

In eighteenth-century London, watchmaking was known for its high-quality craftsmanship, but by the mid-nineteenth century it had virtually disappeared from the capital. With it went the fortunes of those workers in Clerkenwell and St Luke employed in the trade.[37] This situation arose largely because of structural changes in the nature of the product and geographical variations in the costs of manufacturing. The growing awareness of time and the need for accurate timekeeping, especially with the spread of turnpikes and the development of stage-coaches from the 1750s, created a market for cheaper and more portable watches and clocks.[38] As the size of component parts was reduced, their value in relation to weight increased: watch springs, for example, were literally worth their weight in gold. Two outcomes ensued. In view of high London wages, and the fact that watch parts were so valuable that they could bear the additional costs of transport, it became more economic to transfer production away from London to areas where labour costs were lower, notably the Midlands and Lancashire.[39] Similarly, the reduction in the size of watches made them easier to conceal and larger quantities began to be smuggled in from abroad, especially Switzerland.[40] Manufacturers were squeezed both by cheaper domestic and foreign production and their situation became increasingly untenable.

London watchmakers responded by intensifying an already highly differentiated division of labour. According to Adam Smith, the division of labour had reduced the cost of a watch movement from £20 in the seventeenth century to little more than 20s. by the 1760s.[41] By this time many watchmakers merely assembled the movement, using parts made in small local workshops or provincial towns, and engraved the watchcase adding their name as proof of authenticity.[42] Even so, the degree of fragmentation possible in London was still more limited than that in provincial towns where artisan restrictions on the subdivision of work and employment of cheaper labour were weaker. In Coventry, for example, at the start of the nineteenth century, watchmaking was subdivided into over a hundred component tasks, whilst the London trade comprised only fifty different branches. With the exception of the finisher, who assembled the watch, and the watchmaker, who coordinated the various tasks, none could be considered to have been complete masters of the trade.[43]

For all but the most highly skilled watchmakers in the capital, these changes were catastrophic. Both manufacturers and the London Company of Clockmakers blamed the decline on cheap forgeries.[44] William Pitt's imposition of the Watch and Clock Tax in 1797, though hastily repealed in the following year, elicited further complaints from London watchmakers about the parlous state of trade in the capital.[45] Wartime blockades offered a brief respite from smuggled foreign goods but once hostilities ceased Swiss watches reappeared in the domestic market, adding to the growing flood of cheaper provincial goods.[46] After the Napoleonic Wars, the situation of London watchmakers again worsened. In 1816, seven thousand watchmakers were unemployed in Clerkenwell and St Lukes, with the remainder working short time. In the following year a committee of master watchmakers found that large numbers of workers had pawned their tools and were therefore unable to resume work. Although on this occasion the depressed state of trade was blamed on several causes, including the employment of larger numbers of apprentices following repeal of the Elizabethan statutes in 1814, the imposition of a tax on silver plate and the 'Jew system' of reducing prices and screwing down wages, the problems were evidently more deep rooted.[47] The lesson for the capital's trades was clear:

wherever value was high in relation to weight, and whenever market conditions altered to favour mass demand, London manufacturers found it increasingly difficult, if not impossible, to compete.

Silk weaving

During the eighteenth century, as Peter Linebaugh has remarked, silk was the 'fabric of power and class command'.[48] Like watches, however, its value was high in relation to weight and silk weaving struggled in similar fashion to maintain a foothold in the capital. Because of the large numbers involved, when the trade collapsed in the second quarter of the nineteenth century, the impact was even greater and by the early 1840s Bethnal Green and Spitalfields had become synonymous with impoverishment.[49]

The problems of silk weaving in London have been well documented elsewhere and here we need only recount the broad outline.[50] As with watchmaking, the main problems faced by metropolitan manufacturers were foreign competition and cheap provincial production. Although the 1773 Spitalfields Act had prohibited manufacturers from sending work out of the capital, evasion of the Act was commonplace.[51] After repeal of the Act in 1824 it became clear that large numbers of looms existed in the surrounding rural districts, notably in Essex, and in Midland towns such as Coventry, Macclesfield, Manchester and Stockport. In Manchester, for example, the first steam-powered mill for throwing silk was opened in 1819, and by 1830 about a dozen integrated spinning and weaving mills were in operation.[52] Technological change was also evident in Coventry where larger Jacquard and engine looms were replacing the smaller, single hand looms.[53] In London such changes came about more slowly.

What these provincial towns could offer above all was cheap labour, the one commodity that was in short supply in London. The cost of living in the capital was partly responsible, but so too were the Spitalfields Acts which not only regulated wages but also limited weavers to two apprentices and thus restricted entry to the trade. In contrast, no such regulations tied the hands of provincial manufacturers. In 1815, for example, employers in Manchester and Coventry succeeded in introducing large numbers of 'half pay' apprentices to the trade, despite opposition from the weavers' union.[54] Wage costs in both Midland and southern counties were at least a third lower than in London and this fact alone drew the industry away from the capital. In 1833, Thomas James, a London wholesale silk manufacturer, described how he had reduced his dependence on Spitalfields and instead imported about half his goods from Manchester. He was by no means an isolated example and many others followed his lead. Carriers from Manchester were said to be extremely busy, sending about a quarter more goods to London than had been the case in previous years.[55]

Manufacturers in the capital responded by focusing more closely on the production of finer, more fashionable silks rather than the coarser materials woven in the provinces. To some extent this reflected the role of the luxury market in the capital and the importance of fashion. However, such a concentration brought London silks into direct competition with cheaper French fabrics. As long as foreign imports were prohibited, or disrupted by war, the Spitalfields trade clung on. Smuggling had always been a problem but in 1826 import duties were lowered and larger quantities of French silks began to undercut the luxury domestic trade. Spitalfields weavers were forced back towards the production of coarser fabrics and simpler patterns but this then brought them into direct competition with the provinces. In 1832 a witness before the Select Committee on the silk trade stated:

> Spitalfelds has lost its trade in rich silks, especially fancy and figured silks, and in some instances it has adopted the low Manchester trade as a miserable substitute for what it has lost; if I may use the term I will say that Manchester has travelled to London, and hence a competition has arisen between those places, Manchester and Spitalfields, which was not felt before, or at least not to the same extent.[56]

Hemmed in by foreign imports and cheaper provincial production, silk weaving in London collapsed and by the end of 1825, when downturn struck the metropolitan economy, the distress in Spitalfields was acute. In February 1826, over 8600 looms were idle, throwing an estimated 30,000 persons out of work.[57] Three years later reports noted that 7000 looms were again stopped in Spitalfields, prompting the weavers to cut silk from looms and smash machinery that belonged to those 'unprincipled' masters responsible for underpaying their workforce.[58] This forlorn gesture of defiance did little to stem the inexorable decline in the silk weavers' fortunes. Between 1826 and 1832 the price of silk halved and wages fell in proportion.[59] In 1833 John Ballance, a local silk manufacturer, described conditions:

> Every excessive relapse aggravates the distress, because the poor become if possible poorer, have less furniture and less means of rallying; the poor in Spitalfields at this moment, are far more destitute than they were in 1826; then they had some little means to fall back upon but now they have none.[60]

When Henry Mayhew visited the district in 1849 conditions had deteriorated even further. As one weaver ruefully remarked, 'Every year is getting worse in our trade, and in others as well. What's life to me?

Labour – labour – labour – and for what? Why for less food every month.'[61]

Clothing

In eighteenth-century London, two types of tailors and two branches of clothing manufacture existed in London. In terms of workers, there were the foremen who measured and cut the cloth and finished the work. Besides the customary 'cabbage', such skilled artisans received good wages and the occasional tip from a grateful customer.[62] Then there were the sewing tailors, 'as poor as rats' and 'as plentiful as locusts', according to Campbell's *London Tradesman*. Their task was more mundane, to sew seams and buttonholes and prepare the work for finishing. Wages were lower and during the three or four months they were idle these sewing tailors subsisted on credit from publicans and their house of call.[63] A similar division also characterized clothing manufacture itself.[64] On the one hand, bespoke tailors catered for the wealthy London élite. These were initially located in the City but as the wealthy moved westwards so did their tailors, and bespoke workshops were increasingly found in the West End. Then there was the wholesale and ready-made slop sector catering initially for large government or institutional orders but subsequently for a growing middle-class market. In the first half of the nineteenth century, as the middle class grew in size and wealth, this ready-made sector expanded. In doing so, the methods adopted to lower costs in this cheap sector spread into other branches, slowly undermining the basis of skilled work even amongst bespoke tailors.

From an early date the clothing trade was concentrated north of the Thames in a belt stretching from Westminster to Whitechapel. However, evidence from trade directories mapped in Figures 6.7, 6.8 and 6.9 show that important spatial distinctions existed between the bespoke and slop sectors of production. In 1790 tailors were concentrated in western and central districts, including the City itself, with the largest numbers being found closest to the élite West End districts of St George Hanover Square, St James, St Martin's and the Strand. Even from this date, however, the distinction between bespoke tailoring workshops and the wholesale slop trade, located mainly in eastern districts and the City, was clear. By the 1830s tailoring had spread westwards and northwards, notably along Oxford Street and into the fringes of St Marylebone. The bespoke trade, however, remained focused in and around Savile Row in the aristocratic quarter of St James.[65] The slop trade, on the other hand, was firmly entrenched in eastern districts and the City, with Whitechapel, in particular, containing the largest numbers of wholesale warehouses. From the late 1830s the directory evidence suggests that this

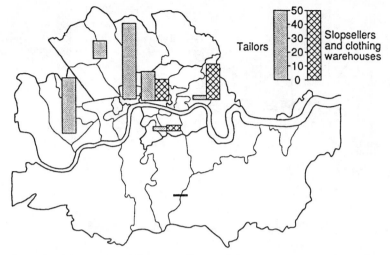

Source: Wakefield's Merchants and Tradesman's Directory, 1790

Figure 6.7   The clothing trade, 1790.

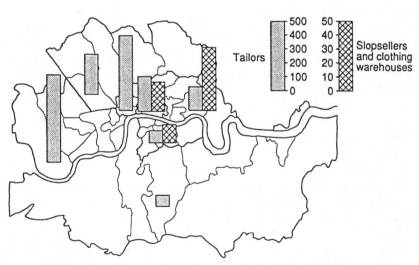

Source: Robson's London Directory, 1832

Figure 6.8   The clothing trade, 1832.

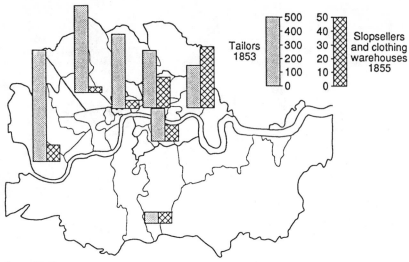

Source: Watkin's London Directory, 1853; Post Office Directory, 1855

Figure 6.9   The clothing trade, 1853–1855.

cheap ready-made sector was beginning to invade districts that traditionally had been the preserve of the bespoke trade and by the 1850s, as Figure 6.9 shows, clothing warehouses had become even more widespread, notably in central, western and northern districts.

The expansion of ready-made firms into districts hitherto the preserve of the bespoke trade was a significant shift in the pattern of production and a sharp break in the experiences and livelihoods of artisan tailors. 'Show shops', in which samples of garments were displayed and priced in glass-fronted premises to be made up later either in the shop or more commonly by outworkers, had begun to appear from the early 1800s along prominent shopping streets.[66] Strictly speaking, such show shops were neither part of the bespoke trade nor the ready-made sector. They stood midway, adopting some of the practices of bespoke work, such as choosing the cloth and measuring the customer, but also breaking with the tradition of indoor work by having garments finished off the premises. If Francis Place was anything to go by, the trade proved to be lucrative. In 1801 he prided himself that his glass-fronted shop at 16 Charing Cross was the first and largest in London.[67] Evidently business prospered, for not only did Place himself make more than a comfortable living, but by the 1830s others had followed his example, and by mid-century show shops were common throughout the West End.[68]

A second and more important change was also taking place,

consisting of the growth of 'slop shops' belonging to large, ready-made wholesale firms. By aggressive advertising and ruthless cost-cutting, these firms had managed by 1850 to corner a large section of trade, amounting to perhaps as much as a third of all business. [69] Three firms were exceptionally large, Hyams, Moses and Nicholls, and each employed hundreds of outworkers through an extensive web of subcontractors and sweaters that, although densest in eastern districts, nevertheless stretched across the entire city. [70] The structure of each firm was similar: it was common to have large retail premises or emporiums in the West End, one or more warehouses in the City which was supplied by an army of outworkers in the eastern districts, and workshops in provincial centres such as Leeds or Manchester. In 1850, for example, Hyams brashly advertised the fact that it had a West End shop, as well as a City warehouse and no less than 11 provincial branches. [71] Moses operated on a similar scale, claiming immodestly that it was the first to have introduced ready-made clothing for sale. [72] The firm had adjoining premises located on the border of Whitechapel and the City, and by 1852 two more shops had been opened in New Oxford Street and Tottenham Court Road, as well as branches in Bradford and Sheffield. [73] Taking no prizes for poetry, the advertising puff for the company proclaimed:

> Eight houses in a splendid style,
> This extensive range discloses;
> And all who view the buildings, smile
> Approvingly on Moses
>
> Moses and son are just famed
> For such a trading mansion;
> And not a warehouse can be named
> With such a vast expansion. [74]

The success of these brash new forms of enterprise depended entirely on their ability to sell cheaply and this in turn relied primarily on their seemingly infinite capacity to pay poorly. It was claimed that large slop-sellers could produce at two-thirds the cost of small independent masters: compared with the usual 'respectable' price of 19s., for example, Moses paid outworkers 12s. for the best dress coats, out of which they had to find their own trimmings, candles and coals. [75] Fines for late delivery, imperfections in workmanship or any sign of infestation further reduced the price paid to workers. Economies of scale and the ability to shift the costs of production onto sweated domestic labour, thereby saving on rent, light and heat, were also important additional means of reducing costs. In this respect, Mayhew estimated that Nicholls, who employed as many as 1200 outworkers, saved nearly £20,000 a year. [76] Given the range of savings, it was little wonder that such large firms grew at the expense of smaller, master tailors.

Large firms were also in the forefront of technological change and were the first to use sewing machines from the early 1850s.[77] Cost at first restricted the spread of machines, but by 1861 they could be bought for as little as £9, and rented for even less. Although it was claimed at the time that machines were not present in large numbers in London, and that they were confined mainly to the export market and the manufacture of coarser clothing, by 1855 machine-made clothing 'made at a considerable reduction in price' was being advertised by Hyams in their Oxford Street showroom.[78] Reductions in the cost of machine-made clothing gave these large firms a competitive edge over their more traditional rivals and they were thus able to expand at a faster rate. By contrast, machines were much slower to spread in the luxury bespoke trade where hand sewing remained the norm. However, whilst the spread of sewing machines was of enormous significance in increasing the speed of production and so forcing down the cost of clothing, the main impact was only felt in later decades once they had diffused more widely through the trade.[79] We must therefore look to other means whereby slopsellers were able to reduce costs, and for this we need to consider the geography of employment and the dismantling of the barriers of skill.

Clothing manufacture played a particularly significant role in the capital's industrial structure. Indeed, events in London were of national importance since nearly one in five of all adult male tailors in 1851 were located in the capital.[80] In the first half of the nineteenth century, clothing was the largest manufacturing trade in the city, accounting for one in seven male handicraft workers in 1831 and about 10 per cent of the total metropolitan workforce in 1851. The census, however, reveals marked spatial variations in the structure of employment. In 1841, the first date for which female occupations were recorded, the census figures in Table 6.4 indicate that male workers outnumbered female by over two to one. Even allowing for a considerable under-enumeration of women's occupations, a clear gender division of labour existed between eastern and western districts. In the City and Holborn districts, men outnumbered women at least threefold, whilst in Westminster, the centre of the bespoke trade, the ratio was more than four to one. In contrast, the majority of the workforce in the eastern Tower division were women, confirming the directory evidence cited above relating to the location of the slop sector of production.

With the 1851 census we are on firmer ground, both in terms of a better coverage of female occupations and a more detailed geographical breakdown of employment. By then the number of women employed in clothing had risen to a total of 25,935 compared with 20,957 men. Although it would be unwise to compare the 1841 and 1851 census figures directly, the large increase in the number of women hints at their

Table 6.4   Employment in clothing,* 1841

District	Male	Female	Male : female ratio
Kensington	588	225	2 : 6
Westminster	4,562	1,044	4 : 4
Holborn	4,915	1,654	3 : 0
Finsbury	1,124	486	2 : 3
City of London (within)	693	197	3 : 5
City of London (without)	1,225	463	2 : 6
Tower	2,946	3,201	0 : 9
Southwark, Bermondsey, Rotherhithe	1,057	689	1 : 5
Greenwich	490	219	2 : 2
Lambeth	280	176	1 : 7
Total	17,880	8,354	2 : 1

*Tailors, seamstresses, shirtmakers

Source: Census, 1841

growing importance in the workforce. A clearer picture of the sexual division of labour emerges from Figure 6.10, showing the gender breakdown of employment. This confirms the sharp distinction between male-dominated bespoke production in the west and the predominantly female slopwork of the east. In areas dominated by the bespoke trade, such as St James, men were up to three times as numerous as women but in eastern districts the reverse held true. In Stepney and St George-in-the-East, women outnumbered men by as many as five to one, reflecting the overwhelming dominance of sweated domestic labour. Above all, it was the ability of large wholesalers and slopsellers to tap into this vast army of under-employed and low-paid female domestic workers that enabled them to undercut competitors and so stave off cheaper competition from the provinces.

Whilst clothing manufacturers turned to eastern districts for supplies of cheap labour, once the ready-made slop trade gained a foothold in western districts, price competition ensured that methods of work and levels of pay adopted by slopsellers spread relatively quickly. Slopworkers interviewed by Mayhew in 1849 claimed that prices had been halved in the previous ten years and the reason was plain to see:

> The masters have now learned that tailoring work, under the sweating system, can be done at almost any price; and hence those

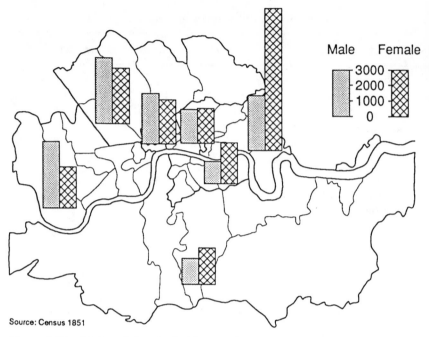

Source: Census 1851

Figure 6.10   Male and female clothing employment, 1851.

who are anxious to force their trade by underselling their more
honourable neighbours advertise cheap garments, and give the
articles out to sweaters to be made up by women and girls. By such
means the regular tailor is being destroyed; indeed a man's own
children are being brought into competition against himself, and the
price of his labour is being gradually reduced to theirs.[81]

Complaints from honourable West End tailors were voiced with
increasing frequency from the 1830s and although it was claimed in 1843
that there were very few sweaters in the West End, it was nevertheless
evident that the system was spreading rapidly.[82] Society tailors interviewed
by Mayhew claimed that the number of dishonourable West End masters
had doubled whilst those in the honourable sector had fallen from 72 to
about 60. The number of outdoor workers had risen in similar fashion
whilst the number of society men had fallen in equal proportion.[83] As
Mayhew somewhat ruefully remarked, 'The quiet, unobtrusive place of
business of the old-fashioned tailor is transformed into the flashy palace
of the grasping tradesman.'[84]

   This transformation did not occur without a good deal of conflict
during which the barriers of skill were overthrown and the tailors' trade
unions, deemed to have been the most militant and effective in the
eighteenth-century, were destroyed.[85] Structural division of the trade was

paralleled by contrasting levels of organization between skilled society men, known as 'flints', and those less skilled outworkers, or 'dungs', who operated outside the union in the cheaper branches of trade.[86] In 1833 the First Lodge of United Tailors described the contrasts between the two sets of workers:

> The honourables are those who are enlisted in the books of what is called a house of call – these alone are permitted to work in the shops of the masters, and have regular stated wages; the dishonourables are those who do not belong to a house of call but take in work at home and are free to accept any remuneration which they can obtain for their labour. The two parties are at war; the former will not work with the latter.[87]

From the 1820s and 1830s, strains between flints and dungs reflected the existence of mounting pressures that threatened to undermine customary practices of work. In 1827 a strike in the West End trade failed to prevent the spread of women outworkers and, following the death of George IV in 1830, the tailors were again defeated when masters refused to pay the traditional double pay during periods of official mourning.[88] These defeats, small in themselves, were more significant for the light that they shed on the waning power of artisan tailors, a situation thrown into sharp focus during the disastrous events of 1834.

In that year, as part of the agitation associated with Robert Owen's Grand National Consolidated Trades Union, the tailors prematurely embarked on an ill-conceived and contentious strike. At the centre of the dispute was the attempt to restrict the spread of outwork and prevent further erosion of wages and artisan status at the workplace.[89] The dispute ended in dismal failure and in the aftermath of defeat tailors lost the remaining vestiges of protection which their union had provided. The house of call system, so admired by Place, was dismantled and replaced instead by a system of 'call houses' shorn of any trade-union functions and under the control of bespoke employers.[90] Piece wages based on a 'log' of prices replaced daily rates of pay, thereby adding to the growing uncertainty of employment. Although in theory the new log mirrored the old daily wage rates, in practice, as the men fully appreciated, it was a very significant change – by legitimizing piece work it encouraged the spread of subcontracting and the use of outdoor, sweated labour.[91]

From this time on, conditions in the bespoke trade deteriorated in parallel with those in the slop sector of production and attempts to reunite the trade met with little success. Continuing distrust between the remaining bespoke tailors and the growing number of outdoor workers undermined efforts to form a trade union in both 1844 and 1858.[92] It was not until 1865, with the formation of the London Operative Tailors

Protective Association, that attempts at unification bore fruit.[93] With the barriers of artisan control in disarray, the path was cleared for the rapid spread of cheaper forms of production using less skilled and poorly paid domestic outworkers. By the 1860s as many as 80 per cent of those employed in clothing manufacture were outworkers and the centre of production had moved firmly eastwards.[94] Meanwhile, the expanding webs of subcontracting and sweating ensured that competitive pressures on the wages of artisans and outworkers moved freely across the capital. The barriers of skill, gender and geography were all but overthrown and workers in the east competed openly with those in the west.

Shoemaking

In terms of the numbers employed, shoemaking was second only to clothing manufacture and faced similar problems. The trade was divided into bespoke and wholesale sectors, both of which had specific patterns of employment and distinct geographies of manufacturing. From an early date, as shown in Figure 6.11, the bespoke retail trade was concentrated in and around the West End, notably St George Hanover Square and St James, whilst the cheaper, wholesale sector, indicated by the presence of shoe warehouses, was located in the City and eastern districts. By the early 1850s this spatial distinction had intensified, as Figure 6.12 confirms, with warehouses largely confined to the City,

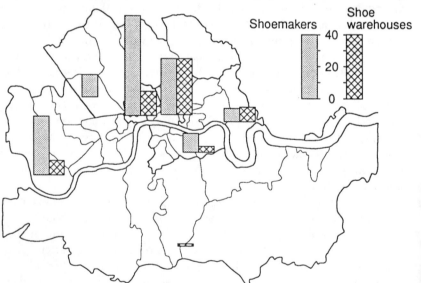

Source: Wakefield's Merchants and Tradesmans Directory, 1790

Figure 6.11 The shoemaking trade, 1790.

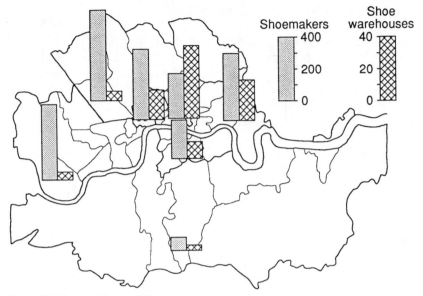

Source: Watkin's London Directory, 1853

Figure 6.12   The shoemaking trade, 1853.

eastern and, to a lesser extent, central districts, and the bespoke sector focused in western and northern areas.[95]

Although the structural divisions of clothing and shoemaking were similar, and both shared a common geographical distribution, the pattern of production was different in one important respect. Unlike clothing, the distinction between bespoke and wholesale shoemaking rested primarily on rates of pay and quality of work rather than on the distinction between indoor and outdoor production. Although some bespoke masters made shoes on the premises according to the specifications of individual customers, the usual method was for the leather to be cut out by 'clickers' in a workshop and for the tasks of stitching and finishing to be given as outwork. Within the bespoke sector, therefore, domestic production was far more common than was the case with clothing. Women and children frequently worked alongside their male partners or fathers, a fact recognized by the inclusion of the category 'shoemakers' wife' in both the 1851 and 1861 censuses. Indeed, according to the former, women enumerated in this manner comprised over 40 per cent of the total workforce.

For small masters, or 'chamber masters', who often took orders from wholesale warehouses, the availability of female labour was crucial and in this respect the sexual division of labour operated in a similar manner to clothing. According to the census data mapped in Figure 6.13, the main

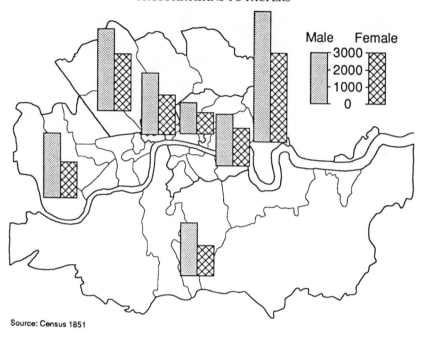

Source: Census 1851

Figure 6.13   Male and female shoemaking employment, 1851.

focus of employment was in eastern districts, despite the fact that trade directories listed more employers and retailers in western and central parts. This discontinuity merely confirmed the geographical distinctions between bespoke workshops in the west and much larger wholesalers in eastern areas and the City. The significance of female outworkers, however, and the contrasts between wholesale and bespoke production, are brought out most clearly by considering the sexual division of labour at the level of registration districts, as illustrated in Figure 6.14. In élite West End districts at the centre of the bespoke trade, such as St Martins and St James, male artisans outnumbered women by about two to one. In eastern districts, on the other hand, notably in Bethnal Green, Whitechapel and St George-in-the-East, the sexual composition of the workforce was more evenly balanced. It was rare for women to outnumber men in any manufacturing trade, but in shoemaking in these districts they came close to doing so.

As with clothing, these distinctions were paralleled by contrasting patterns of unionization. In common with the tailors, workers were divided into 'flints', who belonged to the shoemakers' union and were paid according to an agreed scale of prices, and 'scabs', who worked outside these formal agreements.[96] From the early 1800s, shoemakers' unions were divided by type of work and locality. Separate societies existed for mens' and womens' shoes, as well as for the 'strong' trade

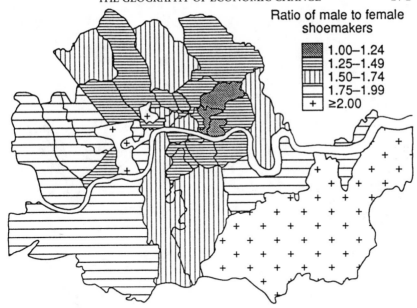

Source: Census 1851

Figure 6.14   Ratio of male to female boot- and shoemakers, 1851.

making rougher boots, and these were further divided into separate West End and City societies, each with different rates of pay.[97] This geographical separation had arisen in 1812 during a dispute over wages when West End masters conceded to a rise whilst those in the City refused. Thereafter, two different price lists operated depending on where the work was undertaken, a distinction that was subsequently formalized by the separation of shoemakers' unions into West End and City societies.[98] In 1824 John Alexander, secretary to the London Boot and Shoemakers' Society, estimated that between 700 and 800 men were members of the West End society compared with about 600 in the City.[99] By the 1840s union memberships had hardly changed, despite considerable growth in the number of workers. At the national conference of trades held in London in 1845, union delegates from the capital claimed a total membership of at least 2000 men which at a conservative estimate represented less than 10 per cent of the adult male workforce.[100]

Union membership, moreover, was overwhelmingly concentrated in western and central areas, as the distribution of meeting houses in 1861, shown in Figure 6.15, suggests. Despite the large numbers of workers employed in eastern districts, only five out of a total of 37 trade-union houses were located in eastern areas, of which three belonged to the strong trade. By contrast, St James alone contained seven trade-union houses. Whilst many East End workers no doubt frequented meeting

Source: Burn, 1861

Figure 6.15   Boot- and shoemakers' trade-union meeting houses, 1861.

houses in the City, the absence of a network of trade unions in eastern districts suggests that the barriers of skill and trade unionism were particularly weak. This factor, coupled with the importance of female domestic workers, ensured that wages and conditions of employment were far worse there than in other parts of London.

From the 1820s pressures mounted on metropolitan shoe manufacturers to reduce prices. Cheaper provincial shoes from Northampton and Leicester made inroads in the ready-made market, whilst in the bespoke trade the reduction of import duties made French boots and shoes more competitive.[101] Added to this were changes in fashion and methods of manufacture that increased the pressures to lower costs. In 1838, for example, 'blind rands' involving less work were introduced in place of stitched work, resulting in reductions in the price of shoes. Retail shops also began to give out bulk orders to warehouses, which in turn relied on the availability of cheap labour in eastern districts:

> Employers at the East-end, who buy of the chamber-masters, supply some of the best shops at the West-end, and many of the better kind in the country parts. The reason why the chamber masters are able to get up goods at a less price than the usual rate, is on account of the number of boys, and girls, and women, and all kinds of cheap labour they employ.[102]

Prices indeed were far lower in the East End: 'sew around' shoes, for example, which fetched 1s.4d. a pair in the bespoke trade, cost between 5d. and 10d. from wholesale warehouses.[103] Faced with such pressures, there was little that respectable masters could do but follow suit and screw down wages. This was only possible, however, where the barriers of skill and artisan opposition were weak and nowhere were they less firm than in the East End trade.

Furniture making

Furniture making was the fourth largest of the capital's manufacturing trades, behind clothing, shoemaking and textiles, and like these it too faced intense pressures during the first half of the century. The fall in house building after 1825 dampened demand and in the following years the furniture trade stagnated. However, the recovery in building from the 1840s, coupled with sharp falls in the price of furniture brought about by cheaper wood, the introduction of veneers and the spread of machinery, provided both the conditions for growth as well as the impetus for change.

In this competitive economic environment, furniture manufacturers also turned eastwards in search of cheaper forms of labour. Between 1831 and 1851 adult male employment in the trade grew by over 55 per cent, as shown in Table 6.5. This increase, however, was accompanied by an important geographical shift in production. Although the regional classification adopted in the 1831 census was altered in subsequent censuses, it remained sufficiently close to allow comparison with the other trades so far examined. The changes in location mirror what was fast becoming a common pattern. In 1831 one in three workers were located in the Holborn division, comprising mainly those areas immediately to the west of the City. During the 1840s the industry shifted eastwards and by 1851 the centre was no longer in Holborn but further east in the Tower district, especially in and around Curtain Road in Shoreditch.[104] This eastwards shift accounted for over 60 per cent of the growth in furniture employment. Directory evidence confirms this geographical realignment.[105] In 1811 there were 80 furniture makers in the West End, compared with 20 in Bethnal Green, Shoreditch and Stepney. By 1847 the numbers had risen to 269 and 176 respectively and by 1859 the two sets of districts were approximately even, with 380 manufacturers in the west and 350 in the east. In the 1860s the balance shifted even further and the *Post Office Directory* of 1872 shows an absolute fall in the number of West End firms compared with an increase of over 80 in eastern districts.

This geographical shift was accompanied by a significant restructuring of production. As with clothing and shoemaking, supplies of cheap labour were most abundant in eastern districts where the

Table 6.5   Employment in furniture making, 1831–1851 (adult males)

Division	1831		1851	
	Number	Per cent	Number	Per cent
Holborn	3,118	36.4	3,214	24.1
Tower	1,651	19.3	4,548	34.1
Finsbury	964	11.2	1,550	11.6
Westminster	1,108	12.9	1,756	13.2
Southwark	703	8.2	796	6.0
South	550	6.4	568	4.3
City	475	5.6	892	6.7
Total	8,569	100.0	13,324	100.0

Source: Census, 1831, 1851

barriers of protection were weakest. By 1850, there were fewer than 650 members of the Cabinet-makers' Society, out of an estimated total of over 5200 workers in London.[106] But even these figures, are somewhat misleading since geographical variations existed in the level of unionization. As Mayhew observed:

> There is among the East-end cabinet makers no society, no benefit or sick fund, and very little communion between different classes. The chair maker knows nothing of the table maker next door, and cannot tell whether others in his calling thrive better or worse than he does. These men have no time for social intercommunication. The struggle to live absorbs all their energies and confines all their aspirations to that one endeavour.[107]

Thus, of the seven trade-union meeting houses belonging to the furniture trades in 1861, only one was located in east London, the remainder being centred around Soho and Tottenham Court Road.[108]

Differences in the level of unionization were accompanied by different rates of pay. Even amongst society cabinet makers, wages in eastern districts were approximately 10 per cent lower than those in the west.[109] But the difference between these levels and those in the unregulated sector was even greater. Prices paid to workers sometimes covered little more than the cost of the materials. Mayhew was told that the price of a Pembroke table was 12s. but that materials alone cost between 9s. and 10s. The price for 'loo tables', which took two days to make, was about £1 of which 12s. or 13s. was the cost of wood, nails and glue.[110] Working six days a week, and always managing to sell such tables at the best price, a cabinet maker in the cheap trade would have earned little more than about 21s. to 24s. a week in full employment but this was the exception rather than the rule and more often that not earnings fell well short of this amount.

By the 1840s three distinct sectors of furniture making had emerged. A small number of bespoke cabinet makers were still found in the West End, producing exquisitely crafted pieces for the capital's élite. The growing middle-class market, however, was served in a different manner. The publication of standard pattern books and the fall in prices brought about by the introduction of sawing machinery, which reduced the cost of veneers from 6d. to 1d., encouraged an increase in demand. From the 1840s furniture stores, such as Heals and Maples in Tottenham Court Road, began to cater for this demand by subcontracting orders to numerous small masters working in the immediate vicinity or in some cases buying directly from East End workers.[111]

Of even greater significance was a third sector of production based in eastern districts and relying in familiar fashion on cheaper forms of manufacture and a web of wholesalers and middlemen. Costs of entry were low, amounting to no more than a few pounds, and by concentrating on one item of furniture alone, workers could make do with a modicum of skill. In and around Curtain Road, cheap furniture was turned out in quantity by several hundred 'garret masters' relying on the domestic labour of wives, children and learners. Although these small masters were blamed for 'crushing down the men', a more material cause was the control of prices exerted by wholesalers, or 'slaughterers' as they were sarcastically called.[112] By the 1840s most of the East End trade had fallen into their hands and they were primarily responsible for screwing down prices. In turn, as noted above, these items of furniture were sold in the West End by 'linen drapers', so bringing cheap eastern workers into direct competition with those artisans in western districts. Together with those masters who employed non-society men, these slaughterers were known by journeymen as 'black masters', and there was nothing more contemptuous in the cabinet-makers' vocabulary than to say 'He's nothing but a black.'[113]

Conclusion

In several respects this chapter has covered familiar ground. That the barriers of skill were weaker in eastern districts compared with the west, and that wages and conditions of employment were worse, was common knowledge at the time. Islands of skill persisted in the west but artisans working in these havens found themselves hemmed in by the swell of unskilled labour that arose in eastern districts and threatened to overwhelm those in its path. Everywhere the barriers that protected skilled artisans were being undermined by this rising tide of cheap manufacture. In the first half of the century, and particularly after the Napoleonic Wars, the pressures mounted. The reduction or removal of import duties during the era of free trade, the growing facility with which goods could be moved both between and within London and the provinces, the dismantling of apprenticeship, falling costs and changing demand all played their part. The production and sale of a wide variety of goods that passed from the hands of London workers to those of the customer were increasingly organized by networks of middlemen and as the points of production and sale moved further apart, so the importance of such middlemen grew.

To say, as Schwarz has recently done, that 'until the 1860s changes in London's manufacturing had tended to be gradual', is therefore to miss the point.[114] In silk weaving and watchmaking those changes were anything but gradual. Indeed, the speed of their demise was little short of catastrophic. Equally, changes in those trades that remained in the capital, notably clothing, shoemaking and furniture, although less obvious were none the less even more significant in view of the numbers of workers involved. In each case, production was restructured along geographical lines and cheaper methods of production spread from eastern to western districts. Workers in both parts of London were brought into direct competition with each other and in this way wages and conditions deteriorated. The complaint voiced by cabinet makers to Mayhew applied equally well to other traditional London trades: 'I don't know that we have any great grievances to complain of except one and that's the East-end.'[115]

Notes

1. Mayhew, 1968, vol. 3, p.233.
2. Young, 1772, pp.337–8.
3. Gilboy, 1934, p.220.
4. PP 1818 IX *SC to consider the … petitions relating to the ribbon weavers*, p.55; PP 1831–32 XIX *SC on the silk trade*, q. 5756–7, 7639, 7737.
5. *Reynolds Newspaper (RN)*, 10 January 1858, 8 September 1867, 2 February 1868; see also Bowley, 1900, Hunt, 1973.
6. Bowley, 1900, p.70.
7. Hunt, 1973, pp.93–104; Crafts, 1982, p.68.
8. Mayhew, 1981, vol. 3, p.127.
9. Green and Parton, 1990, pp.66, 70.
10. Bosanquet, 1841, pp.91–4.
11. Statistical Society, 1848a, pp.201, 209.
12. See Clout, 1991, p.75.
13. Olsen, 1979, pp.129–89. The significance of large landlords in structuring

residential segregation in towns and cities is discussed further by Cannadine, 1977. However, a cautionary note is sounded about the extent to which such landlords in London were able to swim against the tide of market forces. See Cannadine, 1980, pp.394–401.

14. Dyos, 1957, p.264; Jones, 1971, pp.159–78.
15. Dyos, 1955–56, pp.12–14.
16. Fletcher, 1844, pp.70–1.
17. Stamp, 1916, pp.108–10.
18. Data taken from PP 1852–53 XXVIII *Return of the number of houses rated to the house tax.*
19. Statistical Society, 1840, p.17.
20. Weld, 1843, p.17; Statistical Society, 1848a, p.209.
21. Place Coll. Add. Ms. 27800, fol. 3.
22. Mayhew, 1982, vol. 5, pp.153–4.
23. From 1794 the rules of friendly societies could be registered with local magistrates and from 1856 with the Registrar of Friendly Societies. For a discussion of the legal background to friendly societies see Gosden, 1961, pp.173–97. I am most grateful to Dr Southall for permission to use this information.
24. Hobsbawm, 1984, p.142.
25. See Cole and Filson, 1951, p.489.
26. Marx, 1954, vol. 1, p.435.
27. Hobsbawm, 1984, p.142.
28. See Taylor, 1983 for a general discussion of this topic.
29. *The Times*, 27, 30 May 1806, 4, 5, 18 June 1806; Webb Coll. E series A, vol. 14, fol. 29.
30. Schwarz, 1992, pp.45–6. See Chapter 2, pp.24–6.
31. Although many servants did not 'live in', given the lengthy hours of work they still had to remain close to their employers' residence. See Higgs, 1983, for a discussion of the relationships between class and the employment of servants.
32. George, 1966, pp.75–6; Schwarz, 1982, p.172.
33. Burn, 1858, p.12. See Appendix 6.1.
34. Fletcher, 1844, p.80.
35. *ibid.*, p.70.
36. Burn, 1858, p.12.
37. George, 1966, pp.175–6.
38. Landes, 1983, pp.227–8; Thrift, 1977, p.1. Thompson, 1967b, argues for a more general relationship between the diffusion of watches and clocks and the rise of industrial capitalism and consequent demand for the synchronization of labour.
39. Landes, 1983, p.251.
40. Place Coll. vol. 53, p.25.
41. Smith, 1974, p.35.
42. Campbell, 1747, p.251.
43. Wilkes, 1816 (ULMC); Powell, 1819, pp.9–13, 16 (Webb Coll.); PP 1817 VI *SC on the petitions of the watchmakers of Coventry*, pp.357–60, 366.
44. Letter to George Rose, Esq. from the clockmakers' committee, 1789 (ULMC); *Report of the committee appointed by the general meeting of clock and watchmakers*, 1790 (ULMC).

45. *True Briton*, 6 April 1798; *The Case of the Distressed Watch and Clockmakers*, 1798 (ULMC).

46. *Committee of Watch and Clockmakers*, 1814.

47. PP 1817 VI *SC on the petitions of the watchmakers*, pp.290–1. The 'Jew system' apparently included engraving fictitious names on a watch and paying workmen in kind. See *To the watch trades*, 1815 (ULMC). 'Jew' was also used more generally in a pejorative sense to signify a dealer who would not give credit.

48. Linebaugh, 1993, p.256.

49. PP 1840 XXIII *RC on the handloom weavers, reports from assistant commissioners*, part 2, pp.56, 80; Chadwick, 1965, p.251.

50. George, 1966, pp.178–96.

51. See Clapham, 1916, for a discussion of the Spitalfields Acts.

52. PP 1831–32 XIX *SC on the silk trade*, q. 3036, 9323–42.

53. PP 1840 XXIV *RC on the handloom weavers, reports from assistant commissioners*, part 4, pp.21–5, 28.

54. PP 1818 IX *SC on the petitions relating to the ribbon weavers*, pp.9, 67–9.

55. PP 1831–32 XIX *SC on the silk trade*, q. 3250; PP 1833 VI *SC on manufactures, commerce and shipping*, q. 1344, 5102.

56. PP 1831–32 XIX *SC on the silk trade*, q. 8404.

57. *Trades Newspaper*, 8, 22 January, 5 February, 30 July, 3 September, 8 October 1826; Place Coll. vol. 16, pp.32, 58, 69, 79.

58. *Weekly Free Press*, 7 February, 6 June 1829; Place Coll. vol. 16, p.127.

59. *London Dispatch*, 12, 19 March 1837; *London Mercury*, 12 March 1837; *Weekly True Sun*, 16 April 1837; PP 1831–31 XIX *SC on the silk trade*, q. 5751–52, 6023–07, 8357, 8371, 8385, 12693.

60. *ibid.*, q. 8484.

61. Mayhew, 1980, vol. 1, p.59.

62. According to the *Dictionary of the Vulgar Tongue*, 1971, cabbage literally meant 'cloth, stuff or silk purloined by taylors from their employers'.

63. Campbell, 1747, p.193.

64. For a discussion of the situation after 1861 see Hall, 1962b, pp.37–70.

65. Green, 1988, p.181.

66. Place Coll. vol. 53, pp.89–91.

67. Place, 1972, p.215.

68. Mayhew, 1981, vol. 2, pp.106–23, 128.

69. Jones, 1851–52, vol. 1, p.366.

70. See *The Appeal of the Distressed Operative Tailors ...*, 1850.

71. Hyam, 1850.

72. Moses, 1860.

73. *idem.*, 1852.

74. *idem.*, 1849, p.4.

75. Place Coll. vol. 53, p.89; Jones, 1851–52, vol. 1, p.366.

76. *Northern Star* (*NS*), 2 November 1850.

77. The first mention of the use of sewing machines was in 1853 during a strike of seamstresses at a large wholesale clothier in the City. *RN*, 2 October 1853. American machines had first been seen at the Great Exhibition in 1851.

78. *RN*, 2 December 1855, 19 May 1861; Strang, 1858, pp.465–6; PP 1856 XIII *SC on masters and operatives*, q. 993–1001.

79. This issue is dealt with more fully in Schmeichen, 1984, pp.24–49.

80. Schwarz, 1992, p.42.
81. Mayhew, 1981, vol. 2, p.84.
82. Place Coll. vol. 53, pp.91, 123, *idem.*, vol. 56, pp.10–11; PP 1840 XXIII *RC on the handloom weavers*, part II, p.120; *NS*, 9 December 1843, 13 January, 3 February, 13 April 1844.
83. Mayhew, 1981, vol. 2, pp.79, 84, 123.
84. *ibid.*, p.97.
85. Dobson, 1980, p.60.
86. *Craftsman*, 31 January 1801.
87. Webb Coll. E, series A, vol. 14, fol. 60. In the early decades of the century Francis Place described the flints' almost military style of organization based on a network of delegates drawn from thirty or so of houses of call. In turn these delegates elected five of their number to form an executive committee known as the 'Town', who were responsible for formulating wage demands and organizing strikes. See *Gorgon*, 16 September 1818; PP 1824 V *SC on artizans and machinery*, p.45.
88. Jones, 1851–52, vol. 2, pp.363–5. This practice had arisen because the cancellation of social events during periods of official mourning meant that the demand for new fashions ceased and hence bespoke employment fell away.
89. *Crisis*, 30 November 1833, 14 June 1834; *Pioneer*, 10 May 1834; Place Coll. vol. 51, pp. 243, 247; Webb Coll. E, series A, vol. 14 fol. 60; for a discussion of the strike and the events which surrounded it see Parssinen and Prothero, 1977, pp.65–107.
90. PP 1867–68 XXXIX *RC on trade unions*, q. 18189–90, 18217. In 1861 only three tailors' trade-union meetings houses were recorded in the Burn, 1861.
91. Mayhew, 1981, vol. 2, pp.75–80.
92. *NS*, 3 February, 13, 20, 27 April 1844; PP 1867–68 XXXIX *RC on trade unions*, q. 18189–90; Place Coll. vol. 53, pp.88, 123; Prothero, 1971, pp.212–13.
93. *RN*, 12 November 1865.
94. Schmeichen, 1984, p.18.
95. For the later period see Hall, 1962b; Schmeichen, 1984, pp.29–32, 39–41.
96. *True Briton*, 28 February 1799; *London Dispatch*, 21 May 1837. Both 'scab' and 'scamp' appear to have been used interchangeably.
97. PP 1824 V *SC on artisans and machinery*, pp.134, 142; Mayhew, 1982, vol. 5, p.121; Webb Coll. E, series A, vol. 25, fol. 88.
98. O'Neill, 1869, p.314; Mayhew, 1981, vol. 3, pp.146–7.
99. PP 1824 V *SC on artizans and machinery*, pp.134–6.
100. *NS* 29 March 1845; in 1851 the census notes a total of 26,859 adult male shoemakers.
101. Mayhew, 1981, vol. 3, pp.131–3, 147.
102. *ibid.*, pp.162–3.
103. *ibid.*, p.158.
104. For a discussion of the period after 1861 see Hall, 1962b, pp.71–95.
105. The following figures are taken from Oliver, 1961.
106. Mayhew, 1982, vol. 5, p.145. Southall, Gilbert and Bryce, 1994, p. 83 claim that the national membership of the Friendly Society of Cabinet Makers was 455.
107. *ibid.*, p.174.

108. See Burn, 1861.
109. Mayhew, 1982, vol. 5, pp.145–6.
110. *ibid.*, pp.155, 158–9, 178–9.
111. Mayhew, 1968, vol. 3, p.224; Oliver, 1964, p.403 provides a map of furniture shops supplying Heals, Maples and other retail stores in 1872.
112. Jones, 1851–52, vol. 2, p.657.
113. Mayhew, 1982, vol. 5, p.143.
114. Schwarz, 1992, p.40.
115. *ibid.*, pp.143–4.

1 *Reading the paper*, 1855. Following the repeal of stamp duty in 1855, cheap newspapers for a working-class readership were printed in far greater numbers.

2   *Slum tailors in London, 1863.*

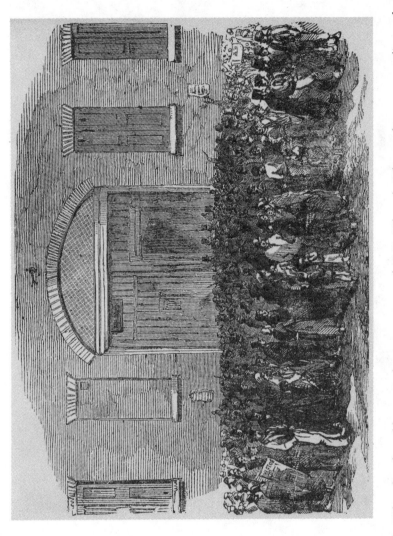

3   *Outside the Whitechapel workhouse in the severe winter of 1855.* When the Thames froze over, applicants for relief besieged workhouses throughout eastern and southern riverside districts.

4 *Death on the parish* by Alfred Elmore, *c.* 1860. Fear of a pauper funeral loomed large in working-class minds.

CHAPTER SEVEN

Into an unknown land: the geography of poverty

In the second quarter of the nineteenth century, middle-class concerns over the threats posed by outcast London gathered strength. Those concerns focused on the dangers to social stability fostered by working-class radicalism and the perceived dangers inherent in the demoralization of the honest poor. Such concerns were thrown into sharp relief in the 1840s as contemporaries began to recognize that as a result of class segregation the social balance between rich and poor within metropolitan parishes, as well as between districts in the east and west, had all but disappeared. Although the map of poverty in 1840 had clear parallels with that of earlier periods, it was this realization that proved to be so alarming.[1]

This shift in the awareness of localized and regional patterns of poverty was accompanied by a corresponding change in middle-class perception of the urban poor, from recognizable individuals to the poor *en masse*. In the course of that transformation of consciousness, new forms of discourse and methods of dealing with the poverty emerged. To the metropolitan bourgeoisie, spatial segregation imposed a barrier that appeared to preclude the possibility of establishing personal ties between the classes, thereby leaving an ideological vacuum into which socialist and atheistic ideas could permeate. It was fear of this vacuum that hastened the development of what became known as the district visiting movement. That this movement gained such prominence in the capital was clear evidence of the extent to which rich and poor had come to inhabit separate spatial worlds. Middle-class visitors to the homes of the poor, particlarly in that dreary region to the east, 'so urgently needing the exercise of Christian liberality – so little known by those who are able to give of abundance', thus entered into a *terra incognita*. Charting the geography of that unknown land, and examining the efforts of middle-class missionaries to explore and colonize the territory of the poor, are the main issues to be addressed.

Overcrowding and the formation of slums

The geography of poverty in nineteenth-century cities operated at two distinct spatial scales. At a neighbourhood level, there were the slums, or rookeries as they became known, pockets of overcrowded and insanitary housing tucked from view behind the main thoroughfares and wealthier streets. Those 'lurking nests of dwellings', as John Hollingshed called them, were by no means new and several could trace their lineage at least as far back as John Stow's sixteenth-century survey.[2] Unless destroyed by street clearances in the nineteenth century, such places clung on tenaciously as the built-up area expanded. There was, however, a second, larger and more novel scale of poverty that emerged during the nineteenth century as a result of the segregation of the classes. As one charity report noted in 1865, 'Not only is London greatly increased in magnitude, but in progress of that extension there is a constant tendency to produce a wider separation of the rich from the poor, and a broader contrast between the abundance of one parish and the destitution of another.'[3] As wealthy residents abandoned central and eastern areas for the West End and suburbs, and as street clearances and demolitions reduced the stock of working-class housing in central districts, so the geographical gulf between the classes widened.

Whilst slums were certainly nothing new, what threw them into sharper focus in ninetenth-century British cities was the fact of urbanization. By the 1840s the age of great cities had dawned, and for the first time, in 1851, the census revealed that more people lived in towns than in the countryside. New and distinctly urban concerns gained prominence, and slums, in particular, highlighted not only the problems associated with overcrowding, lack of sanitation and the spread of epidemic diseases but also drew attention to the social degradation of working-class urban life. Sanitary issues coalesced with bourgeois concern over working-class morality and it was argued that rookeries functioned as much as the foci of disease as the nurseries of vice and disorder.[4]

In London the issues raised by the existence of slums were perceived more acutely by the middle class in central and western districts. Mindful of the threat that poor housing posed for the spread of epidemic disease, Edwin Chadwick in 1842 noted, 'Immediately behind some of the best constructed houses in the fashionable districts of London are some of the worst dwellings, into which the working classes are crowded.'[5] Higher rents in western and central districts meant that for working-class households one room living in such areas was the norm. Investigations by the Statistical Society of London showed that working-class families in the relatively wealthy areas of St George Hanover Square, and St Margaret and St John Westminster suffered worse overcrowding than those in the much poorer district of St George-in-the-East.[6] In St Marylebone, for example, a survey of 205 houses found that 845 rooms were occupied by 859 families.[7] If anything, therefore, living conditions were worse and poverty more intense in these central rookeries than in working-class areas further east.

The epitome of slumdom was the Irish rookery in and around Church Lane in St Giles. Known variously as 'Little Ireland', or the 'Holy Land', the rookery itself was a maze of interconnecting streets and alleys that lay immediately to the south of the wealthy Bedford estate in Bloomsbury. Even as a new suburb in the seventeenth century it had contained a poorer population than the surrounding area and during the eighteenth century its descent into squalour was rapid. By 1750 it was estimated that one in four houses was a gin shop, as Hogarth vividly portrayed in his drawing of 'Gin Lane'.[8] During the first half of the nineteenth century conditions worsened as the pressures on housing increased and between 1841 and 1847, demolitions for New Oxford Street, coupled with an influx of Irish migrants, resulted in a doubling of occupancy rates.[9] In 1841 the average number of inhabitants in houses along Church Lane stood at 24 – three times the average for London and nearly twice that of St Giles as a whole. By 1851 the situation had worsened and average occupancy rates had reached 46 persons per house.[10] Even this enormous rise hid the fact that lodging houses often contained more than 50 persons. Some houses seemed to have an almost infinite capacity for taking in extra lodgers. The census enumerator who visited Church Lane in 1851 noted that several lodging houses contained over a hundred persons, including one which on the night before his visit had accommodated 140 people. Although the lodgers had already left before he arrived, the beds were still warm and on that basis the count was made.[11]

This exceptional level of overcrowding reflected the growing pressures on working-class housing throughout central districts arising from street clearances, warehouse construction and railway building.[12] From the 1830s and 1840s thousands of households in central and western districts were displaced by clearance schemes designed to rid neighbourhoods of the poor. When Regent Street was finally completed in 1823, for example, the poor were driven from there into the Strand and Westminster from where they were subsequently removed in the 1830s by the building of Trafalgar Square and other road-widening schemes. When New Oxford Street was opened in 1844 the poor displaced from the Church Lane rookery initially moved into neighbouring streets or eastwards towards the slums of Saffron Hill. Thousands of working-class households were displaced between 1832 and 1856 by the construction of Farringdon Street and Cannon Street through the City, Commercial Street through Whitechapel and Victoria Street through Westminster.

Other pressures contributed to the growing shortages of working-class housing. From the 1830s warehouse and office construction in the City began to reduce the housing stock and in the following decades the pressures on housing spread northwards and eastwards into the surrounding areas. Dock construction also reduced the housing supply: the London Docks in St George-in-the-East removed 1300 houses and St Katharine's Dock, completed in 1828, resulted in the demolition of 1033 houses in Whitechapel.[13] No more docks were built in inner areas after this date but the opening of the Royal Victoria Docks in 1855, coupled with the general growth of trade, was accompanied by additional warehouse construction in central districts.[14] Finally, railway building had a traumatic impact on working-class districts. Railway schemes presented to Parliament between 1859 and 1867 involved the displacement of 37,000 people alone.[15] In the west and north, large aristocratic landowners were able not only to block the railway but also to prevent other forms of public transport from crossing their estates. Eastern and southern districts, in which large landowners were conspicuous by their absence, bore the brunt of railway construction. On its way to Liverpool Street in the 1840s, for example, the Eastern Counties railway bisected Bethnal Green, disrupting communities, blocking drainage and intensifying overcrowding throughout the region. The same was true of the Blackwall Railway through Whitechapel and the Greenwich Railway through Bermondsey and Southwark. As each company struggled to gain access to a central terminus, so they ploughed their routes through working-class districts with similar results.

As a result of these developments the housing stock of most central districts began to decline from the 1830s and 1840s. Where this was accompanied by corresponding falls in population, the reduction caused fewer problems. However, where the demand for working-class housing continued to rise, the inevitable outcome was a marked increase in overcrowding and the creation or spread of slums. This pattern is examined in more detail in Table 7.1 which shows the changing balance between housing and population in inner districts. In the two western districts of St Martins and St James, housing decline was more than matched by the loss of population and the number of persons per house dropped accordingly. Elsewhere, housing failed to keep pace with population and most districts experienced higher occupancy rates. In the City, housing supply fell faster than population, resulting in higher levels of occupancy. In other central districts, such as St Luke and Clerkenwell, population growth exceeded the increase in housing and consequently occupancy rates also rose.

The situation was similar in eastern and southern districts bordering the City. With the notable exception of Whitechapel, population growth in such areas clearly outstripped housing supply. Clearances in the City

Table 7.1 Housing and population change in inner London, 1831–1861

	Housing Change (per cent)		Population Change (per cent)		Persons per house	
	+	−	+	−	1831	1861
WEST						
St Martins		4.6		5.3	10.7	10.1
St James		3.7		4.7	11.0	10.6
CENTRAL						
St Giles		5.3	2.2		11.2	11.5
Strand		3.9	2.3		10.7	11.4
Holborn	4.0		17.2		9.8	10.9
Clerkenwell	11.0		37.9		7.9	9.3
St Lukes		1.5	22.4		7.2	9.0
CITY						
East London		6.8		2.6	8.2	9.0
West London		30.7		19.9	9.5	10.5
City of London		26.9		18.3	7.0	7.2
EAST						
Shoreditch	38.2		83.5		6.4	7.6
Bethnal Green	22.3		69.5		5.7	7.1
Whitechapel	22.5		23.1		7.2	7.2
St George-in-the-East		1.1	27.0		6.7	7.9
Stepney and Mile End	34.3		79.0		6.1	7.1
INNER SOUTH						
St Saviour		8.2	14.1		7.0	8.1
St Olave		23.4		4.8	6.8	8.6
St George Southwark	9.6		39.6		6.6	7.7
Bermondsey	54.0		96.2		6.1	7.1
Rotherhithe	41.9		90.3		5.7	7.0
Newington	45.6		84.7		5.7	6.5
REST OF LONDON	86.5		109.9		6.7	7.6

Source: Census 1831, 1861

displaced large numbers of the poor who in turn moved into houses vacated as a result of middle-class suburban flight.[16] In Southwark, Edward Collinson, chairman of the Board of Guardians, remarked, 'Unquestionably the improvements in the City at first tended very much to make poor person's houses, which were formerly shop and dwelling houses, be let out in tenements and as lodging houses, and the consequence is that they are sometimes very closely packed with inhabitants.'[17] By the 1860s over half the housing stock in the area had been subdivided and was being let by the room.[18] In Bethnal Green, which in 1840 already had the dubious reputation of having the lowest value housing in London, a similar pattern of abandonment and subdivision occurred. In parts closest to the city, older housing was subdivided and let to working-class families. Elsewhere flimsy summer houses were made into more permanent accommodation for the poor.[19]

Regions of the poor

Whilst pockets of slum housing existed in most parts of the city, from about the 1820s evidence began to mount of a different and wider geographical pattern of poverty. By 1858, Reverend Frederick Meyrick could point to two distinct spatial scales of poverty: 'Where are the poor? They are close to us, round about us, crowded together within perhaps a few yards of us, and we know it not, or they are congregated together in still greater masses at a few miles distance eastward, and we see them not.'[20] As the geographical divide between rich and poor widened, so it became increasingly difficult for the urban bourgeoisie to grasp the full dimensions of poverty. James Grant was not alone in the view that 'The great mass of the metropolitan community are as ignorant of the destitution and distress which prevails in large districts of London ... as if the wretched creatures were living in the very centre of Africa.'[21] Indeed, as imperial expansion proceeded it sometimes seemed that foreign parts were more conscientiously explored and better known than the nether regions of the capital.

The precise extent to which nineteenth-century cities were spatially segregated by class is still a matter for debate, but contemporary perception was that the divisons were widening and that rich and poor were leading increasingly spatially segregated lives.[22] In Manchester, for example, the young Friedrich Engels noted how 'by unconscious tacit agreement, as well as with outspoken conscious determination', working-class housing was sharply differentiated from those areas inhabited by the middle class.[23] Similar evidence for London was close to hand. Differences in the fortunes of eastern and western districts had long been engraved onto the urban fabric.[24] For much of the eighteenth century, despite the growing attractions of new developments to the west, the City itself retained a core of high-status households.[25] Not until the 1830s and 1840s did middle-class flight finally undermine this residential function, leaving the central districts to a scattering of tradesmen together with large numbers of casual labourers, carmen, porters, hawkers, Jewish peddlars and 'people who do not know, when they rise in the morning, by what chance jobs in the streets or the markets they are to get food for the day'.[26] Those who could afford to leave this decaying residential core did so. As Evans remarked in 1845, 'A dwelling in the City is a thing not now considered desirable – all move either towards the west, or emigrate to the suburbs – the one for fashion, the other for economy and fresh air.'[27]

Those who remained viewed this outward procession of middle-class ratepayers and subsequent inmigration of the poor with growing concern. In Clerkenwell 'Houses which were formerly filled with tolerably well-to-do, are now let out in lodgings, and the lodgers, instead of being able to aid others, sometimes need aid themselves.'[28] A similar pattern occurred elsewhere, notably in eastern districts bordering the City. In St George-in-the-East, Revd George MacGill, an implacable campaigner for poor law reform, remarked, 'Most of the better class of tradesmen have migrated to the suburbs – to Stratford, Bow, Hackney and elsewhere ... Few will be left soon besides the poor, the poor rate collector, the relieving officer, the policeman and the parson.'[29] In the whole quarter of Bethnal Green, one observer claimed, 'There is not one resident whom the world would call respectable.'[30]

Measuring poverty

The extent to which this perception of poverty meshed with reality is difficult to ascertain. Whilst middle-class observers at mid-century became aware of the geographical gulf between rich and poor, no attempts were made to measure poverty or map its distribution until Charles Booth's research in the 1880s and 1890s.[31] Over and above the difficulties associated with establishing a poverty line, lack of evidence for earlier decades clearly prevents us from measuring directly the proportion of families or individuals in poverty. However, by combining and mapping a set of social indicators that collectively reflect deprivation we can nevertheless still establish the spatial pattern of poverty, albeit via a more circuitous route than that taken by Charles Booth later in the century.[32]

The lack of data on household incomes for the period means that we need to approach the problem of mapping poverty indirectly, focusing on a range of measures that are indicative of adverse social conditions.[33] If possible, the social indicators used should mirror the findings of contemporary research and in this respect the causes of primary poverty established by Charles Booth for London, and Seebohm Rowntree for York, shown in Table 7.2, are instructive.[34]

Both studies confirmed that the main causes of poverty were related to questions of employment and the incidence of ill health. The former set of causes accounted for about two-thirds of London poverty and half of that in York whilst ill health was responsible for between a quarter and a third of those who fell beneath the poverty line. In terms of employment, important differences occurred between the two cities, with irregular and casual work of far greater importance in London than York, where the chief problem was low pay rather than no pay. In Booth's analysis, differences also existed between the chronically poor in classes A and B, and the intermittently poor in classes C and D. For the former, the main cause of poverty stemmed from the dependence on casual labour with all the uncertainties and inability to save that that entailed. For the latter, many of whom would have been sweated and seasonal workers, irregular work was of lesser significance than low and uncertain earnings.

Ill health was the other main cause of poverty but by the late nineteenth century sanitation had improved considerably, death rates were falling and therefore the problems of disease were beginning to recede. In earlier decades, when the prevalence of disease was more common and death rates were higher, ill health would probably have been a more significant causal factor in explaining the incidence of poverty.

With Booth's and Rowntree's research as a guide, a total of fifteen social indicators (referred to below in CAPITALS) were examined relating to employment, health, demographic structure, housing and pauperism. These variables were collected for 32 districts in London for two dates centred around 1840 and 1870.[35] The districts themselves are based on the spatial framework adopted in the 1851 census, although in some cases lack of suitable data made it necessary to amalgamate districts.[36] The availability of data for specific years also posed problems and some temporal latitude was necessary in relation to certain social indicators. Thus the analysis of poverty in 1840 also includes variables referring to typhus and consumption mortality in 1838 and to the ratio of female to male clothing and shoemaking workers taken from the 1851 census. Similar problems arose in mapping the distribution of poverty in 1870. Changes in the registration districts meant that the variables relating to clothing and shoemaking had to be measured using figures from the

Table 7.2   Causes of poverty

Cause	Booth (per cent of families)		Rowntree (per cent of households)	
	Class A and B	Class C and D	Cause	
Casual work	52.8		Out of work	2.6
Irregular work, low pay	10.7		Irregular work	3.5
Small profits	3.0	5.3		
Low pay (regular work)		23.5	Low pay (regular work)	43.7
Irregular earnings		49.1	Illness of chief	
Illness or infirmity	12.9	5.7	wage earner	9.9
Illness or large family, combined with irregular earnings	11.2	6.0	Death of chief wage earner	27.5
Large family	9.4	10.4	Large family	12.8
	100.0	100.0		100.0
Total families	1319	2144	Total households	1463

Sources: Booth, 1902, *Poverty* series, vol. 1, p. 147; Rowntree, 1901, p. 120

1861 census, whilst those for pauperism, poor rates, consumption mortality and illiteracy referred either to 1867 or 1868. The remaining social indicators used to map the incidence of poverty all referred to the year of the analysis itself or those on either side.

Employment

In the absence of data on unemployment or rates of pay, patterns of employment and earnings must be measured indirectly. Given the importance of manufacturing within the metropolitan economy, especially clothing and shoemaking, gender patterns of employment in these trades were used to examine the nature of local labour markets. In both trades different labour-market characteristics based on the sex structure of the workforce characterized bespoke and slop production. Thus, the ratio of female to male workers in clothing (TAILOR) and shoemaking (SHOE), were used as surrogate measures for rates of pay and levels of employment.[37] In both cases the presence of women indicated lower earnings and less secure employment. Given the importance of literacy as a defining characteristic of artisan status, a further surrogate measure of skill, based on literacy rates as defined by the number of marriage partners able to sign their name on the marriage register (ILLIT), was also incorporated in the analysis. Although this indicator adopts a narrow definition of literacy and is heavily biased towards young adults, the absence of alternative data for individual districts means that it must suffice as a surrogate indicator of occupational skill.

Health

Both Booth and Rowntree agreed that, after matters of employment, the second main cause of poverty was related to illness or death of the chief wage earner. Differences in the categories and sample populations of each study help to account for the variations shown in Table 7.2.[38] Since death rates were considerably lower towards the end of the century, it is reasonable to assume that in earlier decades the causal relationship between ill health and poverty would have been stronger. Four variables relating to ill health and mortality were used to reflect this situation: deaths per 1000 persons from consumption (TB) and typhus (TYPHUS), infant mortality (INFMORT) and the crude death rate (CDR). Though cholera may have been more shocking, pulmonary tuberculosis was the major adult-killing disease in Victorian cities.[39] It was associated with overcrowded living and working conditions and, because of its debilitating effects over a long period of time, was also closely linked to the onset of chronic poverty. Typhus was the next major killer of adults and it was also associated with insanitary living conditions: the various colloquial names under which it was known – the 'Irishman's itch' and 'gaol fever' – bore witness to the conditions under which it flourished.[40] Infant mortality, the third health-related variable, accounted for approximately 30 per cent of the total mortality during the period and was closely related to social status. In Bethnal Green and other poor districts, Edwin Chadwick discovered that working-class children were twice as likely to die before reaching the age of five as those born to middle-class parents.[41] In terms of both cause and effect, each of these three variables were closely related to poverty. The final variable concerns the crude death rate and provides an overall indication of mortality. However, it suffers from the distortions arising from different age structures of the population and the location of large hospitals, and must therefore be treated with greater caution.

Demographic structure: the family life-cycle

Whilst Booth's work focused on families with children, Rowntree examined a wider age range and therefore appreciated better how changes in the family life-cycle influenced the incidence of poverty. Working-class individuals were likely to experience poverty at three points in the life-cycle: their own childhood, early middle age during which they themselves were raising a family, and finally old age.[42] Three demographic variables were used to gauge the influence of the family life-cycle on the incidence of poverty. The first (FERT) measures the number of births per 1000 women of childbearing age. Chadwick had noted that birth rates tended to be higher in poorer districts, although this was balanced by higher rates of infant mortality.[43] The general fertility rate also gives an indication of the relative frequency of pregnancy, which itself was an important factor in the ability of women to continue working. The second variable (YOUNG) represents the proportion of the population aged below 14 years and is an indication of the relative importance of the dependent population, as well as a measure of family size. The final demographic variable is a measure of old age and refers to the proportion of the population aged 60 years or more (OLD). Although life expectancy varied according to social class, and therefore wealthy areas could be expected to have larger numbers of elderly residents, this was balanced by the fact that such districts also had larger numbers of young adults working as domestic servants. Therefore, whilst the absolute number of the elderly may have been smaller in poorer districts, the proportion of those aged above 60 years in relation to the total population was probably larger.

Housing

Living conditions closely reflected socio-economic status and four variables relating to housing quality were measured. No attempt was made to assess levels of overcrowding because aggregate measures of occupancy rates are meaningless without knowledge of house size. However, population density (POP) measures the number of persons per acre and provides a useful, if general, indication of overcrowding. Because the figures were distorted by non-residential land use, such as warehouses and offices, a further measure representing houses per acre (HOUSE) was also included. Despite reservations about measuring overcrowding, an attempt was made to gauge levels of house occupancy by calculating changes in the number of persons per house for the periods 1831–1841 and 1861–1871 (CHANGE). By controlling for house size, this variable highlights any changes in occupancy rates. Finally, a general measure of environmental quality was examined based on the average net rateable value per inhabited house (VALUE). The main shortcoming of this particular measure was that figures for net rateable value included non-residential property, such as offices and industrial premises. The greatest distortion arose in the City which by 1840 already contained a large concentration of commercial premises. Elsewhere, however, such problems were of lesser magnitude and rateable values reflected more accurately the quality of local environments and housing conditions.

Pauperism

The final group of variables relates to the general incidence of pauperism. Although the precise relationship between poor relief and poverty was in part determined by the policies of local boards of guardians, nevertheless the two were closely related. Unfortunately, counts of those in receipt of poor relief did not become available for individual unions until 1860. Instead, we must rely on measures of expenditure as a means of assessing levels of pauperism, including the level of the poor rate (RATE) and the per capita expenditure on relief (EXPENSE).

Mapping metropolitan poverty in 1840 and 1870

The prime objective in examining the social indicators outlined above is so that we can construct an index of deprivation with which to map the geography of poverty in 1840 and 1870, prior to the period covered by Charles Booth. By combining these indicators, factor analysis allows us to define such an index based on the pattern of factor loadings.[44] Tables 7.3 and 7.4 outline the pattern of loadings on the three main factors for 1840 and 1870 respectively. In both years the first and most important factor (I) was broadly indicative of poverty. In 1840 this factor had high positive loadings on variables relating to the labour market (TAILOR, SHOE, ILLIT), the family life-cycle (YOUNG, FERT) and the level of the poor rates (RATE). In addition it had a high negative loading on rateable value (VALUE). In 1870 a similar set of loadings defined the first factor although the importance of rateable value had declined. For both dates, the pattern of loadings defines a factor that can best be described as a composite index of poverty. Districts with high loadings on this factor were those with relatively large numbers of unskilled and low-paid workers in clothing and shoemaking, low rates of literacy, large families with a high proportion of dependent children, high poor rates and relatively low-value housing. Although it cannot be argued that any given household in these districts conformed to this pattern, the likelihood of these constituent elements of poverty occurring were higher

Table 7.3   Factor loadings, 1840

| | FACTORS | | |
Variable	I	II	III
TAILOR	.62	.09	.26
SHOE	.72	.04	−.19
ILLIT	.73	−.14	.26
TB	−.10	.59	.02
TYPHUS	.29	.82	−.07
INFMORT	−.28	.68	−.24
CDR	.24	.81	.01
YOUNG	.85	−.15	.37
OLD	.17	−.14	.76
FERT	.77	.04	.08
POP	.06	.50	−.69
CHANGE	.23	.13	.42
VALUE	−.75	−.02	−.27
RATE	.79	.37	.05
EXPENSE	−.06	.06	−.08
Eigenvalues	4.806	3.069	1.018

Note: factor loadings significant at the 0.05 level are in bold

in such places than elsewhere.

The second and third factors, though less important in explaining the data, deserve brief consideration.[45] In both 1840 and 1870 the pattern of loadings on the second factor (II) suggests that this was related to mortality. Variables with high loadings included TB, TYPHUS, INFMORT and CDR for 1840 and a similar set, with the exception of TYPHUS, for 1870. In both cases, this factor is best interpreted as indicative of the incidence of disease, and therefore mirrors the findings of Booth and Rowntree in relation to ill health outlined above. The third factor (III), unlike the first two, differed in that the pattern of loadings changed between the two study years. In 1840 this factor was defined in relation to low population densities and a relatively elderly population, suggesting that it was measuring an inner-city/outer-city dichotomy that included an age component. In 1870 the third factor was defined by variables that referred to poor relief. More specifically the loadings suggest that this factor picked out areas with high-value housing and relatively generous levels of poor relief. As such, it was an indication of wealth rather than poverty and can therefore be ignored for the purposes of this research.

Table 7.4 Factor loadings, 1870

Variable	FACTORS		
	I	II	III
TAILOR	.74	.03	.09
SHOE	.65	.19	−.39
ILLIT	.83	.00	.01
TB	−.01	.88	.12
TYPHUS	.29	.31	−.22
INFMORT	.03	.65	−.10
CDR	.16	.95	−.03
YOUNG	.76	−.01	−.48
OLD	−.21	.13	.22
FERT	.54	.19	−.34
POP	.15	.39	.07
CHANGE	.15	−.03	−.40
VALUE	−.34	−.25	.83
RATE	.71	.40	−.13
EXPENSE	.06	.09	.94
Eigenvalues	5.119	2.891	1.438

To map the poverty index we need to examine the district scores on factor I: the higher the score, the greater the importance of that particular factor in the district in question. In other words, districts with high scores were those in which poverty was most prevalent. The ranked district scores on the poverty index for 1840 and 1870 are shown in Table 7.5 and their spatial distribution is mapped in Figures 7.1 and 7.2. From the table it first appears that there was considerable variation in the ranking of districts between the two dates. Of the five poorest districts in 1840, only Bethnal Green retained its position in 1870. By contrast, Bermondsey and St George Southwark fell from first and third place to thirteenth and tenth respectively. Other districts similarly fell in the ranking, including St Luke and Whitechapel, together with the suburban districts of Hackney, Islington and Lewisham. Conversely, several districts moved up the poverty ranking, including the City of London itself and Camberwell, Greenwich and Newington to the south. In some cases these changes reflected sharp differences in the performance of districts with relation to specific social indicators. In Bermondsey, for example, a tighter poor-relief regime after 1840 brought down levels of expenditure, resulting in a marked fall in poor rates. Thus, in 1840 it had the highest rates in London but by 1870 it had

Table 7.5 Ranked scores of districts on the index of poverty

District	1840		1870	
	Factor score	Rank	Factor score	Rank
Bermondsey	2.001	1	0.329	13
Bethnal Green	1.745	2	1.981	1
St George Southwark	1.197	3	0.408	10
Shoreditch	1.191	4	0.586	9
St Luke	1.162	5	0.359	11
St George-in-the-East	1.025	6	1.755	2
Whitechapel	0.899	7	0.250	14
Rotherhithe	0.866	8	1.302	3
Hackney	0.661	9	−0.155	19
Poplar	0.621	10	0.689	7
Stepney	0.465	11	1.294	4
St Saviour and St Olave	0.410	12	0.234	15
Islington	0.219	13	−0.961	29
Lewisham	0.126	14	−0.622	25
East and West London	−0.030	15	0.168	16
Strand	−0.031	16	−0.216	20
Clerkenwell	−0.050	17	−0.304	21
Camberwell	−0.109	18	0.741	5
Holborn	−0.150	19	−0.428	23
Lambeth	−0.187	20	0.031	17
Wandsworth	−0.305	21	−0.144	18
Newington	−0.325	22	0.696	6
Greenwich	−0.385	23	0.642	8
St Giles	−0.460	24	−0.584	24
Kensington	−0.766	25	−0.921	28
City	−0.767	26	0.335	12
St Pancras	−0.934	27	−0.421	22
St John and St Margaret	−1.064	28	−0.645	27
St Marylebone	−1.247	29	−0.637	26
St Martin-in-the-Fields	−1.369	30	−1.537	31
St James Westminster	−1.817	31	−1.512	30
St George Hanover Square	−2.692	32	−2.714	32

fallen to nineteenth position and this helped to account for the relative improvement in the district's position on the poverty index. In St George Southwark and St Luke, the changes were less obvious and reflected a general improvement across a range of social indicators. Clearly, the fortunes of districts could alter and some fluidity existed in relation to the spatial hierarchy of impoverishment in the capital.

At the same time, however, we must be cautious about overestimating the extent of change. Considerable stability existed, particularly at the wealthy end of the continuum. The aristocratic district of St George Hanover Square stood at the pinnacle of wealth in both 1840 and 1870. Indeed, with the exception of the City and St Pancras, the eight wealthiest districts in 1840 retained their broad rankings thirty years later. Viewed as a whole, however, the correlation coefficient of the rankings for the two dates is 0.66, suggesting a broad similarity in the pattern for 1840 and 1870. The geography of the factor scores confirms this view of stability. Figure 7.1 shows that in 1840 the wealthiest districts, defined as those with the lowest scores on the poverty index, were overwhelmingly concentrated in the west. By contrast, the poorest districts, including those with the highest scores, formed a belt surrounding the City stretching from St Luke in the north, eastwards to Bethnal Green and St George-in-the-East, and encompassing the southern riverside districts of Rotherhithe, Bermondsey and Southwark. In 1844 this zone of poverty, which corresponded closely to the inner industrial perimeter outlined earlier, was described by Joseph Fletcher:

> These 'out' parishes ... are the great commercial, manufacturing, artisan, labourer and mariner suburbs; having near the river docks and warehouses, manufactories and places of business of every kind, with shops in the main streeets; but behind these, the parts approaching nearest to the City and Borough are densely populated by dock labourers, coal-whippers, weavers, watchmakers, shoemakers, bricklayers and their labourers, and artisans of every kind; and in such quarters as Bethnal Green, Whitechapel and St Giles by large numbers of persons living in a very low condition, whose honest occupations are not so easy to discover. It is the vast bodies of the labouring classes thus aggregated round the centre of the town and not absolutely in its centre, that are properly the great solicitude in a sanatory view.[46]

If in the 1840s the main distinction in terms of poverty was between a belt of impoverished inner districts surrounding the City and those wealthier areas further out, by 1870 this distinction had become primarily an East-West division. Figure 7.2 shows that the main changes reflected an eastwards shift in the geography of poverty to encompass the riverside districts of Stepney, Poplar and Greenwich, all of which had been seriously affected by the collapse of shipbuilding in 1867. The

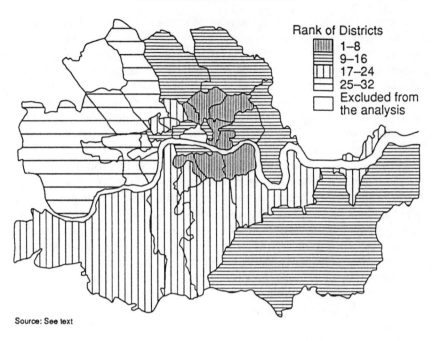

Figure 7.1   Poverty *c.* 1840.

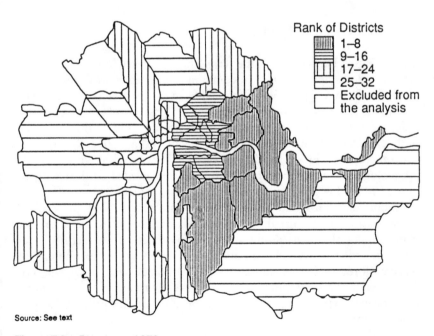

Figure 7.2   Poverty *c.* 1870.

dubious distinction of being the poorest district in London passed from Bermondsey to Bethnal Green, closely followed by its neighbour St George-in-the-East. Southern districts, notably Camberwell and Newington, had also slid down the social scale as poorer populations displaced from the centre moved into these localities. In relation to Camberwell, Harold Dyos observed that by the 1870s parts of that area had already commenced their descent towards slumdom.[47] By 1870, therefore, it is possible to describe the city in terms of two main constrasting zones of wealth and poverty. The West End retained its high-status position, accompanied to a lesser extent by suburban districts to the north and south. Acting as a buffer between the West End and the most impoverished region to the east, stood a central zone comprising the City and surrounding districts. Although some of the worst slums in London were to be found in this inner zone, they remained isolated pockets set amidst an increasingly commercialized urban landscape and as such they were more easily targeted for slum clearance. The main concentration of poverty, however, lay in the east, notably in Bethnal Green, St George-in-the-East and Stepney, and in southern districts bordering the Thames. There the problems of poverty and the existence of slums were too widespread to be dealt with either by sanitary measures or by clearance schemes.

The threat of outcast London

According to Harold Dyos, the term 'slum' appeared in the 1820s and 1830s and by the 1840s was in common usage, along with 'rookery', to describe the wretched conditions of life in the poorer parts of town.[48] From the start, such terms embodied at least two sets of concerns, relating to the insanitary nature of slum housing and to the moral and political threat to social order posed by the urban poor. Whilst street clearances and sanitary legislation were instituted to deal with the threat of biological contagion, other measures were needed to deal with the more intractable problem of social and moral reform.[49]

From the 1830s and 1840s, middle-class fears about the physical degeneration of the urban working class had begun to be expressed. Concern initially focused on the deleterious effects of the factory system in places such as Manchester and Leeds. In 1833, for example, Peter Gaskell forecast that 'A diminutive and ill-shaped race, possessing little muscular strength, and fitted as labourers only to act in subservience to a more powerful agent, will be the product of the present mode of manufacture.'[50] Blame was placed not on the poverty of workers *per se*, but on the disruption of home life and domestic ties that arose as a result of separation of families employed in factories.[51] Pessimism was further compounded by the findings of sanitary reformers who argued that similar problems of degeneration were typical of all large cities and not just the rapidly expanding factory towns. Edwin Chadwick himself cited the physical superiority of rural recruits to the army and Metropolitan Police as evidence of the degenerative effects of town life, particularly in London.[52] Dr Neil Arnott, a strong supporter of the Health of Towns Association and one of the surgeons employed by the Poor Law Commission to investigate the relationships between fever and pauperism in London, argued that the putrid atmosphere in poorer districts affected the constitution and stature of the inhabitants and that its effects were passed down through the generations.[53] William Strang, another strong supporter of the degenerationist view, perhaps expressed these fears most clearly: 'The disordered condition of the parent's system is brought down to positive disease in the offspring: and what was removable in the former, by the operation of better circumstances, can only be palliated in the latter.'[54]

Bourgeois fears of physical degeneration were compounded by a concern over the threat of moral contagion posed by slum life, particularly in relation to the demoralizing effects of overcrowded housing on the honest poor. In expressing these concerns, two broad strands of thought coalesced. The environmentalist position emphasized the role of housing conditions in influencing patterns of behaviour.[55] George Godwin, for example, argued, 'It cannot be too often repeated that the health and morals of the people are regulated by their dwellings.'[56] Hector Gavin, another fervent campaigner for sanitary reform, argued in similar vein that overcrowded housing and the polluted atmosphere of the slums could not but help foster 'idleness and vicious abandonment'.[57] Cleanse the homes and working-class morality could be reformed, so the argument ran.

But a second strand of thought was equally important, resting on the fear of demoralization fostered by proximity between the honest and dishonest poor. In 1858, nearly thirty years before Andrew Mearns wrote *The Bitter Cry of Outcast London*, Reverend Frederick Meyrick first used the term 'outcast' to describe the houseless poor who lived on, and in some case beyond, the margins of respectable society. 'These are the outcast', he claimed, 'such classes as the costermongers and beggars of the street; criminals such as thieves; the vicious, such as the fallen; the ungodly, such as infidels.'[58] By contrast, the respectable poor, whom Meyrick took to include labourers, mechanics, tailors, seamstresses and others struggling to make an honest living, were those who found themselves ground down by competition and forced by poverty to share their dwellings with the 'dangerous class' of outcast poor.[59] In 1850

Thomas Beames had voiced similar concerns over the demoralizing effects of slum life: 'We speak of human masses pent up, crowded, thrust together, huddled close, crammed into courts and alleys and we ask if a malignant spirit wished to demoralise the working classes of the country could he find a plan more congenial to his wishes?'[60]

Such concerns took on added urgency in the light of the growing geographical separation of the classes. With morality debased, religion neglected, the bonds of domestic life destroyed, and a sullen discontent born of squalour, contemporaries argued that slums provided fertile breeding grounds for the demoralization of the honest poor and the subsequent spread of disaffection. Though Marx was dismissive of the very poor, calling them a 'lumpenproletariat' with little or no political consciousness, bourgeois fear in mid-nineteenth century London was that without the moderating influence of persons of rank, the honest working class would be seduced to insurrection by the blandishments of radicals – Owenites, Huntites or 'political desperadoes' as Wakefield called them.[61] Beames echoed this concern when he pointed ominously to the spectre of recent revolution in France. Conjuring up an image in which the supporters of Chartism and the most riotous elements of the masses were recruited from the London slums, he stated, 'Our argument is that Rookeries are among the seeds of revolution; that taken in conjunction with other evils, they poison the minds of the working classes against the powers that be, and thus lead to convulsions.'[62] These fears, by no means unique to Beames, confirmed that from the 1840s and 1850s concern over the existence of outcast London involved more than just a narrow focus on the dangers of biological contagion or the degenerative effects of slum life. It also directed attention to the demoralizing influences of slum life on working-class morality and this set of problems proved to be as pressing as those relating to sanitary reform of the urban environment.

The geography of separation: private philanthropy and the rise of the district visiting movement

If private philanthropy was the barometer of social concern, then the growing flood of charity that began to well up from the 1820s and 1830s signified heightened middle-class awareness of the problems posed by urban poverty.[63] Far from abating, this outpouring of philanthropic endeavour gathered momentum in subsequent decades. So numerous had the channels of almsgiving become that by 1850 they commanded their own directory in which over 490 philanthropic societies were recorded for London. By 1861 this number had risen to 640 with a total annual turnover of £2.5 million, three times the amount spent by metropolitan unions on poor relief.[64] The *Westminster Review*, which interpreted this outpouring of alms and the profusion of charities as evidence that society 'was becoming foolishly soft, weakly tended, irrationally maudlin, unwisely and mischievously charitable', was outspoken in its criticism.[65] Others, including its main rival the *Quarterly Review*, expressed a different and less overtly hostile opinion.[66] All, however, were agreed that if philanthropic efforts were any indication of concern, the condition of the poor had never before occupied such a prominent position in the thoughts of the urban middle-class.

Whilst the establishment and growth of London charities bears witness to the awareness of urban poverty and the strength of bourgeois fears over the threat of outcast London, the objectives of those philanthropic efforts shed considerable light on the nature of those concerns. Whilst each period spawned its own particular set of concerns, from the 1830s it was the district visiting movement that occupied the central role.[67] In terms of the extent and intensity of their activities, district visiting societies, also known as home missionary societies, were unique. Above all, their activities highlighted bourgeois fears of an emerging ideological gulf between rich and poor brought about by geographical separation of the classes.

The immediate context of the rise of the district visiting movement can be traced to the impact of rapid urbanization, particularly the perceived breakdown of face-to-face communication between the classes. From the start, bourgeois concerns for the demise of religion loomed large. Reverend Thomas Chalmers, the movement's main publicist, argued that riots and disturbances, such as those in his native city of Glasgow in 1820, were proof that the poor had been deprived both of the civilizing influence of Christianity and of the example set by their social superiors.[68] Class conflict, he argued, was little more than an urban pathology that arose because of the spatial gulf between rich and poor. It could only be mitigated through the benevolence of 'disinterested agents of Christianity' who would visit the poor in their own homes and dispense, if not alms, then at least a homily on the middle-class virtues of sobriety, thrift and self-reliance. By such means, he argued, could deferential bonds of personal obligation between the classes be forged and class antagonisms be reduced.[69]

Such ideas held intuitive appeal for the London bourgeoisie, for whom spatial segregation of rich and poor seemed to be an alarming prospect. The threat of disorder was much in evidence during the 1820s and early 1830s, as the Queen Caroline affair, the Clerkenwell Riot of 1833 and the great working-class processions associated with the Grand National Consolidated Trades Union demonstrated. Uppermost in middle-class minds was the prospect of an alliance between politically aware working-class radicals and the mass of urban poor.[70] Fiery language was certainly part and parcel of working-class political rhetoric, from the unstamped press through to the reform bill agitation and subsequently to Chartism, and on the surface, at any rate, grounds for concern appeared well founded.[71] Much of the blame for this state of affairs was directed at the impact of rapid population growth and middle-class flight to the suburbs, both of which underlay the failure of church building in poorer districts to keep pace with the increase of population.[72] According to the Association for Promoting the Relief of Destitution in the Metropolis (APRDM), the 'true type of parish comprises both rich and poor, worshipping in the same sanctuary, and appearing on each successive Sabbath as equals and brethren before their heavenly Father'.[73] By mid-century, however, such an image had little relevance in London. As the classes moved apart, what mutual knowledge and personal ties of sympathy may have existed became more difficult to sustain.

As a means of tackling these problems and responding to these fears, the metropolitan bourgeoisie enthusiastically embraced Chalmers' schemes for the organization of district visiting societies. Whilst much personal benevolence undoubtedly occurred outside such formal arrangements, the creation of a formal and organized system of district visiting marked a signficant departure from existing practice. Evangelical concern with working-class irreligion underlay the early formation of the General Society for Promoting District Visiting (GSPDV), founded in 1828. The GSPDV urged the 'aggressive relief' of the London poor based on a regular system of home visiting. But unlike Chalmers' scheme, in which visitors were drawn from the same social strata as the poor themselves, the GSPDV urged that visitors should be recruited from the higher social strata. Only by these means, they argued, could personal ties between the classes be re-established and deferential feelings of gratitude be fostered in the minds of the working class:[74]

> It is, in truth, only by means of a more frequent and friendly interchange of feeling than has hitherto prevailed among the different orders of the community that the bond of social union can be permanently strengthened. Thus alone can the more advanced civilisation of the educated ranks be brought to bear upon the tone of morals and manners which pervade the nation at large ... Few among the rich are aware how easily they might thus surround themselves with an impregnable barrier of attachment – a barrier which no political convulsion would be able to destroy.[75]

Other district visiting societies followed hard on the heels of the GSPDV. In 1835 the London City Mission (LCM) was founded with the explicit aim of spreading Christianity amongst the working class through district visiting. Numerous other local district visiting societies also emerged and in 1843 the APRDM was established, primarily as an umbrella organization for these local societies. Each of these district visiting societies had its own particular characteristics but their basic philosophy and mode of operation were similar and as such they formed a single, coherent movement. The APRDM, in common with most district visiting societies, relied on voluntary lay visitors and disinterested benevolence 'to mitigate the bitterness of present penury and privation by at once exemplifying the fellowship of Christians and recognising the brotherhood of men'.[76] It was not uncommon for alms, often in the form of cast-off clothes, to be dispensed. The LCM employed paid agents, or missionaries, to preach the gospels, particularly in areas where middle-class residents were few in number. Home visits by an LCM missionary usually entailed a scripture reading and large numbers of bibles and religious tracts were distributed to working-class homes by various societies.[77]

As a means of providing access to working-class homes, visits formed the basis upon which middle-class philanthropists could foster bonds of personal obligation and preach the virtues of sobriety, thrift and self-reliance. Such visits also addressed the problems posed by the outmigration of wealthy residents from working-class areas which many felt had left an ideological vacuum into which socialist or insurrectionary ideas could permeate. Robert Owen's views, in particular, were condemned by the LCM, whose committee regarded them as a 'foul system of atheism, irreligion and immorality'.[78] Sabbath-breaking was specifically condemned on the grounds that spiritual destitution and the spread of socialist ideas were intimately linked. With the popular Sunday lectures at the Rotunda given by Robert Owen and Richard Carlisle, and the publication of unstamped newspapers, uppermost in his mind, Reverend Baptist Noel, a leading supporter of the LCM and a committee member of the APRDM, argued that on Sunday 'the thieves, and profligates of the metropolis, the Unionists, Owenites and the needy of every class, overlooked and neglected by the Establishment, are taught by the apostles of mischief to consecrate to revolutionary musings and to the schemes of violence and spoliation.'[79] Whilst explicitly instructing its agents not to enter into any political discussions, the LCM, in common with other societies, none the less were quick to denounce working-class radicalism. Nor were they in any way shy to preach the benefits of religion as opposed to the apparent evils of socialism on countless occasions in innumerable homes of the London poor.[80]

The extent of the district visiting movement and intensity of operations should not be underestimated, as the activities of the two

largest societies, the LCM and the APRDM, testified. During its first year
of operations in 1836 the LCM supported 40 agents but by 1864 this
number had risen to nearly 400, and included, amongst others, special
missions to gypsies, cabmen, bakers and 'Orientals'. In the same period
the number of house visits rose from nearly 56,000 to just under 2
million a year.[81] Agents normally had about 500 families under their
care, each of which was visited once a month for about half an hour. At
the height of its operations the LCM estimated that its missionaries
visited about 200,000 families on a monthly basis.[82] Each week, a
missionary was expected to devote approximately 36 hours to visiting
and to hold at least two public scripture readings.[83] According to the
schedule of one such missionary, Joseph Oppenheimer, who operated in
the St Giles rookery in 1861 and 1862, this set of duties was followed
closely. Oppenheimer himself had over 650 families in his care, a large
number of which were Irish Catholics and were often less than
sympathetic to his own evangelical Christian faith. Despite the hostility
he encountered, he still spent over 30 hours a week on home visits, in
addition to distributing tracts and visiting public houses.[84] Whilst no
society could match the intensity of the LCM's system of paid
missionaries, other district visiting societies were able to operate on a
wider scale by relying on volunteers, rather than having to shoulder the
financial burden of employing visitors. In 1843, its inaugural year, 121
local visiting societies affiliated to the APRDM, and by 1867, there were
154 affiliated societies north of the Thames with those in the south
linked to a parallel organization known as the South London Visiting
and Relief Association.[85]

From the outset, the district visiting movement focused its efforts on
eastern districts, notably Shoreditch, Bethnal Green and Stepney. In 1844
nearly half the grants made to local visiting societies by the APRDM
went to these areas.[86] In Hoxton, for example, 14,000 visits were made
in 1855 and relief given to over 750 families. A similar number of visits
was also made in Limehouse.[87] In Whitechapel and Bethnal Green
working-class families were visited on a weekly basis and in the 1850s it
was proudly claimed that no street in Stepney was left unvisited.[88] The
LCM also started operations in Shoreditch and Spitalfields and remained
very active in those districts throughout the 1850s and 1860s.[89] The
salaries of the LCM missionaries, each of whom received £60 a year,
constituted a large proportion of expenditure and at various times lack
of funds forced a reduction of operations.[90] To deal with this problem,
the LCM encouraged the formation of auxiliary societies in wealthier
districts to raise funds in support of their efforts in poorer, eastern
parishes. The West London Auxiliary Society, one of the first to be
formed, soon supported 20 missionaries in Spitalfields and other

auxiliary societies were founded in Hampstead, Chelsea, Islington and Belgravia.[91] The St Marylebone Auxiliary committee alone raised sufficient funds to engage 49 missionaries, a sixth of the total number employed by the LCM.[92]

The same financial problems also undermined the efforts of the APRDM. Although sudden crises, such as a severe frost or the outbreak of food rioting, helped to prise open middle-class purses, the structural problems of providing funds in poor areas were common to all district visiting societies. There were frequent complaints that the outmigration of middle-class residents from poorer districts had resulted in shortages of both suitable visitors and funds.[93] The minister of St Peter's Walworth, echoing a familiar theme, complained to the central committee of the APRDM in 1855 that 'with a neighbourhood which is losing almost every day some of its few remaining gentry, I find it very difficult to make the local resources supply the money wants of so large a district.'[94] In response to these problems, the APRDM itself became the pivot about which money raised in wealthier areas was distributed to local visiting societies in poorer districts. In 1855, for example, the central committee sanctioned additional grants to Shoreditch, Limehouse, St George-in-the-East and Whitechapel, as well as to the South London Visiting and Relief Association under whose auspices Walworth fell. As far as the central committee was concerned, by the 1860s the function of the APRDM had changed from one which coordinated the activities of local societies to that of 'the almoner of the rich, or channel of distribution between the wealthy and the pauperised districts of London'.[95]

Conclusion

This role, forced on the district visiting movement by 'the disparity of condition which exists between the Eastern and Western parts of London – the growing pauperism (comparatively speaking) of the East, and the growing wealth of the West', was indicative of the structural factors that determined the spatial distribution of rich and poor in the capital.[96] There were those who viewed such philanthropic endeavour as a positive encouragement to the spread of pauperism and a contributory factor in the demoralization of the honest poor. However, the structural pattern of poverty was such that marked divisions between east and west were already clearly etched onto the urban landscape by the 1840s, prior to the outpouring of charity that occurred in subsequent decades. If indeed the metropolitan middle class had become 'foolishly soft', as the *Westminster Review* believed, it was in response to the impoverishment of the population in eastern districts. Private philanthropy, as well as the provision of poor relief examined in the next chapter, was thus of minor significance in the manufacture of poverty compared with the structural decline of the local economy. All that charity could hope to do was to breach the social gulf that many felt had emerged between the classes from the 1820s and 1830s. It was, for many, a forlorn task.

Notes

1. See Schwarz, 1976, p.210; *idem.*, 1982, p.173.
2. Hollingshed, 1986, p.7.
3. *Association for Promoting the Relief of Destitution in the Metropolis (APRDM)*, 1865, p.6.
4. Beames, 1850, p.119.
5. Chadwick, 1965, p.232.
6. Statistical Society of London, 1840, p.22; *idem.*, 1848a, p.211; Weld, 1843, p.20.
7. Rawson, 1843, p.44.
8. St Giles was also the setting for John Gay's *Beggar's Opera*, published in 1728, See George, 1966, pp.54, 91–4; Power, 1978, pp.181, 185.
9. Statistical Society of London, 1848b, pp.16–17; Mann, 1848, pp.19–20.
10. Green and Parton, 1990, p.64.
11. See Cooper, 1850, pp.9–24.
12. Dyos, 1957, p.264.
13. Denton, 1861, pp.5–8.
14. Capper, 1862, p.161; see also Pattison, 1964, p.39.
15. Dyos, 1955–56, p.141; Gavin, 1848, p.42; PP 1844 XVIII *RC on the state of large towns*, q. 6029–31, 6050; PP 1861 IX *SC on poor relief*, q. 7372–4, 7433–7.
16. Gilbert, 1857, pp.6–7.
17. PP 1862 X *SC on poor relief*, q. 7348.
18. *ibid.*, q. 7037–8, 7372–4, 7399, 7570, 7770; PP 1866 XXXIII *Eighth report of the medical officer to the Privy Council*, p.504.
19. Gavin, 1848, pp.12–18.
20. Meyrick, 1858, p.119.
21. Grant, 1842a, pp.164–5.
22. See Cannadine, 1977; Carter and Lewis, 1990, pp.125–35; Dennis, 1984, pp.48–55; Gavin, 1850, p.70; Ward, 1975; *idem.*, 1980.
23. Engels, 1973, p.77.
24. Power, 1978, pp.171–5.
25. Schwarz, 1982, p.172.
26. Fletcher, 1844, p.70.
27. Evans, 1845, p.190.
28. *APRDM*, 1857, p.6.
29. *idem.*, 1866, p.6.
30. Morley, 1854, quoted in Flint, 1987, p.207.
31. See Booth, 1902, First series, *Poverty* (4 vols). Booth first presented his findings for Tower Hamlets to the Royal Statistical Society in 1887. Subsequent investigations covered London as a whole, focusing on poverty (first series, 4 volumes), industry (second series, 5 volumes), religious

influences (third series, 7 volumes) and a conclusion (1 volume). The entire series was published in 1902 as *Life and Labour of the People of London*.

32. This section is an amended version of Green, 1984. The technique used here to combine a set of indicators is known as 'factor analysis'. It seeks to reduce the data to a series of composite factors, each of which represents a pattern of interrelated variables within the original data set. The statistical aspects of this technique are described in Johnston, 1978, pp.127–82.

33. Because it is difficult to attribute causality to any specific indicators, it is important to examine the measures in combination. For example, high birth rates are not in themselves the cause of poverty since their impact will vary according to the economic status of households. However, taken in conjunction with other factors, such as low incomes, they tended to aggravate social deprivation. For further discussion of this approach see Green, 1984, pp.268–73.

34. Both authors based their work on the concept of absolute poverty, measured against a notional poverty line defined with reference to the minimum income considered necessary for an independent existence. Booth's definition was less systematic than Rowntree's and was by no means consistent throughout the lengthy volumes that constituted the final edition of *London Life and London Labour*. He defined the poor as 'those whose means may be sufficient, but are barely sufficient, for decent and independent life ... [and] living under a struggle to obtain the necessaries of life and make both ends meet'. According to Booth, the minimum income required to remain above this standard was 21s. a week, depending on the size of family. Given that the cost of living at mid-century was similar to that during the 1880s and 1890s, this figure can also be taken as respresentative of the minimum income needed to remain above the poverty line for this earlier period. Rowntree based his poverty line on the cost of diets that would ensure mere physical efficiency. He distinguished between primary poverty, where household income was insufficient to obtain the minimum necessities of life, and secondary poverty, which occurred when household income would have been sufficient were it not that a portion was impecuniously spent on other items, notably drink. See Booth, 1902, First series, *Poverty*, vol. 1, p.53; Rowntree, 1901, pp.86–111. For further discussion see Bales, 1991, pp.66–99; Hennock, 1987, pp.208–16; *idem.*, 1991, pp.190–213; Williams, 1981, pp.309–26, 332–6, 345–51.

35. A full description of the data is provided in Appendix 7.1. A more detailed discussion is provided in Green, 1984.

36. See Appendix 1.1 for a description of the districts. Hampstead was omitted due to lack of data.

37. Variables are referred to in the text by small capitals.

38. Booth's sample population was drawn from families with children of school age and therefore contained a larger proportion of young and thus comparatively healthy adults. In contrast, Rowntree's research focused on a sample drawn from income groups and therefore covered a wider age range, including older persons. For this reason, death of the main wage earner was far more important than in Booth's work.

39. Cronjé, 1984, p.83; Wohl, 1983, p.130. The social stigma of the disease meant that the cause of death was often certified as respiratory rather than pulmonary tuberculosis.

40. Creighton, 1965, pp.188–214; Luckin, 1984, pp.102–4.

41. Chadwick, 1965, p.228.
42. Rowntree, 1901, p.137.
43. Chadwick, 1965, pp.242–5.
44. Factor loadings can best be explained as correlation coefficients between individual variables and separate factors. The factors themselves are defined with reference to the pattern of high and low loadings. In this study high loadings have been interpreted as those having values significant at the 0.05 per cent level. Eigenvalues are a measure of the relative importance of factors and, in keeping with convention, only factors with eigenvalues greater than 1.00 have been included.
45. Discussions of the remaining factors can be found in Green, 1984, pp.309–10, 326–32.
46. Fletcher, 1844, p.80.
47. Dyos, 1977, pp.109–13.
48. *idem.*, 1967, pp.8–13.
49. Roberts, 1859; Wohl, 1977, pp.73–92, 109–20.
50. Gaskell, 1833, p.170.
51. *ibid.*, pp.7–8.
52. Chadwick, 1965, pp.251, 267.
53. PP 1840 XI SC *on the health of large towns*, q. 568–72.
54. Strang, 1845, p.33.
55. For the relationship between environmentalism, the urban environment and social reform see Driver, 1988.
56. Godwin, 1854, p.32.
57. Gavin, 1850, p.75.
58. Meyrick, 1858, p.11.
59. Carpenter, 1851, p.2; Himmelfarb, 1984, pp.371–99; Symmons, 1849, p.1.
60. Beames, 1850, p.5.
61. Wakefield, 1831, p.9.
62. Beames, 1850, p.198.
63. Owen, 1965, p.134–62.
64. Low, 1850, p.453, *idem.*, 1862, pp.vii–xi.
65. Anon, 1853, p.63.
66. Anon, 1855, p.408.
67. During the 1840s, for example, revelations about the insanitary conditions in working-class areas spurred the growth of medical charities. The plight of fallen and destitute women attracted attention in the following decade, stimulated by the revelations of prostitution amongst needlewomen brought to light by Henry Mayhew, and the foundation of several female refuges dates back to this decade.
68. Chalmers, 1821, vol. 1, pp.27–8.
69. Moffatt, 1853, p.146. In his own parish in Glasgow Chalmers introduced a system of lay visitors, or deacons, each of whom was responsible for investigating requests for relief. By regular home visiting, the honest poor were encouraged to rely upon their own exertions whilst careful investigation of applicants was supposed to reduce imposture.
70. Lhotky, 1845; Wakefield, 1831, pp.9–11.
71. Stevenson, 1992, pp.293–5.
72. *District Visitors Record*, 1836, vol. 1, p.1.
73. APRDM, 1855, p.25.
74. *District Visitors Record*, 1836, vol. 1, p.2; *The District Visitors' Manual*,

    1840, p.32.
75. *ibid.*, p.31.
76. *APRDM*, 1844, p.3.
77. *London City Mission (LCM)*, 1841, p.17. In 1838, LCM missionaries distributed nearly 40,000 sets of scriptures. It was ironic that the printing of cheap bibles in such large quantities caused changes in bookbinding that in 1849 resulted in a bitter strike by workers in the firms engaged on contracts for the British and Foreign Bible Society. See *Appeal of the Journeymen Bookbinders*, 1849.
78. *LCM*, 1839, p.18; *idem.*, 1840, p.20.
79. Noel, 1835, p.77.
80. Unstamped newspapers and other working-class weekly papers were usually distributed on Sunday.
81. *LCM*, 1837, p.6; *idem.*, 1864, p.2.
82. *idem.*, 1854, p.5; *idem.*, 1858, p.xxviii.
83. *idem.*, 1840, p.27.
84. He normally began his visits in Dudley Street at the start of the month and worked his way through to Monmouth Court by the end, visiting the same house on the same day of each month. See Oppenheimer, 1861–62.
85. *APRDM*, 1844, p.29; *idem.*, 1845, pp.45–6; *idem.*, 1867, p.5.
86. *idem.*, 1844, p.29; *idem.*, 1848, p.10.
87. *idem.*, 1855, pp.19–20.
88. *idem.*, 1850, p.12, 20, 29; *idem.*, 1856, pp.5–6.
89. *LCM* minutes, 16 May 1835; *idem.*, 1844, p.17.
90. *LCM*, 1851, p.38; *idem.*, 1863, p.6.
91. Weyland, 1884, p.126.
92. *LCM*, 1852, p.32.
93. *APRDM*, 1845, p.11.
94. *idem.*, 1855, p.15.
95. *ibid.*, pp.25–6. For the activities of the Charity Organisation Society see Jones, 1971, pp.241–80.
96. *ibid.*

CHAPTER EIGHT

'No powers of expansion': the crisis of poor relief

Introduction: the New Poor Law

The history of poor relief in the nineteenth century is dominated by the changes brought about by the 1834 Poor Law Amendment Act.[1] The old Poor Law, with its generous scales of outdoor relief, was swept away, albeit to differing degrees and in some places not without a struggle. In its place came the New Poor Law, focused more closely on the provision of relief inside the workhouse and overseen by a centralized bureaucracy in the form of the Poor Law Commission and, from 1847, the Poor Law Board. The history of this change and the subsequent development of the New Poor Law has been told on numerous occasions and it is not the intention here to review that discussion.[2] However, despite attempts by the central Poor Law to impose uniformity on the provision of relief, the network of local authorities and the discretionary powers of expenditure they retained after 1834 ensured that the map of poor relief comprised a mosaic of contrasting, and in some cases, competing policies. The balance between indoor and outdoor relief, treatment of different categories of paupers, and the role of the workhouse could and did vary markedly between places according to local circumstances. For these reasons, as others have pointed out, there is no single history of the New Poor Law but instead several different histories of distinctive institutional and regional practices and it is an important aspect of analysis to locate such practices in their geographical context.

In this respect there was no greater variation than that which existed within London, where the juxtaposition of wealth and poverty meant that conditions in neighbouring districts, and consequently Poor Law policy, differed widely. The proximity of such social contrasts, together with the large number of separate Poor Law unions in the capital, added a uniquely metropolitan dimension to the London Poor Law that was missing from other towns and cities of the period. It is the purpose here to investigate that uniqueness and to examine more specifically the difficulties in providing relief encountered by Poor Law unions in eastern districts of London.

The two pillars of Poor Law policy: the workhouse and removals

Rising costs of poor relief, particularly in southern counties, and labour shortages in Midland and northern towns, provided the immediate geographical context for the recommendations made by the Royal Commission appointed to reform the old Poor Law. Under the influence of Edwin Chadwick, the New Poor Law aimed to deter the abuses that had characterized the old Poor Law, particularly the practice of providing outdoor relief to able-bodied paupers. Chadwick believed that this not only encouraged pauperism but also hindered the free flow of labour by ensuring that unemployed and under-employed labourers remained tied to their place of settlement.[3] Like free trade, which aimed to remove impediments to the flow of goods and commerce, so the New Poor Law sought to encourage the free flow of labour from over-populated southern counties to the burgeoning Midland and northern regions. An awareness of this geographical context necessarily informs our understanding of the operation of the New Poor Law, and in particular the problems that arose in London as a result of its implementation.

The two central instruments of Poor Law policy after 1834, the workhouse and the removal of paupers, were designed to meet two specific needs. The first related to the problem of the over-supply of agricultural labour in southern counties and the growing demand for labour in Midland and northern regions. The second concerned the need to protect urban ratepayers from the burden of having to support a potentially much larger pauper population that could have arisen as a result of the influx of rural labour. The workhouse was crucial to the first, removals essential for the second. The construction of new workhouses and the strict enforcement of indoor relief was aimed primarily at encouraging agricultural labourers to migrate to areas of high labour demand, notably those towns and cities undergoing rapid industrialization. To achieve this end, the Royal Commission argued that outdoor relief to the able-bodied poor should cease and they should only be relieved within the workhouse. At the same time, adherence to the principle of less eligibility demanded that the workhouse should become 'an uninviting place of wholesome restraint ... thus making the parish fund the last resource to the pauper and rendering the person who administers the relief the hardest taskmaster and the worst paymaster that the idle and dissolute can apply to'.[4] Indoor relief thus became the cornerstone of Poor Law policy whilst outdoor relief, particularly any form of aid in place of wages, was strongly discouraged. Such measures, it was hoped, would go far towards restoring a measure of equilibrium in the labour market.

By way of a counter-balance, the removal of paupers without a settlement protected urban Poor Law guardians from any excessive demand for relief arising from a disproportionate influx of impoverished rural labourers or as a result of cyclical unemployment. Although attempts were made to abolish powers of removal prior to 1834, no changes were made when the New Poor Law was first introduced.[5] Indeed, given the emphasis on indoor relief, to have done so would have placed urban guardians in an extremely difficult position. Thus the laws of settlement and the powers of removal, so disliked by Adam Smith and Thomas Malthus, remained as a counterbalance to the impact of the New Poor Law's insistence on enforcing indoor relief and the emphasis on less eligibility. To a large extent, it was the growing imbalance between these powers of removal and the provision of indoor relief that triggered the crises of Poor Law expenditure in mid-nineteenth century London.

Poor relief: regional contrasts

The Poor Law Commission, and its successor, the Poor Law Board, struggled with varying degrees of success to impose a degree of uniformity on local relief expenditure and practices. Their powers, however, were circumscribed by the independence of local guardians and the strength of opposition, and this, together with differing economic and social circumstances, meant that regional experiences under the New Poor Law varied considerably.

In terms of expenditure, supporters of the New Poor Law could claim with some justification that initially the reforms were a success. Throughout England and Wales, including London and the industrial regions of Lancashire and the West Riding, expenditure fell sharply after 1834, as shown in Figure 8.1.[6] In Middlesex, where the rise in expenditure after 1825 had been particularly steep, the New Poor Law had a dramatic impact. In real terms, expenditure was brought down to similar levels to those which had existed at the end of the Napoleonic Wars, despite the increase in population. After 1834 real expenditure in general grew more slowly than population but from the late 1840s regional experiences began to diverge. In England and Wales, excluding London, population rose by about 63 per cent between 1834 and 1868, more than three times the real increase in poor relief. In the West Riding, the rate of population growth was more than double the increase in relief expenditure. Elsewhere the picture was less clear. In Lancashire, for example, where the fortunes of the cotton industry largely dictated the demand for relief, expenditure rose more rapidly than population and in

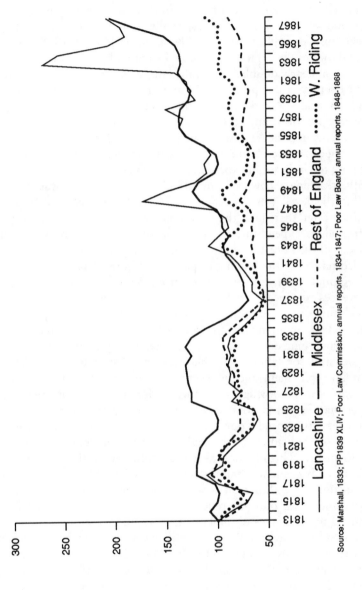

Source: Marshall, 1833; PP1839 XLIV; Poor Law Commission, annual reports, 1834-1847; Poor Law Board, annual reports, 1848-1868

Figure 8.1 Poor Law expenditure by county, 1813–1868 (1813=100).

London there was little to choose between the two.[7] Thus, although we can speculate about general trends in poor relief expenditure, in reality the national picture is a more complex mosaic of regional experiences.

The situation in London, which prior to the 1834 reforms had contained more than a hundred separate authorities responsible for the provision of poor relief, was especially complex and the patterns of expenditure difficult to unravel. Between 1834 and 1868 Poor Law expenditure in the capital as a whole increased by 79 per cent whilst the population nearly doubled. From the late 1830s, in common with the rest of the country, real expenditure began to rise, peaking during the crises of 1842–43 and 1848–49. From the mid-1850s, however, experiences between London and the provinces began to diverge. Although fluctuations in poor relief were far greater in Lancashire than London, in both regions expenditure outpaced the national rate of change. In London, the increase in expenditure was particularly marked in the mid-1850s, reaching a new peak in 1858, at which point it was more than double the level it had been in 1834. Although the rate of increase declined after that date, the economic crisis of 1867–68 again pushed metropolitan expenditure to unprecedented levels, bringing about the collapse of the Poor Law in several eastern districts and hastening much-needed reform of the funding of poor relief in the capital.

Regional contrasts in expenditure were paralleled by similar differences in local relief policies. As we have already seen, the workhouse was designed primarily to deal with permanently overstocked labour markets in southern counties rather than the needs of an urban industrial economy characterized by cyclical fluctuations in the demand for labour.[8] Workhouses were incapable of dealing with mass unemployment and in several northern towns outdoor relief and allowances in aid of wages continued to dominate relief practice.[9] George Boyer has recently pointed out for such places that where large employers influenced Poor Law policy, outdoor relief was used as a means of subsidizing the labour force during downturns in employment.[10] This practice, as well as antipathy to the interference of a centralized bureaucracy and the reluctance of local Poor Law authorities to sanction expenditure on workhouses, meant that in many northern towns and cities outdoor relief to the able-bodied remained in place contrary to the wishes of the Poor Law Commission.

In London, however, Poor Law policy was different from that in other industrial regions. From 1849 the Poor Law returns distinguished between expenditure on indoor and outdoor relief and these figures show that indoor relief was of far greater importance in the capital throughout the period compared with either Lancashire or the West Riding. The data in Table 8.1 suggest that during the 1850s and 1860s

Table 8.1 Categories of poor relief expenditure (per cent of total)

| | 1850 | | | 1860 | | |
	Indoor	Outdoor	Other	Indoor	Outdoor	Other
London	34.1	34.5	31.4	32.7	25.0	42.2
Lancashire	16.6	54.0	29.4	19.1	41.1	39.8
West Riding	9.5	73.2	17.3	13.0	61.5	25.5

Source: Poor Law Board, annual reports, 1850, 1860

indoor relief as a proportion of total expenditure was consistently higher in London than other regions whilst outdoor relief was always lower.[11] This may be explained partly by the different methods of classifying paupers, particularly in London where those who were relieved on account of sickness were included in the total of outdoor paupers.[12] Nevertheless, the disparity between the capital and elsewhere is too large for this explanation to be anything more than of minor significance and the figures suggest that distinctive relief policies were being pursued in each region. In London this meant a greater emphasis on indoor relief, a policy that the figures in Table 8.1 confirm was followed with increasing diligence from the 1850s. Indeed, as the data plotted in Figure 8.2 show, from 1853 the balance of expenditure in the capital shifted decisively towards indoor relief. London guardians thus appeared much more willing to implement the workhouse test than their northern counterparts, and this in turn tied them irrevocably into an expensive and inappropriate system of poor relief. The financial implications of this policy had much to do with explaining why the metropolitan Poor Law was at the centre of the growing crisis of relief expenditure in the 1860s.[13]

Indoor relief and workhouse construction

If indoor relief was the cornerstone of Poor Law policy after 1834, the construction of new workhouses was its physical manifestation. The Poor Law Commission was anxious to build new institutions as soon as possible, as much for symbolic reasons as for practical considerations, and within six years of the Poor Law Amendment Act, the majority of new workhouses had been built.[14] Initially the rate of construction was most rapid in southern rural unions but in the 1840s and 1850s building slowed and focused more on urban areas.[15] It is important, however,

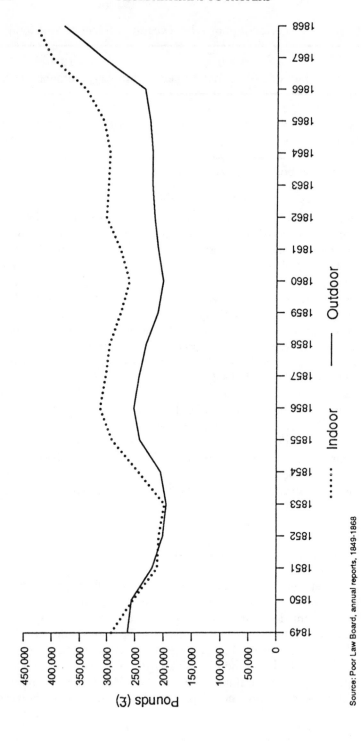

Source: Poor Law Board, annual reports, 1849-1868

Figure 8.2   Expenditure on poor relief in London, 1849–1868.

particularly in London, to draw a distinction between the provision of indoor relief and the construction of new workhouses. Although the two were closely related, they were by no means synonymous. First, metropolitan guardians often argued, rightly or wrongly, that workhouse provision in their locality was adequate. In rural districts, where new Poor Law unions were created from several parishes, an argument could be made for building a large, centrally located institution. Such reasoning was less relevant to London where over a third of Poor Law authorities were single parish unions with little to gain from erecting a new central workhouse. Secondly, workhouse construction in the capital was especially costly and guardians were reluctant to burden ratepayers with any unnecessary expenditure. Where possible the old workhouse was altered, or pauper children farmed out in order to relieve pressure on space. Symbolic importance or not, the general rule in London appeared to be to avoid additional expenditure and build afresh only when absolutely essential.

This did not necessarily mean, however, that indoor relief was any less important. Indeed, as we have seen, the opposite was the case. What it did mean was that after 1834 workhouse construction in London was both slow and incomplete. By 1847 only eight unions had sought permission from the Poor Law Commission to build new workhouses, although a far larger number had spent money on alterations, as the expenditure data shown in Figure 8.3 makes clear. The depression of the late 1840s and the ensuing rise in pauperism prompted a surge in construction but even by 1854 less than half the metropolitan unions had built a new workhouse.[16] In 1861 Henry Farnall, the Poor Law inspector for London, reported that 16 of the 42 existing workhouses were inadequate both in terms of size and internal arrangements.[17] Partly because of increased demands on relief during the economic downturn of the early 1860s, and partly because of renewed central pressure to stem the tide of outdoor relief, authorizations for workhouse expenditure increased sharply after 1864 reaching a peak of £208,258 in 1868. Even at that point, however, 10 of the 39 metropolitan unions, including several in the centre, steadfastly refused to construct a new workhouse.

The geography of workhouse construction in London illustrates effectively the differences in poor relief policy between metropolitan districts. Those authorities that built new workhouses were mainly located either in the rapidly growing suburbs, such as St Marylebone or Lambeth, or in eastern districts. Table 8.2 shows that of the eleven workhouses in 1857 that could hold over a thousand paupers, five were in the east whilst four were located in the suburbs. The remaining two, belonging to the City and Southwark unions, were built not because

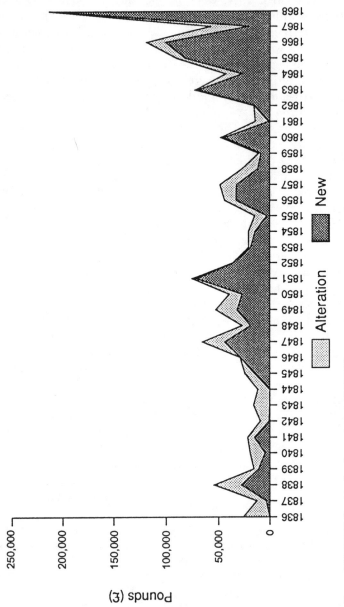

Figure 8.3   Workhouse construction in London, 1836–1868.

Source: PP 1866 LXI; Poor Law Board, annual reports, 1867-1868

Table 8.2   Workhouse accommodation in London, 1857 (over 1000 people)

District	Workhouse Accommodation (1857)	Size of Population (1861)
St Marylebone	2,000	161,680
Lambeth	1,730	162,044
St Pancras	1,393	198,788
St George Southwark	1,255	55,510
St George-in-the-East	1,250	48,891
Shoreditch	1,230	129,364
Stepney	1,204	56,572
Whitechapel	1,050	78,970
Greenwich	1,044	85,975
Bethnal Green	1,016	105,101
City	1,010	45,555

Source: Lumley, 1858; Census 1861

population was expanding but in order to accommodate much larger numbers of paupers. Thus, in relation to the population, the workhouses in the City, St George-in-the-East, Stepney and Southwark were particularly large. If the large, integrated workhouse reflected the symbolic triumph of the New Poor Law, then the victory appeared to be most complete in inner districts to the east and also in the expanding suburbs. As we shall see, however, that victory entailed a heavy cost, borne relatively easily in the more affluent districts but with increasing difficulty in the east.

Whilst new workhouses may have reflected a commitment to the principles of the New Poor Law, in reality relief policies varied widely between metropolitan unions. Disparities in social and economic conditions, coupled with the attitudes of local guardians, meant that relief policies in neighbouring unions often differed considerably. From 1849 we can gauge those differences in terms of the balance between indoor and outdoor relief. Broadly in keeping with the central Poor Law policy, most parishes and unions spent more on indoor than outdoor relief. However, wide variations existed as shown by the mosaic of relief practices mapped in Figure 8.4. Contrary to the recommendation of the New Poor Law, several districts, notably Poplar, Rotherhithe and Lewisham, consistently spent more on outdoor than indoor relief. The

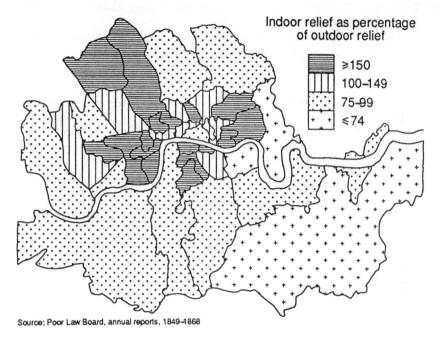

Source: Poor Law Board, annual reports, 1849–1868

Figure 8.4   Indoor relief, 1849–1868.

Poplar guardians led the way, normally spending between 50 and 75 per cent more on outdoor relief than indoor, rising to over 300 per cent during the crisis years of 1867 and 1868. In Rotherhithe and Lewisham, although such variations were less pronounced, the policy of providing outdoor rather than indoor relief was applied with equal consistency. Somewhat less clear-cut outdoor policies also prevailed in several other districts, notably in the suburbs and the City of London.

Relief policies, however, were always subject to change and marked reversal occurred in several places. A good example of this was the City of London union, the policies of which were of particular importance in relation to the surrounding districts. Over the period as a whole, the City union spent more on outdoor than indoor relief, but this trend masked a sharp change in policy from the late 1850s when outdoor relief to the non-resident poor was discontinued and the ratio of indoor to outdoor relief shifted in favour of the former.[18] Similar shifts in relief practices also occurred in the mid-1850s in St Marylebone, St Pancras, and the East and West London unions. In Wandsworth and Chelsea the policy of providing outdoor relief was also replaced from the early 1860s by one favouring the workhouse. With the exception of Islington no set of guardians altered policy in the opposite direction, from favouring indoor to outdoor relief. In that respect, even well before the crusade against outdoor relief of the later 1860s and 1870s, metropolitan unions had made the workhouse test a pivotal part of Poor Law policy.

This situation was particularly true of those districts in which outdoor relief was the exception and indoor relief the rule, shown in Figure 8.4 as those in which indoor relief was at least 50 per cent higher than outdoor relief. This group actually consisted of contrasting sets of districts and included some of the more affluent West End parishes and suburbs together with several poor districts in the inner industrial perimeter, notably East London and Southwark. The wealthy inner West End districts, consisting of St George Hanover Square, St James and St Martin's, each operated an indoor policy despite the fact that they had relatively small workhouses. The same policy was also adopted in Hampstead and St Pancras, although in both cases the emphasis on indoor relief was less pronounced. With the exception of St Pancras, the affluence of the resident population in such areas meant that the demand for relief was relatively small and there was little need either for large workhouses or for heavy expenditure on outdoor relief. Since manufacturing and casual labour were of lesser importance as a source of working-class employment than domestic service, fluctuations in the demand for relief were less pronounced and even relatively small workhouses normally had sufficient capacity to deal with any sudden increase in the number of paupers.

By way of a contrast, the second set of districts where indoor relief was the rule mainly comprised those located in the inner industrial perimeter surrounding the central core. In the west, St Giles, Holborn and St Luke contained pockets of the poor as well as significant concentrations of wealthier residents. None of these districts built new workhouses, despite the fact that expenditure on indoor relief was relatively high. St Giles in particular kept to a strict indoor policy throughout, its guardians mindful of the potentially large demand for relief from the slum population of the Church Lane rookery and Seven Dials. To the south, the hard-pressed ratepayers of Southwark kept a similarly tight rein on expenditure.

The last set of indoor unions, and in many ways the most significant, was a group of relatively poor eastern districts comprising Bethnal Green, St George-in-the-East, Stepney and Mile End. Unlike indoor unions elsewhere, this group shared a common problem of balancing a rising demand for poor relief with a relatively small and ever-diminishing ratepayer base. Pinched by poverty, boards of guardians in these districts followed the New Poor Law to the letter, and sometimes beyond, and here the workhouse test was enforced most rigorously. Bethnal Green stands out in this respect by virtue of the vigour with which its guardians embraced a strict policy of indoor relief. Indeed, they had the dubious reputation of being the strictest in London, a belief borne out by the figures. Between 1854 and 1866, with the exception of one year, indoor expenditure in the district was more than four times higher than outdoor relief.[19] Given the structural decay of silk weaving, the lack of alternative employment and the casual nature of dock work, demand for relief was considerable. To the extent that the population was so poor, and the ratepayer base was shrinking, there was justification for exercising prudence over Poor Law expenditure. However, the reputation for harshness and penny-pinching gained by the Bethnal Green guardians far exceeded even the bounds of prudence.

During the 1840s, for example, in defiance of explicit instructions by the Poor Law Commission to provide a night's lodging for tramps or casuals without money, the Bethnal Green guardians steadfastly refused to give any form of casual relief. In 1842 they relieved a mere 386 casual poor, compared with 5559 in neighbouring Whitechapel and 10,385 in St George-in-the-East.[20] When asked to justify this policy by the Poor Law Commission, the guardians merely stated that Bethnal Green was 'not a casual parish ... and therefore the evil is not so extensive with reference to vagrants'.[21] Clearly, ratepayers in neighbouring districts forced to bear the brunt of their actions would not necessarily have agreed.

Paupers in Bethnal Green who suffered at the hands of guardians told a similar story of niggardly relief and harsh treatment. An elderly silk weaver called Daniel Bush, for example, complained bitterly to the Poor Law Board about the guardians' refusal to grant him outdoor relief: 'I was once cast away in Africa in the Caffers Country and traveled 1000 miles and found more humanity among the Caffers and Hottentots than I find among thies Jacks in office,' he wrote.[22] Nor was his complaint an isolated incident, as the bundles of letters sent to the central Poor Law Board testify.[23] In each case the guardians justified their strict indoor policy, pleading 'that if they were to deviate from the rule, in one case, a vast influx of similar applications would soon be the "order of the day"'.[24]

It was precisely to avoid such an influx that guardians in eastern districts, with the exception of Poplar, strictly enforced the workhouse test and carried the principle of less eligibility to its limits.[25] Conditions in the workhouse were harsh and the regime was strict. Complaints about damp and overcrowded accommodation, lack of heating during winter, unwholesome food and restriction of liberties were common.[26] Moreover, even a strict policy was liable to be tightened as a result of the need to reduce overcrowding. So, when the Poor Law Board instructed guardians in St George-in-the-East to reduce numbers in the workhouse, they responded by tightening rules, removing pauper indulgences and restricting visiting hours, thereby eliciting a flurry of complaints from the indoor poor and their relatives.[27] Repetitive and laborious work was demanded even of elderly paupers: stone breaking, wood chopping and oakum picking were standard tasks, whilst tailors, seamstresses and shoemakers were required to exercise their trades to make workhouse clothes and shoes. In some eastern unions, such as Whitechapel, clothes made by paupers were sold to slopsellers, thereby driving down even further the pitifully low prices paid for such items outside the workhouse. In August 1849 paupers in the Bethnal Green workhouse collectively complained to the Poor Law Board about unwholesome food and restrictions on their liberty: 'But Sirs, their chief complaint is the Pump, the ever lasting pump with a cistern that is never satisfied ... the men positively declare it to be a system of murder which it appears neither age nor affliction will excuse them [sic].'[28] Evidently these harsh conditions persisted for in 1858 the Poor Law Board were told that as a result of continued cruelties, 'A general feeling of discontent prevails throughout the house.'[29] But as long as the Bethnal Green guardians behaved in this manner, neighbouring Poor Law authorities could ill afford to waver from a similarly strict policy. It was quite literally the very epitome of a 'beggar thy neighbour' policy in which none dared deviate for fear of being swamped by the flood of paupers that threatened to overwhelm each and every poor law authority.

Removal and irremovability

Whilst the construction of workhouses and the provision of indoor relief comprised one-half of Poor Law policy, removals constituted the other, acting as a counterbalance for urban unions against the influx of poor from rural areas. The weight of poor relief policy, however, was unequally distributed. Removals were both cumbersome and costly and boards of guardians were often reluctant to act. In some cases 'friendly orders' between reciprocal pairs of parishes rendered unnecessary the expensive and time-consuming process of obtaining court orders for removals. However, where no such arrangements existed, guardians were obliged to follow a lengthy and cumbersome procedure. First, the parish to which the pauper belonged had to be established, by no means an easy task given the complexity of the laws of settlement and the difficulty of communicating with distant officials. Guardians then had to appeal to a magistrate for an order allowing them to pass the pauper back to his or her place of settlement. In practice, the delay in obtaining an order often meant that paupers disappeared before a conclusion was reached. In the case of Irish and Scottish paupers this cumbersome process was revised in 1845 when officials were allowed to dispense with prior investigations before appealing for a removal order. The impracticality of operating even this simplified procedure in London and other large towns was obvious and in 1847 relieving officers were given speedier means of applying for a removal order. Nevertheless, between being summonsed and appearing before the court, many paupers still made themselves scarce and the considerable work involved in investigating their case thus went to waste.

Once a removal order had been obtained, expense itself became a significant issue. In 1861 the average per capita cost of indoor relief in London was estimated to have been 4s.½d. a week compared with outdoor relief of 1s. 4.½d.[30] In contrast the cost of removing paupers from districts north of the Thames back to Ireland was between 22s. and 38s., and to Scotland between 22s. and 60s. In southern unions the practice of transporting Irish paupers overland to a seaport, usually Bristol, rather than placing them directly on a ship in London, doubled the cost of removals.[31] Consequently, only those paupers likely to have been a continual burden on the rates, notably widows with children, the aged, lunatics and the chronically ill, rather than the able-bodied poor, were likely to have been removed and even those may have escaped removal depending on the distance of their place of settlement.[32]

Further evidence that removals were only of limited importance in London came after 1845, when the cost of passing a pauper back to his or her place of settlement was transferred from the county to the individual parishes.[33] This was particularly important in the case of Irish and Scottish paupers where cost was a major consideration in the decision to enforce a removal order.[34] As a result of this change the number of removals to Ireland and Scotland declined dramatically. In the 12 months prior to 1845 the St George-in-the-East guardians removed 819 Irish and Scottish paupers but in the following year they removed none. The situation was similar in several other unions, notably the City, East London, Shoreditch and Whitechapel north of the Thames, and Camberwell and St George Southwark to the south, all of which became known after 1845 as non-removing authorities.[35] Indeed, by 1861 Robert Warwick, deputy chairman of the City union, reckoned that because of the expense and uselessness the practice of removing paupers had been abandoned altogether in London.[36]

Providing that the grounds for receiving relief remained unchanged, guardians could still remove non-settled paupers back to their place of settlement, although as mentioned above, considerations of cost meant that removals were used selectively. The situation changed in 1846, however, with implementation of the Poor Removal Act which created a new category of non-settled but irremovable poor.[37] This new status was conferred on widows within a year of their husband's death and most significantly on those applicants for relief who had been resident in the parish for five continuous years. This was a crucial change in the rights to receive relief and shifted the burden of provision from the pauper's place of settlement to that of residence. In effect it transferred the cost of relief from the countryside to the towns, particularly those places, such as London, that attracted large numbers of rural migrants.[38] At first the cost of providing this additional relief was borne by individual parishes but Bodkin's Act of 1847 shifted the burden to the common fund of the union according to the relative expenditure of each parish.[39] Poor parishes within a union thus paid more for the support of the irremovable poor than their wealthier neighbours. In 1861, when the period of residence conferring irremovability was reduced from five to three years, the cost was shifted from expenditure to rateable value, thereby relieving the poorest parishes in a union from shouldering the major financial burden.[40] Finally in 1865 the Union Chargeability Act reduced the period of irremovability to one year's continuous residence in a union, as opposed to a parish.[41]

The implementation of the Poor Removal Act was initially surrounded by confusion, notably whether the five-year clause applied retrospectively and if it included Scottish and Irish paupers. Where reciprocal arrangements could be agreed, guardians continued to pay relief to their non-resident poor living outside the district, though there were some notable exceptions to this policy, such as St James Westminster and Whitechapel.[42] Nevertheless, from 1846 guardians in inner districts were faced with an immediate flood of applications for relief from irremovable paupers which was further exacerbated by the large number of Irish who arrived in the capital after fleeing the potato famine. In St George Southwark, for example, an estimated 900 additional persons were relieved as a result of this influx and the operation of the Act.[43] Faced with these potentially huge increases, the Poor Law Commission hastily advised guardians that although the legislation applied to Irish and Scottish paupers it was not retrospective and therefore the residency requirement would only come into effect five years hence.[44] This ruling removed much of the immediate pressure and allowed guardians to withdraw relief to many non-settled but resident poor. But the reprieve was temporary and the message was clear: once the five-year clause became operative, districts in which the poor resided could expect a huge increase in the burden of relief. Guardians in these unions braced themselves for the deluge.

From the early 1850s, as the Poor Removal Act took effect, the precarious balance in several districts between relief expenditure and income from the rates was overturned. In central areas, such as the Strand, St Martin-in-the-Fields, and the City, all of which were losing population from mid-century, irremovable poor constituted only a small proportion of the total number of paupers and the changes made little difference.[45] John Rowsell, clerk to the City of London union, estimated that there were no more than 40 irremovable, non-settled poor in the district compared with between 1500 and 1600 paupers with settlements in the City but resident in adjacent parishes.[46] Thus, the decision of the City guardians to continue to pay for their non-resident poor was of enormous significance for the surrounding districts.[47] In western areas, where working-class housing was in short supply, the number of irremovable poor was similarly low and the problems created by irremovability less important. However, districts in which the poor resided, or into which they had moved as a result of slum clearance, experienced sudden increases in the number of irremovable paupers and correspondingly sharp rises in expenditure. In eastern districts, notably the East London union, Whitechapel, Poplar, and in the southern districts of St George Southwark, St Olave and St Saviour, a third or more of the total Poor Law expenditure from the mid-1850s was committed to relief of the irremovable poor.[48] It was in the context of this worsening situation that guardians in such districts set about tightening relief practices and enforcing stricter workhouse regimes.

The rating problem: structural factors

For ratepayers, rising expenditure inevitably meant higher rates. But the rate burden was distributed unequally, falling with greatest severity on poorer districts, notably those in the east and the inner south. For a brief period after 1834, falling expenditure masked these inequalities but once expenditure began to rise from 1838, the disparities in rating assumed greater prominence. The variations between districts were indeed large. Data for 1840, mapped in Figure 8.5, show clearly the spatial distinction between highly-rated central and eastern districts and those parishes in western and suburban areas with much lower rates. Rates in Bethnal Green, for example, were 2s.1d. compared with 5½d. in St George Hanover Square.[49] In the mid-1850s, as the full impact of the Poor Removal Act began to be felt and as economic

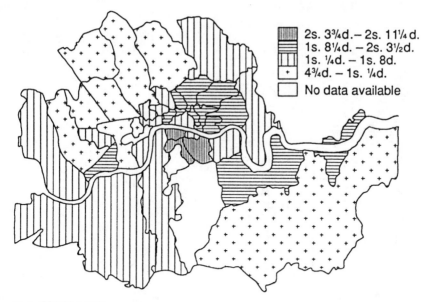

2s. 3¾d. – 2s. 11¼d.
1s. 8¼d. – 2s. 3½d.
1s. ¼d. – 1s. 8d.
4¾d. – 1s. ¼d.
No data available

Source: PP 1857–8, XLIX

Figure 8.5   Rate for poor relief, 1840.

downturn threw large numbers of workers onto the Poor Law, those disparities widened. The range of districts shown in Figure 8.6 bear witness to the extent of this rating inequality. In wealthy districts, such as St Marylebone, St Pancras and St George Hanover Square, rates remained low throughout the period and barely moved even at the height of economic downturn. In contrast, in Bethnal Green, St George-in-the-East and St George Southwark, guardians struggled in vain to keep rates low. The inexorable upward trend in these districts was unmistakable, punctuated by the impact of periodic downturns. Thus, although the geography of the rate burden appeared to change very little, as confirmed for 1860 by Figure 8.7, the disparities themselves were widening. Indeed, the basic similarity in the spatial pattern of the rate burden between 1840 and 1860 masks the fact that the range in the level of rates had increased substantially.

Several factors helped to account for this situation, over and above any increases in the demand for relief caused by the Poor Removal Act. In particular, social segregation and the outmigration of middle-class ratepayers from central areas compounded the problems of poverty. Throughout the inner districts, housing abandoned by the middle class was subdivided and sublet to working-class households.[50] In St George-in-the-East, in common with other areas, such outmigration threatened

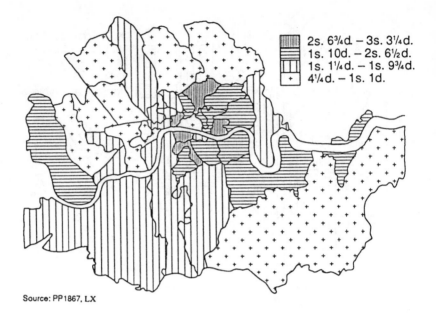

2s. 6¾d. – 3s. 3¼d.
1s. 10d. – 2s. 6½d.
1s. 1¼d. – 1s. 9¾d.
4¼d. – 1s. 1d.

Source: PP1867, LX

Figure 8.6   Rate for poor relief, 1860.

to undermine the Poor Law. George MacGill ruefully remarked that 'Few will be left soon besides the poor, the poor rate collector, the relieving officer, the policeman and the parson.'[51] Similar concerns were voiced throughout the riverside districts, notably in Southwark. James Blake, clerk to the St Saviour's Board of Guardians, noted that street clearances in the centre, coupled with the availability of cheaper housing south of the Thames, had attracted a large number of poverty stricken Irish into the district. The same situation arose in neighbouring St George's where middle-class housing and shops had been subdivided and let out as tenements or lodging houses.[52] By 1865 over half the housing stock in the district was let out by rooms and as the property further depreciated in value, so the remaining middle classes took flight for the suburbs.[53]

The extent to which wealthier ratepayers had abandoned eastern and southern riverside districts can be gauged with reference to Charles Booth's investigations later in the century, the results of which are shown in Table 8.3.[54] Although the study itself was undertaken in the late 1880s and 1890s, the broad spatial pattern of poverty was similar to that which had existed in the middle decades of the century.[55] The most obvious contrast is the distinction in the proportion of class A to D, those families in chronic or intermittent poverty, between the Inner

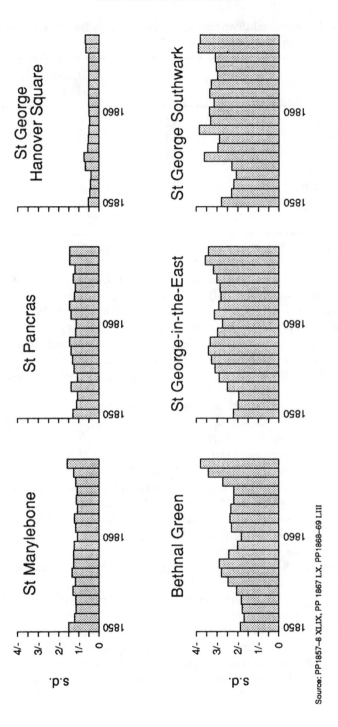

Source: PP1857–8 XLIX, PP 1867 LX, PP1868–69 LIII

Figure 8.7   Rate for poor relief, 1850–1868.

Table 8.3 Regional distribution of classes according to Charles Booth (per cent of families)

	Classes		
	A–D	E–F	G–H
Inner South	42.8	51.6	5.5
Central	41.6	46.8	11.6
East	38.2	56.8	4.9
City	31.5	53.9	14.6
Outer South	27.5	51.3	21.2
North	27.5	51.0	21.5
West	24.1	48.5	27.4

Source: Booth, 1902, *Poverty*, first series, vol. 2, appendix A, table 2, pp. 61–2

South, Central and Eastern districts and the rest of the city. But a second, and somewhat different contrast existed in relation to the distribution of categories G to H, defined by Booth as the middle classes. Compared with elsewhere, eastern and southern riverside districts contained relatively few middle-class households. Indeed, according to Booth's research, the defining characteristic of the East End and the Inner South, was not so much the proportion of the population in poverty but the lack of a resident middle class. This social imbalance, which was becoming increasingly evident from at least the 1840s, underlay the structural problems of financing the Poor Law in these penurious districts.

Serious concern over the level of rating inequality between eastern and western districts, and the inability of ratepayers in the former to sustain high levels of expenditure, began to be voiced from the 1850s. Surveying the scene in 1855, Robert Warwick, a City guardian and active supporter of rate equalization, noted that as a result of the Poor Removal Act 'the burdens of supporting the poor have been removed from one class of ratepayers to another, and that the class which are sufferers are those who occupy property in those parishes where the labouring man can obtain a residence.'[56] Suspicion also existed that as a result of the Act, ratepayers in wealthy districts had become keener to displace the poor as a means of shifting the burden of relief.[57] Although such an accusation is difficult to prove, the Act may indeed have hastened slum clearance in wealthy districts. Before irremovability was introduced, support for the settled but non-resident poor of wealthy areas would still have been the responsibility of local ratepayers. After the Act this was no longer true and guardians from wealthy parishes were at liberty to throw the costs of poor relief onto the districts into which the poor themselves had been displaced. Thus, when the City guardians chose to discontinue relief to their non-resident poor in 1857, the burden thrown onto surrounding districts into which the poor had moved was considerable and added significantly to the mounting difficulties faced by ratepayers in such areas.[58] It was little surprise that in some eastern and riverside districts in the 1860s up to a third of ratepayers were being summonsed for arrears.[59] Clearly, relief in these districts had reached the limits of expansion.

The recurrent crises of poor relief

In the long term, the balance between supply and demand for poor relief was becoming increasingly untenable. In the short term, providing there was no excessive demand for relief, the situation could be managed by judicious and prudent use of the rates. However, when cyclical downturn coincided with high prices and adverse weather, the inherent weakness of the Poor Law in eastern and inner riverside districts became obvious. Such crises recurred with growing frequency from the late 1840s and 1850s and as the abyss of pauperism yawned ever wider, the Poor Law stood in imminent danger of being overwhelmed.

The conjuncture of high prices, economic downturns and cold winters was relatively rare and Figure 8.8 shows that during the 1840s the only occasion on which high prices and cold winters coincided was in 1847. Although the clouds of commercial gloom were already gathering, the harvest of that year was exceptionally good allowing prices to fall sharply later in the year.[60] Thus, when the economic crisis spread at the end of 1847 and the start of 1848, guardians were largely able to cope with the pressure on relief, helped also by an extremely mild winter. Although much distress occurred the local Poor Law managed to contain it without undue difficulty.

The situation in the mid-1850s was very different. By then the Poor Removal Act had opened the floodgates and the burden of supporting large numbers of paupers had been thrown onto many hard-pressed eastern and southern unions. Matters were made worse by a poor harvest in 1853, followed by the outbreak of the Crimean War in 1854, which together fuelled steep price rises. The total number of outdoor paupers in Middlesex on 1 January rose by nearly 40 per cent from 33,869 in 1853 to 47,097 in 1855, with the steepest increases in eastern and riverside districts.[61] Figure 8.8 shows that the winter of that

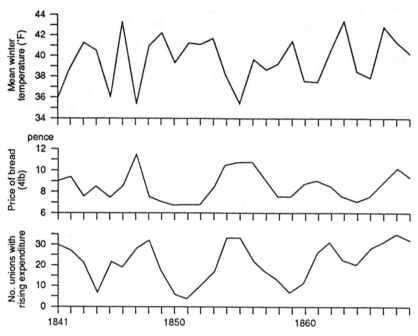

Source: Drummond, 1943; Poor Law Commission, annual reports, 1841–1847; Poor Law Board, annual reports, 1848–1868; Mitchell and Deane, 1962

Figure 8.8   Conjunctural crises in London, 1841–1868.

year was exceptionally severe and in February the Thames froze over, stopping all traffic on the river and halting work at the docks. A report in *Reynolds Newspaper* noted that '... there are not fewer than 50,000 men out of employ, who have been for several days past subsisting on the scanty relief doled out by the parishes and unions'.[62] On 16 February the St George-in-the-East workhouse ran out of bread and a few days later, upon being refused relief at the Whitechapel workhouse, a crowd ransacked food shops in the vicinity.[63] Food riots broke out in other eastern districts and in Bermondsey and for a week the situation remained tense.[64] Extra police were drafted in to protect property whilst alms from the West End bourgeoisie swelled the coffers of philanthropic societies for distribution in the impoverished east.[65] The rioters themselves received little mercy at the hand of magistrates. In Bethnal Green, four labourers who had attacked bakers' shops and stolen bread to the value of 3s., were each sentenced to six months' hard labour.[66] Although a thaw brought a sudden end to the immediate difficulties, it had become abundantly clear that under a combination of adverse circumstances guardians in the poorer districts were unable to cope.

For the remainder of the decade, warm winters and cheap bread alleviated the pressure of distress and the Poor Law in eastern districts was able to manage. Mass applications for outdoor relief, organized by the National Association of Unemployed Operatives in 1857, failed to engender any comparable crisis.[67] In early February the relieving officer in St Marylebone struggled under the daily burden of between 2000 and 4000 applicants.[68] The situation was mirrored in neighbouring St Pancras where the labour yard was swamped with applications for work and the casual wards were overfilled. Other mass applications for relief organized by the National Association of Unemployed Operatives were made at workhouses in Islington, Clerkenwell, St Luke and St Giles and also spread to southern and eastern unions.[69] But unlike the situation in 1855, the winter was mild and bread prices were falling and as a result there was no repetition of the previous shortages.[70] Reports of disorder were confined to isolated attacks on food shops in the East End and Clerkenwell and, except for a handful of extra police stationed at workhouse gates, no extra precautions were taken.[71] Peace was preserved, Poor Law authorities coped and the crisis passed.

The respite was brief for on 17 December 1860 the Thames again froze over and all navigation was halted. Of a dock workforce of 30,000 only between 4000 and 5000 men were kept on.[72] Outdoor work stopped throughout London and the threat of another flood of pauperism resurfaced. In eastern districts crowds of unemployed dockers awaiting hand-outs from the poor box besieged police courts. The Mendicity Society was swamped by a threefold rise in the number of applicants. The number of outdoor paupers relieved on 1 January rose by over 10 per cent between 1860 and 1861, and it was reported that in the third week of January, at the height of the crisis, over 130,000 persons had received parochial relief.[73]

The Poor Law in eastern districts bore the full brunt of the distress. Competition from the newly opened Royal Victoria Docks in Poplar had begun to erode the profitability of the older St Katharine's and London Docks, resulting in reduced work for casual labourers in St George-in-the-East, Whitechapel, Bethnal Green and Stepney.[74] In 1861 matters were further exacerbated by the collapse of the contractor engaged on building the new mains sewer in eastern districts which left 3000 men without work. In St George-in-the-East, Reverend George MacGill estimated that a quarter of the population were in need of relief and that the Poor Law was unable to cope.[75] In January 1861 magistrates' courts were again besieged by crowds demanding relief and bread shops were ransacked in eastern districts.[76] Workhouses rapidly filled to capacity and sheer pressure of numbers prevented the application of any labour test for outdoor relief. Surveying the situation at the end of January, MacGill concluded that:

> The history of the last month shows that the Poor Law has broken down, that it is utterly incompetent under its present constitution to relieve the London poor. It has no powers of expansion to meet an emergency which is almost certain to occur every winter season ... It would be desirable that a rate-in-aid should be levied over London for the relief of such cases as those which are now so rife. Or, better still, that the whole of London should be regarded as one parish and all be made to contribute equally to the relief of the poor.[77]

Difficulties continued in eastern districts for the remainder of 1861 and 1862. The outbreak of the American Civil War further disrupted trade in the docks and reduced the demand for shipbuilding. In May 1861 barely 900 men, out of a normal workforce of 2500, were employed at the Thames Iron Works in Poplar.[78] In addition to dock labourers and shipbuilders, sugar bakers, needlewomen, silk weavers, fellmongers and shoemakers all felt the chill of economic downturn.[79] Falling food prices helped to stave off collapse of the Poor Law, but as MacGill and others recognized, the respite was temporary. In the years that followed, a series of milder winters, low bread prices and the availability of work reduced levels of distress but in 1865 the situation again worsened. Bread prices began to rise and the outbreak of cattle plague resulted in sharp increases in the price of meat. Buoyant employment initially masked the effects of these price rises but in the summer of 1866 the collapse of Peto and Betts, one of the largest building firms in London, followed shortly after by the failure of the finance house of Overend and Gurney, was the signal for the onset of widespread commercial panic. The tightening of credit, coupled with growing provincial competition, hastened the collapse of the Thames shipbuilding industry. By September, the main shipbuilding districts of Millwall, Poplar and Deptford had been plunged into depression and by the end of the year shipbuilding in London had all but ceased.[80] In January 1867 as much as half of the male labour force in eastern districts was without work. By June only one gunboat was being built in the Poplar shipyards and an eerie silence had settled over the district: 'If any person were to walk around the Isle of Dogs and Millwall during the working hours they would almost fancy it was Sunday as there is hardly the sound of a hammer to be heard and nothing but the bare scaffold poles to be seen in most of the shipbuilding yards.'[81]

As the second winter of hardship approached, those who had managed to subsist on their savings and credit were forced to seek relief. Counts of the number of paupers relieved on the last day of the Christmas quarter, shown in Table 8.4, reveal the extent of the problem. Between 1865 and 1867 the number relieved rose by over 43 per cent and in eastern districts the increase in pauperism was nearly double that for the city as a whole. In Poplar, the district most affected by the collapse of shipbuilding, the numbers relieved rose from 3462 in 1865 to 9617 in 1867.[82] On this occasion the crisis overwhelmed the local Poor Law. Relieving officers were unable to cope with the flood of applicants and workhouses throughout the East End and southern riverside districts were filled to over-capacity, making enforcement of the indoor test impossible.[83] In St George-in-the-East, for example, over 4000 able-bodied men applied for outrelief in the last two weeks of January and the guardians openly admitted they were unable to cope.[84] The costs of poor relief in London escalated from £905,640 in 1865 to £1,316,759 in 1868, of which nearly one-third was accounted for by the rise in expenditure in eastern districts.[85] Ratepayers from these districts pleaded in vain for assistance from the Poor Law Board.[86] Poor rates, already high in eastern unions, rose even further and arrears mounted. In Shoreditch, by no means the poorest district, 15,000 summons were issued in 1868 for non-payment of rates and similar stories were repeated elsewhere.[87] The Poor Law in these areas, as George MacGill had remarked in 1861, 'had no powers of expansion' and as ratepayers themselves were dragged into poverty, so the system collapsed.[88]

Table 8.4 Paupers relieved in London on the last day of the Christmas quarter, 1865–1867

	1865	1866	1867
West	13,633	15,597	21,005
North	19,241	23,186	26,448
Central	17,538	19,139	21,953
East	19,988	27,508	36,407
South*	32,792	37,839	41,797
Total	103,192	123,269	147,610

*Includes Inner South and Outer South

Source: Poor Law Board, annual reports, 1865–68

The struggle for rating reform

The New Poor Law created unions of parishes as the basic unit of
expenditure but it left untouched the parochial basis of raising revenue
from the rates. Providing that some semblance of social balance between
rich and poor was maintained at the parish scale, this situation posed no
serious threat to the provision of relief. From the 1840s, however, stresses
imposed on the system of parochial rating began to appear in the capital.
Changes associated with the Poor Removal Act of 1846 highlighted the
fact that in eastern and riverside districts class separation had eroded the
ratepayer base and thereby undermined the local Poor Law. As segregation
proceeded, and any semblance of social balance within these districts
disappeared, so the problems of raising local revenue gained in urgency
and the need for reform grew more pressing. This issue took three main
forms: union chargeability, parochial assessment and rate equalization.

Union chargeability

The question of union chargeability was initially raised in London
during the 1840s in the contexts of the provision of district asylums for
the casual poor and in relation to the debate over settlement and
removals.[89] In the context of casual relief, supporters of centralization,
notably Edwin Chadwick and Richard Hall, the Poor Law
Commissioner for London, argued that the profusion of separate
authorities aided deception by 'crafty paupers' who were thus able to
claim relief from more than one district.[90] The solution they proposed
was to centralize casual relief in a smaller number of large district
asylums based on groupings of unions and this in turn implied a
widening of the geographical basis of raising revenue for the purpose.
    Vigorous opposition to this scheme came from several quarters.[91]
Many boards of guardians and directors of the poor, fearful that
expenditure would rise if new district asylums had to be constructed,
petitioned Parliament and the Poor Law Commission against such
proposals.[92] Such groups argued that only the self-interest of local
ratepayers could keep rates down and so prevent the profligate use of
funds. They feared that if responsibility for expenditure was divorced
from that of raising revenue, as would have been the case if District
Asylum Boards had been created, costs would rise thereby forcing an
increase in the rates.[93] It was further argued that widening the
geographical basis of chargeability was but the thin end of the wedge
and that the next stage was a national fund administered by a
centralized, unrepresentative and extravagant bureaucracy. Mindful of
the threats this would have posed for local self-government, powerful

ratepayer delegations, notably from those wealthier districts with most to lose, successfully blocked the proposals, much to Chadwick's chagrin.

The issue, however, was wider than just district asylums and thus did not disappear with the defeat of Chadwick and Hall's proposals. The question of union chargeability was again raised in the context of the Poor Removal Act of 1846. As we have already seen, this Act conferred irremovable status on paupers resident in a parish for five continuous years. But whilst confirming the parish as the unit of administration insofar as removals were concerned, it was unclear whether the increased burden of relief should fall on the parish or union. Bodkin's Act of 1847 temporarily clarified the situation by transferring the cost of the irremovable poor from the parish to the union, a proposal that had first been made in 1844 by Sir James Graham, the Home Secretary, in conjunction with the initial reform of settlement and removals. Payment of the new union charges, however, was based on average Poor Law expenditure over the previous three years and therefore fell more heavily on poorer parishes. It was, in effect, a tax on poverty rather than property and as such raised strong objections on the part of ratepayers in poorer parishes. But the true significance of Bodkin's Act was that it set a precedent for union chargeability and thus represented an important breach in the parochial system of rating.[94]

In 1848 Charles Buller, chairman of the newly-created Poor Law Board, suggested shifting the basis for relieving the irremovable poor from expenditure to rateable value. As on previous occasions, when the matter came before Parliament it was opposed by country MPs who feared that it would undermine the system of close parishes, and Buller was forced to withdraw his scheme.[95] For a few years the issue was laid to one side but in 1854 the new President of the Poor Law Board, Matthew Baines, reopened the topic of union chargeability by introducing a bill to abolish removals and establish the union as the area for rating. Yet again, concerted opposition from country members and Irish MPs, fearful that the bill would exclude Irish immigrants and therefore do nothing to ease their own situation, defeated the proposals.[96] After more than a decade of attempts to reform the parochial system of rating and introduce some form of union chargeability, little or nothing had been achieved.

Parochial assessment

In Parliament union chargeability aroused strong opinions, not least because of the implications it had for the system of open and close parishes in rural areas. In London, however, whilst important issues were raised, a third of the unions were single parishes and therefore unaffected by the debate. What was of more interest was the complex question of parochial assessment. Although the Poor Law Amendment Act had settled the general principle of valuation as the net annual value of property, in practice there was little uniformity in the way that property was assessed resulting in gross inequalities both within and between parishes.

For shopkeepers and local tradesmen, whose property was more highly rated than residential uses, the question of assessment was of immense importance. Indeed, it was one reason why such persons were attracted on to the boards of guardians. As the rates rose to accommodate the additional burdens that were thrown on to the common fund of the union, notably the cost of the irremovable poor, Irish and Scottish removals, and the relief of vagrants and the casual poor, so the vexed question of parochial assessment gained urgency. Smaller property owners, who were more likely than larger owners and major employers to bear the full burden of the rates, felt particularly aggrieved.[97] In 1850 a Select Committee to investigate the assessment of railway companies noted the difficulties associated with the assessment procedure but failed to recommend any significant reforms.[98] The first change to the system came in 1862 when Boards of Guardians were instructed under the Union Assessment Act to conduct new valuations of property in their district. As far as London was concerned, a more significant change was that the responsibility for payment of rates was switched from property owners to occupiers. This alteration inevitably fell with greatest severity on poorer occupiers and the fact that tenants were far less able than property owners to accumulate sufficient savings to pay a quarterly rate merely added to the already rising number of arrears.[99] In combination, inequalities in the pattern of parochial assessment and the manner of payment of the rates helped to compound further the difficulties faced by the Poor Law in London.

Rate equalization

The third, and in some ways the most significant, aspect of rating reform was the question of rate equalization, particularly in those poorer districts in which demand for relief had outstripped the capacity to raise revenue on the rates. As the problems of the Poor Law gathered urgency from the mid-1850s, ratepayers' associations emerged to press for metropolitan equalization of the rates. Support coalesced in 1854 around the Metropolitan Association for the

Abolition of Poor Removals and the Equalization of the Poor Rates, which in 1857 became known as the Association for Promoting the Equalization of the Poor Rate and Uniformity of Assessments throughout the Metropolitan Districts.[100] Support came primarily from the poorer districts such as Shoreditch, Southwark and Whitechapel, whilst similar associations were formed in Stepney and St George-in-the-East.[101] In 1857 these ratepayers' associations petitioned Parliament to implement some form of equalization. However, opposition from wealthy metropolitan parishes and Irish MPs proved too strong and the bill was withdrawn.[102] Instead, the Select Committee appointed to consider the operation of the Poor Removal Act recommended that the period of irremovability be reduced from five to three years, a measure that was confirmed in 1861 by the Irremovability Act.[103] In order to protect poorer parishes from again being submerged by a flood of newly irremovable paupers, the Act also touched on the question of union chargeability and established rateable values rather than expenditure as the basis upon which parishes should contribute to the union common poor fund. Although the change was irrelevant for single union parishes and the need for full metropolitan equalization was still pressing, none the less the Act succeeded where others had failed and by establishing the principle of union chargeability it created an important precedent for subsequent reform.[104]

Encouraged by these successes, and spurred by the growing problem of pauperism in the early 1860s, ratepayers' associations in the poorer districts continued their campaign for rating equality.[105] Union chargeability was seen as the first step towards the greater goal of metropolitan equalization of the rates. Pressure brought some rewards in 1864 when the Metropolitan Board of Works was temporarily given limited powers to reimburse boards of guardians for the cost of building casual wards and in 1865 these arrangements were made permanent by the Metropolitan Houseless Poor Act.[106] It was not the total amount of money involved that was significant but the fact that a precedent had been set for the redistribution of funds by a centralized authority for certain categories of poor relief.[107] At a meeting of metropolitan guardians in December 1865, amidst claims that measures provided under the Houseless Poor Act had broken down, Henry Farnall, the Poor Law Inspector for London, claimed, 'It was to remedy the injustice of poverty stricken parishes having a burden from which rich parishes were free that the legislature passed the Act.' He elicited enthusiastic cheers from his audience when he stated that as a result of the changes 'payment for the houseless was spread over the whole of the metropolis instead of some poor parishes being burdened and others getting off'.[108]

That opinion was beginning to turn towards rate equalization was now becoming clear. The Houseless Poor Act laid the ground for a more centralized system of redistribution of Poor Law funds within the metropolis. However, it was rapidly overtaken by events. The financial panic of 1866, which hastened the structural decline of traditional trades in eastern and riverside districts, resulted in a huge increase in pauperism, as the figures examined in Table 8.4 above have already shown. Throughout these districts, the volume of applications made it impossible to implement either a workhouse or labour test, thereby laying guardians open to the criticism that it was the indiscriminate nature of poor relief that was responsible for encouraging pauperism and not vice versa. This, it was argued, coupled with the flood of charitable donations from the West End bourgeoisie, merely encouraged thriftlessness, facilitated the crafty pauper and demoralized the honest poor. The central Poor Law noted 'The class of ordinary labourers, many of them already half pauperized, and others only just removed above pauperism, soon learn the advantage of living in a district where the alms of the benevolent flow in to eke out the legal provision from the poor rates.'[109] Without additional expenditure on larger workhouses, and continued vigilance to reduce outdoor relief, the Poor Law Board, abetted by the newly-established Charity Organisation Society, could see little prospect of stemming the tide of pauperism.[110] Indeed, both argued that a positive inducement to grant outdoor relief would exist as long as the lack of workhouse accommodation made it impossible to impose a strict relief test. This, of course, was totally anathema to the New Poor Law and the Charity Organisation Society alike.

The problem was that without some form of fiscal redistribution, hard-pressed ratepayers in eastern and riverside districts were incapable of supporting any extra expenditure, let alone the additional cost of building or enlarging workhouses. In Bethnal Green, for example, rates had risen from 2s. 2½d. in 1864 to 3s. 10½d. in 1868, and those in neighbouring Stepney from 2s. 5½d to 3s. 7d.[111] In these and other surrounding districts, the growing burden of higher local taxation was threatening to drag the ratepayers themselves towards the unwelcoming embrace of the workhouse. For many, the view expressed by the Metropolitan Board of Works in 1865, and reiterated by the Poor Law Board, that 'So heavy is the charge of local taxation become in the less wealthy districts ... that direct taxation of the occupiers of property there had reached its utmost limits', was very close to the truth.[112]

It was to extend those limits and to tackle the growing problem of pauperism that the Metropolitan Poor Act was passed in 1867. The Act attempted to streamline and improve the administration of relief as well as providing some relief for hard-pressed eastern districts. The remaining local act parishes, which were considered as obstacles to the efficient administration of poor relief, were finally brought under the terms of the Poor Law Amendment Act and new boards of guardians were elected. By doing so, it was hoped that the Poor Law Board could exercise closer control over the provision of relief. It was also argued that because middle-class flight had deprived poorer districts of respectable persons suitable to act as guardians, administration of the local Poor Law had fallen into the hands of tradesmen, publicans and shopkeepers, each of whom had a vested interest in providing out relief as a means of encouraging custom. The Act addressed this problem by giving the Poor Law Board powers to nominate guardians who would be more mindful of the need to enforce a stricter policy of indoor relief.

In the context of rate equalization, however, a far more significant measure was the creation of the Metropolitan Common Poor Fund (MCPF). This was intended to redistribute money from wealthier to poorer districts and was funded by contributions from individual unions according to their rateable value. Initially, the cost of maintaining lunatics, pauper children, and the casual poor, in addition to the salaries of Poor Law officials and various forms of medical expenditure, were transferred to the MCPF. In 1870, however, an additional subsidy equivalent to 5d. per day was provided for the cost of each adult indoor pauper. These sums made possible another spate of workhouse construction in poorer districts, without which Henry Farnall's campaign against outdoor relief during the 1870s could not have been undertaken. In terms of rate equalization, the net result of the Act was an immediate transfer of funds from wealthy districts to poorer eastern and riverside unions. Between 1867 and 1877 the four districts that received most from the MCPF were Shoreditch, Whitechapel, St George-in-the-East and Bethnal Green. Over the same period some 25 per cent of poor relief expenditure in St George-in-the-East and 33 per cent in Bethnal Green came from the MCPF. By contrast, wealthier districts were net contributors to the MCPF, the largest of which, as befitted their financial status, were the City of London and St George Hanover Square. As a result of the Act, rates fell in the poorer districts and rose in the wealthier to accommodate this net transfer of funds and in this somewhat indirect manner a measure of rate equalization was finally achieved.

Conclusion

The crisis of poor relief in mid-nineteenth century London was the result of a complex set of interlocking factors rather than the simple outcome of rising levels of pauperism and we need to draw the strands together. It was true that the conjuncture of adverse weather, high prices and rising unemployment triggered general crises of pauperism, and it was equally true that the impact was greatest where local industries were in structural decline or where large numbers were dependent on casual labour, such as at the docks. That the Poor Law had difficulties in coping with these problems is hardly surprising. However, the metropolitan crisis of poor relief had other causes, associated both with the geographical pattern of social segregation and the administration of poor relief itself.

The problems associated with implementing the Poor Removal Act of 1846, coupled with the inadequacy of the remaining removal procedures, meant that in London, and particularly in working-class districts, the balance between expenditure on poor relief and the provision of funds was undermined. Whilst demand for relief rose in poorer districts, it fell in wealthy areas as the poor were displaced by slum clearance and as ratepayers were relieved of the responsibility of supporting even their own settled but non-resident poor. Indeed, it could be argued that the changes may even have exacerbated social segregation by encouraging further clearances of working-class housing from wealthy districts.

Faced by a rising tide of pauperism, boards of guardians throughout the capital, but especially in eastern districts, turned increasingly towards a stricter policy of indoor rather than outdoor relief. But the workhouse was poorly designed to deal with volatile urban labour markets characterized by cyclical and seasonal unemployment. It was, after all, intended primarily as a means of tackling structural unemployment in agricultural areas. Moreover, although removals were designed as the means whereby urban Poor Law authorities could redress imbalances in the cost of relief, as we have seen, once the Poor Removal Act came into force they were neither used widely nor were they of any great importance The outcome was that the poorer metropolitan unions, notably those in the east, were locked into an expensive and inappropriate system of indoor relief that they found increasingly difficult to sustain. Indeed, with the exception of Poplar, far from being profligate in the provision of outdoor relief, guardians in those eastern districts clutched desperately to the workhouse test as a means of stemming the tide of pauperism that periodically swept across London. It was, however, an impossible task, for by the late

1860s, the administrative structures of poor relief in London had been hopelessly outpaced by events.

Notes

1. 4 & 5 Will IV. c. 76.
2. See Boyer, 1990; Driver, 1993, pp.36–53; Fraser, 1976; Rose, 1972; *idem.*, 1985; Webb and Webb, 1929; Williams, 1981.
3. Poor relief was granted on condition of the pauper having a settlement in the district. The grounds for attaining a settlement were complex but the most important were by birth or inheritance from the father, by being hired for one year or through apprenticeship. On marriage, women took the settlement of their husbands. For further discussion see Rose, 1976, pp.25–7.
4. PP 1834 XXVIII *RC into the administration and practical reform of the poor laws*, appendix A, part 3, p.281.
5. Rose, 1976, p.28.
6. Real expenditure is calculated by deflating current expenditure by the Crafts-Mills cost of living index. For the index see Crafts and Mills, 1991, pp.25–9.
7. Poor law expenditure for individual London parishes are only available from 1825. Between 1825 and 1868 the London and Middlesex series move in a virtually identical fashion with a correlation coefficient of 0.986. The Middlesex series can therefore be substituted for London. The population figures are those for London.
8. Ashforth, 1976, pp.134–5; For a detailed discussion of workhouse policy see Crowther, 1983; Driver, 1993.
9. Ashforth, 1976; pp.134–8; Rose 1966, pp.609–10.
10. Boyer, 1990, pp.233–9.
11. Pashley, 1852, pp.36–42. The 'other' category includes the repayment of workhouse loans, the salaries of officials, the cost of maintaining lunatics and other miscellaneous expenditure.
12. Webb and Webb, 1929, vol. 2, p.1052.
13. Rose, 1981, pp.54–8. For the period 1865–1905 Mackinnon has suggested that the proportion of adult indoor paupers was higher in London than in northern or southern counties. See Mackinnon, 1986, p.303.
14. Driver, 1993, p.59.
15. *ibid.*, pp.75–9; Williams, 1981, pp.77–9, 220.
16. Authorizations for workhouse expenditure were published in the annual reports of the Poor Law Commission and the Poor Law Board.
17. PP 1861 IX *SC on poor relief*, p.116.
18. Until the Poor Removal Act of 1846, guardians were responsible for paying relief to those paupers with a settlement in their parish or union. In some cases, paupers resided elsewhere but relief was still paid by the union in which the settlement existed. Such paupers were termed non-resident.
19. PP 1861 IX, *SC on poor relief*, pp.118, 176–7.
20. Poor Law Commission (PLC), 1846, p.107.

21. Public Record Office (PRO) MH12, 6844, 25 February 1844.
22. PRO MH12, 6846, 3 August 1851.
23. See for example, PRO MH12, 6845, 14 January 1848; 22 August, 1849, 6 February, 1850.
24. PRO MH12, 6846, 8 March 1853.
25. The stringency of the workhouse regime had its limits. Deaths in the workhouse or through the neglect of Poor Law officials were frequently reported and on several occasions coroners took to task relieving officers and workhouse employees for dereliction of their duties. Thomas Wakeley, the Middlesex coroner, was particularly vociferous in his condemnation. See *The Times*, 10, 13 February 1840, 12 January, 19 February, 13 March 1844. Anxious to avoid such public condemnation, particularly after the scandals of the Andover workhouse, the central Poor Law paid close attention to conditions in the workhouse and regularly monitored overcrowding. Despite their vigilance numerous examples of neglect and harsh treatment persisted, examples of which were collected in *The Book of the Bastilles* by G. W. R Baxter in 1841.
26. PRO MH12, 6845, 6, 15 February 1850; MH12, 6847, 30 October, 10 November 1857, 22 March, 19 April, 26 July 1858; MH12, 7916 29 June 1849; MH12, 7919 14 December 1855; MH12, 7920 12 October 1856 .
27. PRO MH12, 7105, 27, 29 June, 17, 27 July, 2 September, 14, 17 October, 21 November, 5 December 1857.
28. PRO MH12, 6845, 22 August 1849.
29. PRO MH12, 6847, 22 March 1858.
30. PP 1861 IX *SC on poor relief*, q.2989–91.
31. PP 1847 XI *SC on settlement and removal*, q.6629; St Giles in the Fields, Directors of the Poor minutes, 6th July 1852.
32. PP 1854 XVII *SC on poor removal*, q.7279, 7536, 7571–2; PP 1859 VII sess. 2, *SC on the irremovable poor*, q.47, 1687.
33. The only exceptions were those parishes which had a population of less than 30,000. The costs in this situation were still borne by the county rate.
34. In 1851 Irish and Scottish migrants constituted less than one per cent of the capital's population, although the Irish in particular comprised a disproportionately large number of paupers. In St Giles, for example, they comprised about 11 per cent of the population but over 40 per cent of all paupers. In St George-in-the-East, as much as a third of those in the workhouse were Irish, and they comprised an even greater proportion of the casual poor. See PP 1854 XVII *SC on poor removal*, q.7110–11, 7628–9, 7652–4; Green and Parton, 1990, p.77.
35. PP 1847 XI *SC on settlement and removal*, q.2992–8, 6686; PP 1854 XVII *SC on poor removal*, p.553.
36. PP 1861 IX *SC on poor relief*, q.8125.
37. 9 & 10 Vict. c. 66.
38. The politics of the period meant that this measure was offered as a sop to landowners fearful of the effects on prices and profits that would ensue from removal of the Corn Laws. See Pashley, 1852, p. 275; Rose, 1985, p.9.
39. 10 & 11 Vict. c. 110.
40. 24 & 25 Vict. c. 66.

41. 28 & 29 Vict. c. 79.
42. PRO MH12, 7916, 20 October 1846; St George-in-the-East, Guardians' minutes, 9, 30 October, 20 November 1846; St Giles and St George, Directors of the Poor minutes, 15 December 1846; PP 1847 XI *SC on settlement and removal*, q.151, 179–82 .
43. *ibid.*, q. 470, 486–8, 518; see also Nicholls, 1904, p.352.
44. PLC, 1846, p.9; Webb and Webb, 1929, pp.423–4.
45. PP 1859 sess. 2 VII *SC on the irremovable poor*, q.444, 455, 848, 1022–3.
46. PP 1847 XI *SC on settlement and removal*, q.158–62.
47. *ibid.*, q.151.
48. PP 1859 sess. 2, VII, *SC on the irremovable poor*, q.915, 936, 1139–40, 1300–43, 1441; PP 1860 XVII *SC on the irremovable poor*, q.2147, 2157; Lumley, 1858, p.195.
49. The figures refer to the amount per pound assessed on the rateable value of property.
50. *Association for Promoting the Relief of Destitution in the Metropolis (APRDM)*, 1858, p.6.
51. *idem.*, 1866, p.6.
52. PP 1862 X *SC on poor relief*, q.7082–91, 7372–4, 7381–90.
53. *ibid.*, q. 7037–8, 7117, 7372–4, 7399, 7570, 7770; PP 1866 XXXIII *Eighth report of the medical officer to the Privy Council*, p.504.
54. The very poor, comprising class A included occasional labourers, loafers and semi-criminals whilst class B covered casual labourers. The poor belonged to class C, covering those with intermittent earnings, and to class D, including those with small but regular incomes. Working-class families above the poverty line were classified as class E, which included those with regular earnings, and class F, which referred to higher-paid labour. The wealthy were divided into class G, the lower middle class, and class H, containing the upper middle class. See Booth, 1902, First series, *Poverty*, vol. 1, pp.33–53.
55. See Chapter 7, pp.194–8.
56. Warwick, 1855, p.13
57. Gilbert, 1857, p.19.
58. See St Giles and St George, Directors of the Poor, minutes, 16 October 1857.
59. PP 1861 IX, *SC on poor relief*, q. 3423, 3569, 3578–80; PP 1862 X, *SC on poor relief*, q. 7443, 7588–9; MacGill, 1858, pp.31–4.
60. Evans, 1848, pp.55–74.
61. Poor Law Board (PLB), 1853; *idem.*, 1854.
62. *Reynolds Newspaper*, 25 February 1855.
63. St George-in-the-East, Board of Guardians, minutes 16 February 1855.
64. *The Times*, 23 February 1855; *Reynolds Newspaper*, 25 February 1855.
65. *The Times*, 23 February 1855; APRDM, 1855, p.5.
66. *Reynolds Newspaper*, 18 March 1855.
67. The National Association of Unemployed Operatives consisted mainly of building workers. See *Reynolds Newspaper*, 11, 18, 25 January 1857.
68. *The Times*, 3, 6 February 1857.
69. *Reynolds Newspaper*, 1, 8, 19, 22 February, 1 March 1857; *The Times*, 3, 5, 6 February 1857.
70. *The Times*, 6 February 1857.

71. *Reynolds Newspaper*, 8 February 1857.
72. Hollingshed, 1986, pp.46, 63, 89.
73. PLB, 1860, p.185; *idem.*, 1861, pp.185–6. The total number of paupers relieved on 1 January in 1860 was 94,774 and 103,936 in 1861. The number of outdoor paupers was 67,601 and 74,500 respectively. See also *The Times*, 18 January 1861; *Reynolds Newspaper*, 20 January 1861.
74. *APRDM*, 1861, p.12; PP 1861 IX, *SC on poor relief*, q. 3423; Capper, 1862, pp.161–3, 179.
75. PP 1861 IX *SC on poor relief*, q. 3248–56; *The Times* 11, 23 January 1861.
76. PP 1861 IX *SC on poor relief*, q. 3672–95; *Reynolds Newspaper*, 20 January 1861; *The Times* 19, 21, 22 , 23 January 1861.
77. *The Times*, 23 January 1861.
78. PP 1861 IX, *SC on poor relief*, q.13449.
79. *ibid.*, q. 3424–5, 4159, 4174; PLB, 1861, p.14; *idem*, 1862, p.148; *APRDM*, 1861, p.12; *idem*, 1862, p.12.
80. *Reynolds Newspaper*, 23 September, 21 October 1866; *East London Observer*, 8 December 1866; Pollard, 1950, p.72–89.
81. *Reynolds.Newspaper*, 20 January, 2 June 1867; PLB, 1868, pp.28–30, 119–22.
82. Figures refer to the last day of the Christmas quarter. See Poor Law Board (PLB), 1866, p.347; *idem.*, 1867, p.365.
83. *ibid.*, p.14, 126.
84. St George-in-the-East, Board of Guardians' minutes 18, 25 January, 1 February 1867.
85. *Reynolds Newspaper*, 5, 12 January 1868.
86. PLB, 1868, pp.28–9.
87. *Reynolds Newspaper*, 8 March 1868.
88. *The Times*, 23 January 1861.
89. For a detailed discussion see Caplan, 1978.
90. Eleven districts initially refused to adopt the Poor Law Amendment Act and continued to administer relief under separate local acts. These included Clerkenwell, Islington, Shoreditch, St George Hanover Square, St Giles, St James, St John and St Margaret Westminster, St Lukes, St Marylebone, St Mary Newington and St Pancras. The independence of these local act parishes was a continuous annoyance to the central Poor Law authorities. See PLC, 1836, p.13; *idem.*, 1837, p.5; *idem.*, 1841, pp.28, 142–4; *idem.*, 1842, pp.30–1; *idem.*, 1843, pp.19–26, 95–115; *idem.*, 1845, pp.27–8.
91. PP 1847 XI *SC on settlement and removal*, p.31, 293.
92. See PP 1846 VII *SC on district asylums*, pp.447–523.
93. Head, 1848, p.463.
94. Caplan, 1978, p.276.
95. *ibid.*, pp.277–8. Close parishes were those in which one or a small number of landowners could prevent the poor from residing, thereby reducing the cost of poor relief. Providing that expenditure remained the basis for determining the cost of irremovable relief, ratepayers in such parishes faced little or no extra expense. The proposal to alter the basis for determining the cost from expenditure to rateable value would have meant substantially higher expenditure in these parishes.
96. Rose, 1976, p.30.

97. In addition to the influence that large firms and property owners could bring to bear on local vestries, they were also able to compound the rates; i.e. pay a single discounted rate on their combined properties. Smaller property owners were unable to benefit from compounding.
98. See PP 1850 XVI *SC of the House of Lords on parochial assessments*.
99. PP 1867–68 XIII *SC on poor rate asssessment*, q.2617, 2637, 2645–57, 2745.
100. The earliest reference to the Society for the Equalization of the Poor Rate occurs in a letter to the St George-in-the-East, Board of Guardians' minutes, 10 February 1854; Warwick, 1855; APRDM, *Address*, 1857
101. *The Times* 23 February 1857; *East London Observer*, 5, 19 December 1857; Gilbert, 1860, p.4.
102. *Reynolds Newspaper*, 16 May 1858; According to George MacGill, 70,000 signatures were collected. See MacGill, 1858, p.30.
103. 24 & 25 Vict c. 66.
104. PP 1862 X *SC on poor relief*, q.7621–3.
105. *The Times*, 22 January 1866, *East London Observer*, 27 April 1861.
106. By the Poor Relief (Metropolis) Act (27 & 28 Vict c. 116) and the Metropolitan Houseless Poor Act 28 Vict c. 34.
107. 27 & 28 Vict. c. 116.
108. *The Times*, 1 January 1866.
109. PLB, 1868, p.14
110. See Local Government Board, 1873–74, p.140–1; see also Driver, 1993, pp.53–6, 59–66.
111. Figures from PP 1867 LX *Return relating to poor relief (metropolitan)*, p.109 and PP 1868–69 LIII *Return of poor rates levied*, p.36.
112. PLB, 1866, p.17.

CHAPTER NINE

Conclusion: London in the age of great cities

By the 1870s the age of great cities had come to maturity. In the 1840s little more than a handful of cities existed with populations of over 100,000; by 1870 the number exceeded thirty. The 1871 census showed that nearly one in three of the population of England and Wales lived in these large cities, almost as many as lived in rural areas. As the countryside emptied, so the vision of a rural nation dimmed and the focus shifted irrevocably to urban centres as the crucible in which modern society was being forged. The pressing problems encountered in the course of modernization not surprisingly took on a distinctly urban dimension: the spread of epidemic disease, insanitary and overcrowded housing, the growing concentration of poverty on the one hand and rising affluence on the other, inefficient urban government and the dissolution of social relationships brought about by the weight of numbers. Existing structures of urban government proved incapable of dealing with these emergent problems and in the course of the nineteenth century new institutional bodies, administrative frameworks and urban infrastructures were created to tackle these concerns. Sanitary authorities were established, philanthropic housing trusts founded and legislation introduced to curb the worst excesses of slumdom. The Poor Law was reformed not once but several times. The physical infrastructure of cities was transformed and public utilities created: new means of transporting goods, people, water, sewage and gas reshaped the city both above and below ground. Qualitative change as much as quantitative growth characterized the coming of age of great cities.

London stood, indeed towered, at the apex of the urban hierarchy and served both as a focus of social concern and as an interpretive framework for understanding the changes in nineteenth-century society. In the 1830s and 1840s contemporary awareness that life in great cities was a harbinger of wider currents of social change was only dimly perceived. Britain was, after all, still a rural nation and in most cities size had yet to disrupt patterns of social awareness and class relationships. But in London the processes of urban aggregation and social dissolution were already clearly marked. The press of the crowd, the volume of people and the heterogeneity of life meant that social relations in the capital were more complex and therefore more difficult to comprehend than elsewhere. The view that urban life was chaotic, disorderly and formless was more keenly felt in London than in other cities of the age. It was, as Henry Mayhew remarked, the 'monster city', difficult if not impossible to grasp in its entirety, understandable only as a fragmentary collection of fleeting impressions.

Efforts to comprehend the nature of metropolitan society in the early decades of the century focused on the almost infinite variety of circumstances and range of occupations found in the capital. This concern with individuals is evident, for example, in the novels of Charles Dickens and in the four volumes of Henry Mayhew's *London Labour and the London Poor*. By the 1870s, however, further population growth and the widening geographical gulf between rich and poor had eroded the possibilities of personal acquaintance between the classes. Social relations in cities, especially London, were being transformed by the anonymity of numbers. As individual acquaintance between rich and poor receded, so it was replaced by an awareness of numbers, of the city crowd, of the mass of people who inhabited the nether worlds of the urban poor, and above all, of the social contrasts between East and West.

As awareness of this transformation sharpened, so London became a metaphor for the nation as a whole. Thus, when William Booth wrote *In Darkest England* in 1890, his focus on London revealed a widely held view that the problems of metropolitan life were identical to those of the nation. In particular, the social contrasts between East and West were seen as a reflection of deeper divisions in class relations in society as a whole. For the metropolitan middle class, the contrasts between the darkness and gloom of eastern districts and the glittering brilliance of metropolitan culture in the West End could not have been sharper. The blue and black of Charles Booth's poverty-stricken classes in the east and the red and gold of the servant-keeping class to the west was thus no mere cartographical convention but reflected a deeper understanding of social relations in the metropolis and, in more general terms, the nation as a whole.

This social chasm which, as Weber remarked at the end of the century, 'yawned widest in the cities', and most widely of all in the capital itself, had been developing for some time.[1] Indeed, in terms of geographical contrasts, the social distinctions between East and West had already been sketched out during the eighteenth century and we should be careful not to claim for a later period the start of a process that was in fact already underway. By the 1840s the map of poverty had been set and, although changes occurred in later decades, these were relatively minor and did little to alter the overall pattern of impoverishment. Charles Booth himself would certainly have recognized strong similarities between his findings and the poverty map of London sketched out for the 1840s.

Bourgeois fears over the effects of this geographical separation had already begun to crystallize in the 1820s and 1830s around the district visiting movement which embodied many of the concerns that later in the century were incorporated into the settlement movement. If we are to seek the origins of middle-class concern over outcast London, therefore, we must concentrate on the first half of the century rather than the second.

In economic terms, fundamental changes occurred in the first half of the century which amounted to a restructuring of manufacturing in the capital. By the 1850s some trades, such as watchmaking and silk weaving, had shrivelled to minor proportions. London's position as the centre of watchmaking was usurped by Midland towns and by its European rivals. The same pressures imposed themselves on silk weaving, despite desperate attempts to keep the industry alive, and poverty was never far from those who depended on the trade. Some trades, such as bookbinding and building, remained competitive by intensifying the division of labour and deskilling production. Mechanization was important in the former, economies of scale and closer supervision in the latter and in both cases large firms gained a leading edge over small. Other trades, such as clothing, shoemaking and furniture making, only survived by restructuring the labour process through the imposition of piece work and the spread of subcontracting. This was accompanied by spatial shifts in the geography of production: first, from masters' workshops to workers' homes, thereby transferring many of the costs of production initially borne by the employer onto the shoulders of domestic labour; and, secondly, from high-cost locations in the west to cheaper districts in the east. By mid-century, therefore, all the elements of sweating were in place and what followed in later decades was merely an intensification of this ongoing process.

To understand how this engine of change roared into life we need to be aware of the specificities of period and place, the conjuncture of history and geography. What was of crucial importance during this period was the impact of falling prices on the costs of metropolitan production. As the price of commodities fell in the second quarter of the century, profit margins were squeezed and metropolitan manufacturers stood in danger of being undercut by cheaper competition unless commensurate savings could be made in the costs of production. In London, where the characteristics of locality, the pattern of demand and the nature of handicraft production itself precluded the development of a factory system, the main thrust of savings fell on labour costs. This involved a twofold process: on the one hand, wages could be reduced, although there were limits as to the extent to which this could be achieved, and, on the other, cheaper forms of labour could be employed depending on the division of labour and the strength of resistance mustered by skilled artisans.

In each instance, these changes in production resulted in growing uncertainty and irregularity of employment for all but the most skilled workers and this, rather than any fall in wages, constituted the main threat to working-class living standards in the capital. The extent to which workers were able to cushion the impact of these changes and to retain control of the labour process depended on several factors, including the nature of production itself and the solidarity and strength of the associational structures based around friendly societies, trade unions and houses of call. The downward pressures on skill and wages were not felt by all in equal proportion. Some trades expanded, notably engineering and printing, whilst in others new skills were required as the labour process itself was transformed. It was not simply a matter of de-skilling in response to rising competition. In the traditional trades, notably clothing, shoemaking and furniture making, it was more difficult to stem the rising tide of competition and those who were least able to offer resistance experienced the greatest levels of exploitation. Thus, workers in eastern districts, especially women and children who had little in the way of protective barriers, fared worst and consequently it was in these districts that the problems of poverty were most acute.

In the first half of the century both the Poor Law and private philanthropy were forced to confront the problems posed by this process of economic change. In particular, they struggled to come to terms with the widening gulf between the classes. Geographical separation of rich and poor proceeded with such speed and to such an extent that it undermined the efforts of district visiting societies to establish paternalistic ties of deference based on bourgeois benevolence. Ultimately their role was reduced to little more than an almoner of the rich, a role which laid them open to the biting criticism of indiscriminate alms-giving voiced towards the end of the period by supporters of the Charity Organization Society.

As well as undermining the efforts of private philanthropy, class separation cut the ground from under the feet of the local Poor Law. As ratepayers fled from eastern and inner districts, so their place was taken by displaced workers and the urban poor and as the social balance shifted, so local boards of guardians found it increasingly difficult to meet the rising demand for relief. But this situation was not merely the outcome of demand exceeding supply. The fragmented administrative map of the metropolitan Poor Law, evidence of a profound distrust of centralism and witness to the narrow parochialism of the vestries, also had a part to play. Without some measure of fiscal redistribution to mirror the spatial relocation of the classes, the difficulties of providing relief in the poorer districts inevitably multiplied. This was particularly true from the 1850s as a result of administrative changes in the eligibility of the urban poor to receive relief. The fact that many districts relied heavily on the workhouse test to stem this tide of pauperism, notably those in which poverty was greatest, meant that the Poor Law in such districts was locked into an expensive and inappropriate system of relief. Belief that pauperism could be tackled by enforcing the principle of less eligibility may have had a small element of truth, but it was hopelessly inadequate in the structural context of metropolitan poverty. New problems required new measures and the crisis of pauperism that swept across the capital in the late 1860s proved to be a turning point in Poor Law policy as well as in the basis whereby poor relief was financed. That story, however, belongs to a different period and to a second generation of outcast Londoners.

Notes

1. Weber, 1899, p.427.

London registration districts, 1851

The geographical division of London is based on the 36 registration districts contained in the 1851 census. This spatial framework provides the basis for the regional classification used throughout this study.

West	Chelsea, Kensington, St George Hanover Square, St James Westminster, St John and St Margaret, St Martin-in-the-Field.
North	Hackney, Hamsptead, Islington, St Marylebone, St Pancras.
Central	Clerkenwell, Holborn, St Giles, St Luke, Strand.
City	City of London, East London, West London.
East	Bethnal Green, Poplar, Shoreditch, Stepney, St George-in-the-East, Whitechapel.
Inner South	Bermondsey, Newington, Rotherhithe, St George Southwark, St Olave Southwark, St Saviour Southwark.
Outer South	Camberwell, Greenwich, Lambeth, Lewisham, Wandsworth.

In the factor analysis described in Chapter 7 the following districts were amalgamated: Kensington and Chelsea, East and West London, St Saviour and St Olave Southwark. Hampstead was omitted because of lack of data.

Bankruptcy Series, 1800–1860

Several methodological problems exist with the bankruptcy data. There is, firstly, the question of who could be sued for bankruptcy. Prior to 1825 only traders, defined as those engaged in buying and selling, who owed at least £100 could be dealt with by the law as bankrupts. From that year, however, the scope was widened to cover a broader range of activities, including various manufacturing occupations, such as builders, carpenters, printers and shipwrights. Between 1825 and 1842 over thirty new occupations were specifically added to the bankruptcy laws. In the latter year the ceiling of debt was lowered to £50. Such changes inevitably meant that more businesses fell within the remit of the legislation and without these changes the flattening of the curve of bankruptcies from about 1810 would probably have been more pronounced. Significant changes were made in the 1861 Bankruptcy Act, which allowed debtors to file their own bankruptcy petition, and this led to a sharp rise in the number of recorded bankruptcies.[1] After this date it is hazardous to draw direct comparisons with the totals for earlier years. In general, alterations in the legal framework of insolvency make it difficult to rely on comparisons of absolute totals over time, although relative levels of bankruptcies can still be used to examine broad patterns of economic activity.[2]

The second difficulty with the data relates to the bankruptcy figures themselves which exist in various forms according to the stage of the insolvency proceedings. The first stage involved the striking of a docket (or fiat of bankruptcy) by creditors, thereby rendering a debtor bankrupt. In many cases, this was sufficient to persuade a recalcitrant debtor to settle with his or her creditors and the matter proceeded no further. If payment was not forthcoming, creditors could petition the Lord Chancellor to hear their case. If at that stage there was a case to answer, commissioners of bankruptcy were appointed and the debtor notified by an advert placed in the *London Gazette*. Thus, three distinct sets of figures were produced, referring to the striking of a docket, the petition before the Lord Chancellor and the opening of a commission in the *Gazette*. Between 1817 and 1826, for example, only 72 per cent of dockets struck ever reached the pages of the *Gazette*.[3] Thus, depending on which series is used, considerable differences can exist in relation to annual totals of bankruptcies.[4]

Since our main concern is to get as close as possible to the pattern of economic activity, the series for London is based on the final stage of bankruptcy proceedings concerning the opening of a commission. The data are compiled from entries in the *London Gazette* and from *Perry's Bankruptcy and Insolvency Register*. The geographical area covered is the London division as described in the 1851 census.

Bankruptcies in London

Year	London	Rest of England and Wales	Total	Per cent London
1800	291	660	951	30.59
1801	327	872	1199	27.27
1802	334	756	1090	30.64
1803	374	840	1214	30.81
1804	349	768	1117	31.24
1805	332	797	1129	29.41
1806	372	797	1169	31.82
1807	396	966	1362	29.07
1808	410	1023	1433	28.61
1809	460	922	1382	33.28
1810	758	1556	2314	32.76
1811	775	1725	2500	31.00
1812	767	1461	2228	34.43
1813	669	1284	1953	34.25
1814	458	1154	1612	28.41
1815	561	1723	2284	24.56
1816	562	2169	2731	20.58
1817	458	1469	1927	23.77
1818	399	846	1245	32.05
1819	580	919	1499	38.69
1820	447	934	1381	32.37
1821	435	803	1238	35.14
1822	356	738	1094	32.54
1823	425	550	975	43.59
1824	447	660	1107	40.38
1825	534	697	1231	43.38
1826	1005	1578	2583	38.91
1827	474	847	1321	35.88
1828	469	720	1189	39.44
1829	600	1022	1622	36.99
1830	503	878	1381	36.42
1831	567	865	1432	39.59

1832	517	872	1389	37.22
1833	364	647	1011	36.00
1834	384	713	1097	35.00
1835	366	668	1034	35.40
1836	335	621	956	35.04
1837	347	1139	1486	23.35
1838	186	640	826	22.52
1839	305	775	1080	28.24
1840	324	1060	1384	23.41
1841	375	988	1363	27.51
1842	361	924	1285	28.09
1843	322	788	1110	29.01
1844	343	617	960	35.73
1845	351	649	1000	35.10
1846	419	950	1369	30.61
1847	540	1121	1661	32.51
1848	454	1248	1702	26.67
1849	316	927	1243	25.42
1850	250	584	834	29.98
1851	301	646	947	31.78
1852	294	544	838	35.08
1853	282	470	752	37.50
1854	425	810	1235	34.41
1855	467	934	1401	33.33
1856	391	797	1188	32.91
1857	471	987	1458	32.30
1858	363	976	1339	27.11
1859	284	659	943	30.12
1860	422	867	1289	32.74

Source: London Gazette, 1800–26, *Perry's Bankrupt and Insolvent Gazette*, 1827–60

Notes

1. Lester, 1990, pp.118–19.
2. See Duffy, 1980, pp.293–304; Hoppitt, 1987, pp.35–41; Lester, 1990, pp.2, 156–76.
3. Lester, 1900, pp.76–8.
4. Mariner, 1980, p.354–5; Duffy, 1973, pp.331–3.

Labour disputes in London, 1790–1870

1791	Woolstaplers' journeymen
1792	Shoemakers
	Curriers
1793	Rope makers
	Lamplighters
	Carmen and coal porters
	Tailors (leather breeches)
1795	Millwrights
	Caulkers
	Tailors
	Coalwhippers
1796	Brickmakers
1798	Printers
	Shoemakers
	Sugar coopers
1799	Bakers
	Rope makers
	Shoemakers
1800	Cabinet makers
	Tailors
1801	Biscuit makers
1802	Hat makers
	Shipwrights
	Caulkers
	Fellmongers
1804	Bombazine weavers
	Watermen
	Shoemakers
	Hat makers
	Fellmongers
	Mastmakers
	Saddle tree makers
1805	Printers
	Stonecutters
	Bookbinders

1806	Tailors
	Shoemakers
1807	Tailors
	Coalheavers
1808	Coopers
	Curriers
1809	Compositors
	Pipemakers
	Coalheavers
	Packers
	Brushmakers
1810	Coachmakers
	Tailors
	Carpenters
	Carpenters
	Compositors
	Carpenters
	Dock labourers
	Machinists
1811	Saddlers
	Shoemakers
	Masons
	Turners
	Coopers
	Farriers
	Bakers
	Bakers
	Bakers
	Cardmakers
1812	Coopers
	Shoemakers
	Plumbers
	Saddlers
	Turners
	Bookbinders
	Plasterers
	Painters
	Bookbinders
	Whitesmiths
	Shoemakers
1813	Shoemakers
	Tailors
	Coopers

	Bootmakers
1815	Carpenters
1816	Caulkers
	Coopers
	Shoemakers
1817	Canal excavators
1818	Type founders
	Coachmakers
	Carpenters
	Pipemakers
	Coachmakers
1819	Coopers
	Hat makers
	Cabinet makers
	Iron founders
	Silk weavers
	Shoemakers
	Hat makers
1820	Silver platers
	Silk weavers
	Coopers
1821	Hat makers
	Canal labourers
1822	Coalheavers
	Shoemakers
	Carpenters
	Shoemakers
1824	Shipwrights
	Carpenters
1825	Carpenters
	Shoemakers
	Shoemakers
	Bargebuilders
	Carvers and guilders
	Shipwrights
	Shipwrights
	Shoemakers
	Coopers
	Carpenters
1826	Shipwrights
	Upholsterers
	Compositors
	Shoemakers

	Bookbinders
	Silk weavers
1827	Carpenters
	Tailors
	Silk weavers
1829	Shoemakers
1830	Tailors
	Hat makers
	Hat makers
1831	Bookbinders
1832	Stonemasons
1833	Marble masons
	Hat makers
	Washerwomen
1834	Builders
	Shoemakers
	Washerwomen
	Coal whippers
	Stovemakers
	Tailors
	Hat makers
	Coopers
	Tanners
	Labourers
	Bookbinders
	Gas stokers
	Bakers
1835	Carpenters
1836	Goldbeaters
	Engineers
	Silk weavers
	Corkcutters
	Type founders
1837	Stonemasons
	Shoemakers
	Cabinet makers
	Shoemakers
	Compositors
1838	Bookbinders
	Rope makers
	Shoemakers
	Railway excavators
1839	Rope makers

	Builders
	Stonemasons
1841	Metalworkers
	Seamen
	Coalwhippers
1843	Type founders
	Coalwhippers
	Compositors
1845	Type founders
	Compositors
1846	Carpenters and joiners
1847	Engine drivers
1848	Builders
	Stonemasons
	Bookbinders
1849	Engine drivers and firemen
1850	Sawyers (mill)
	Glaziers
	Type founders
	Engine drivers and firemen
1851	Compositors
	Builders
	Seamen
	Builders
	Shoemakers (strong)
1852	Compositors
	Engineers
	Coalwhippers
	Shoemakers (strong)
1853	Lightermen
	Cloak and mantle makers
	Hairdressers
	Brass and iron founders
	Bakers
	Seamstresses (slop trade)
	Building navvies
	Basket makers
	Plasterers
	Dock labourers
	Carpenters and joiners
	Coal porters
	Hearthrug makers
	Policemen

	Bricklayers
	Dock labourers
	Shoemakers
	Market garden labourers
	Lamplighters
	Bootmakers
1854	Bricklayers
	Corkcutters
	Seamen
	Engine drivers
	Bootmakers
1855	Builders
1856	Builders
	Ironfounders
	French polishers
	Rug and matting weavers
	Shipwrights
	Sailors
1856	Omnibus workers
1857	Furriers
	Bricklayers
	Coalwhippers
	Bricklayers (railway)
1858	Coalwhippers
1859	Gas firemen
	Brickmakers
	Builders
	Carpenters
	Shoemakers (strong)
	Clogmakers
1860	Coopers
	Silk weavers
	Shoemakers
	Builders
	Builders
1861	Stonemasons
	Builders
1862	Carpenters
1863	Brickmakers
1864	Dockers
	Canal boatmen
	Stevedores and dockers
1865	Ironworkers

Carpenters
Builders
Carpenters
Building navvies
Engineers (pattern makers)
Shoemakers (strong)
Coalbackers
Sawmill labourers
Railway porters
Builders' labourers
Carpenters and joiners
Engineers
Coalheavers
Organ builders
Bargebuilders

1866   Stablemen
Basket makers
Seamen
Tailors
Wireworkers
Tailors
Bootmakers
Builders
Cabmen

1867   Sailmakers
Engine drivers
Engine drivers
Coopers
Packing case makers
Brickmakers
Railway navvies
Tailors
Painters
Painters
Masons
Shoemakers

1868   Cabmen
Butchers
Cabmen
Painters
Painters
Matmakers
Builders

Location quotients, 1851

	West	North	Central	City	East	Inner South	Outer South
Clothing	.84	.93	1.16	1.23	1.19	1.15	.73
Building	1.13	1.25	.86	.45	.79	.90	1.16
Boot and shoemaking	.74	.88	1.17	1.16	1.33	1.20	.71
Textiles	.39	.58	.72	1.28	2.61	.73	.41
Wood and furniture	.56	.84	1.23	.83	1.56	1.26	.72
Metal and engineering	.68	.70	1.42	.76	1.13	1.20	1.27
Printing and paper	.58	.77	1.88	1.98	.71	1.80	.60
Leather and hides	.23	.53	1.33	.73	.92	4.15	.45
Coachmaking and saddlery	1.06	1.39	1.52	.68	.59	.79	.81
Jewellery	.70	1.10	2.97	1.16	.71	.52	.35
Chemical and allied trades	.46	.71	1.05	1.25	1.53	1.26	1.02
Precision industries	.40	.73	3.03	1.12	1.40	.40	.35
Shipbuilding	.09	.03	.09	.09	2.82	1.78	1.56
Glass and eathenware	.46	.96	1.48	.60	1.20	1.15	1.13

Source: Census, 1851
For constituent districts see Appendix 1.1
Values more than 1 indicate a greater degree of concentration in that particular district than in London as a whole. Values less than 1 indicate a lesser degree of concentration.

Variables used in the factor analysis

1. TAILOR: Ratio of female to male clothing workers.
   Figures refer to tailors and seamstresses.
   Sources: PP 1852–53, LXXXVII.i *Census of England and Wales for the Year 1851:* population tables II, pp.16–27; PP 1863 LIII.i *Census of England and Wales for the year 1861:* population tables, pp.399–412

2. SHOE: Ratio of female to male shoemakers.
   Figures refer to shoemakers and shoemakers' wives.
   Source: same as TAILOR

3. ILLIT: Percentage of marriage partners unable to sign their name on the marriage register.
   Sources: PP 1842 XIX *Fourth Annual Report of the Registrar General,* p.459; PP 1868–69 XV *Thirtieth Annual Report of the Registrar General,* pp.90–1

4. TB: Deaths from consumption per thousand of the population.
   Sources: PP 1840 XVII *Second annual report of the Registrar General,* pp.104–9; PP 1868–69 XV *Thirtieth Annual Report of the Registrar General,* p.266

5. TYPHUS: Deaths from typhus per thousand of the population.
   Source: same as TB

6. INFMORT: Infant deaths per thousand births.
   Sources: PP 1842 XIX *Fourth Annual Report of the Registrar General,* pp.491–3; PP 1873 XX *Thirty-fourth Report of the Registrar General,* pp.240–1

7. CDR: Crude death rate.
   Source: same as INFMORT

8. YOUNG: Percentage of the population aged 0–14 years.
   Sources: PP 1843 XXIII *Census of England and Wales for the year 1841:* age abstract, pp.126–7, 171–5, 290–5; PP 1873 LXXI.i *Census of England and Wales for the Year 1871,* tables of the ages, pp.3–7

9. OLD: Percentage of the population aged 60 years and above.
   Source: Same as YOUNG

10. FERT: General fertility rate.
    Number of births per thousand women of childbearing age (15–44 years). The number of women was calculated from the censuses of

1841 and 1871. Births were compiled from PP 1842 XIX *Fourth Annual Report of the Registrar General*, p.468; PP 1873 XX *Thirty-fourth Report of the Registrar General*, pp.242–5

11.   POP: Population per acre.
       Source: Price Williams, 1885, pp.404–13

12.   CHANGE: Percentage change in persons per house 1831–1841 and 1861–1871.
       Source: Figures were calculated from the census tables for each year

13.   VALUE: Rateable value per inhabited house.
       Sources: PP 1857–58 XLIX, Return showing gross estimated rental and net rateable value of property; PP 1886 LVI *Returns Relating to the Rates (Metropolis)*, pp.1–5

14.   RATE: Rate in the pound for expenditure on poor relief.
       Sources: PP 1857–58 XLIX *Return showing ... value of property*; PP 1868–69 LII *Return of the Poor Rates levied and the amount thereof expended in relief*, pp.36–7

15.   EXPENSE: Per capita expenditure on poor relief.
       Sources: Poor Law Commission, eighth annual report, 1841, pp.687–719; Poor Law Board, Twenty-first report, 1869, pp.168–72

Bibliography

Primary sources

1. British Library

General Convention of the Industrious Classes, 1839, Additional manuscript 34245 A and B.
Association for Promoting the Relief of Destitution in the Metropolis, annual reports 1844–69.
London City Mission, annual reports, 1835–64.
Society for the Suppression of Mendicity, annual reports, 1819–69.

Place Newspaper Collection
Volume 16, Cotton and silk (1799–1832).
Volume 51, Wages, combinations, machine breaking (1834–41).
Volume 53, Machinery, trade clubs, unions, strikes (1841–44).
Volume 56, Working men (1836–47).

Place Collection Additional Manuscripts
Add. Mss., 27799, 27800, 27803, 27805, Relating to the repeal of the laws against combinations of workmen (1734–1826).
Add. Ms. 27834, Essays for the people, 1834.

2. British Library of Political and Economic Science

Webb Collection, E, series A.
Volume 10, Building trades.
Volume 11, Carpenters and joiners.
Volume 13, Stone masons.
Volume 14, Tailors.
Volume 25, Hand shoemakers.
Volume 31, Compositors.

Webb Collection, E, series B
Volume 6, Powell, J., *A letter addressed to Edward Ellice, Esq. M.P.*

on the general influence of large establishments of apprentices in producing unfair competition, 1819.

3. Public Record Office

HO42/133: *Memorial of the machinists and engineers resident in London respecting combinations and benefit societies,* 1813.
MH12: Correspondence of the Poor Law Commission and the Poor Law Board and the Local Government Board with poor law unions: 6844–7 Bethnal Green (1843–59); 7103–6 St George-in-the-East (1846–63); 7683–4 Poplar (1850–57); 7915–20 Whitechapel (1843–56); 12105–6 Bermondsey (1851–65).
FS2: Register of Friendly Societies.

4. Greater London Record Office

St George-in-the-East, Board of Guardians minutes.
St Giles-in-the-Fields and St George's Bloomsbury, Directors of the Poor minutes.
The Humble petition of John Walker, John Drury, journeymen tinplate workers in the county of Middlesex, 1805, MA/W/26–9.

5. University of London Manuscript Collection

Committee of the clock and watchmakers held at the Queen's Arms Tavern, 11 February 1814, Ms. 755, folio 247–8.
Letter to George Rose, Esq. from the clockmakers' committee, 1789, Ms. 755, folio 10–11.
Meeting of the committee of master manufacturers ... to consider the best means of supporting Mr Sergeant Onslow's intended motion for the repeal of the statute of the 5th of Elizabeth, 1813, Ms. 755, folio 211.
Meeting of master manufacturers of the cities of London and Westminster, 14th January 1814, to take into consideration the notice given by Mr Serjeant Onslow in the House of Commons for leave to bring in a bill for the repeal of part of the statute for regulating masters, journeymen and apprentices the 5th Elizabeth, cap. 4, 1814, Ms. 755, folio 303–9.
Report of the committee appointed by the general meeting of the clock and watch makers of the cities of London and Westminster, convened on the third day of December, 1789, ... to take into consideration the state of trade, 1790, Ms. 755, 17–18.
The case of the distressed watch and clock makers, 1798, Ms. 755,

folio 106–7.

The petition of the masters and journeymen, artificers, handicraftsmen and mechanics, presented to the honourable House of Commons by the Rt. Honourable George Rose on 28th April 1813, signed by 32,735 masters and journeymen, 1813, Ms. 755, fol. 229–39.

To the manufacturers and tradesmen of the United Kingdom, an address of the subcommittee of Manufacturers for obtaining the repeal of the restraints on trade, including a copy of the circular of the journeymen in favour of the retention of the Statute of 5 Eliz. cap. 4 in its entirety, 1813, Ms. 755, folio 214–15.

To the watch trade, 1815?, Ms. 755, folio 339.

Wilkes, J., 1816, *An address on behalf of the distressed poor in the northern half of the metropolis and especially of the watch and clock manufacturers within the parish of St Luke*, Ms. 755, folio 257–9.

6. *Trade directories*

Johnstones London Commercial Guide and Street Directory, 1817.
Post Office London Directory, 1855.
Robson's London Directory, 1832.
Wakefield's Merchants and Tradesman's Directory, 1790.
Watkin's London Directory, 1853.

7. *Poor Law Commission*

Annual reports, 1834–1847.

8. *Poor Law Board*

Annual reports, 1848–1868.

9. *St Giles parish church*

Oppenheimer, J., 1861–62, *Diary of Joseph Oppenheimer*.

Newspapers and periodicals

Artizans London and Provincial Chronicle
Beehive
Bookbinders Trade Circular

Builder
Craftsman
Crisis
District Visitors Record
East London Observer
Friend of the People
Gorgon
Journeymen's and Artizans' London and Provincial Chronicle
Lloyds Evening Post
London Dispatch
London Gazette
London Mercury
National Co-operative Leader
Notes to the People
Northern Star
Operative
Perry's Insolvent and Bankrupt Gazette
Poor Man's Guardian
Pioneer
Red Republican
Reynolds Newspaper
St James Chronicle
Star of Freedom
Statesman
The Times
Trades Newspaper
Trades Newspaper and Mechanics Weekly Journal
True Briton
Weekly Free Press
Weekly True Sun

Parliamentary papers

PP 1812–13 IV Report from the committee to whom the petition of several masters, journeymen, mechanics, artificers and handicrafts-men was referred ... respecting the apprentice law.

PP 1817 VI Select committee on the petitions of the watchmakers of Coventry.

PP 1818 IX Select committee appointed to consider the several petitions relating to the ribbon weavers.

PP 1818 V Report of the House of Lords committee on the poor laws.

PP 1823 IV Appendix to the report from the select committee on the foreign trade of the country: appendix 2, annual accounts of the West India Dock Company.

PP 1824 V Select committee on artizans and machinery.

PP 1825 IV Select committee on the combination laws.

PP 1831–32 XIX Select committee on the silk trade.

PP 1831–32 XXVI Return of the number of friendly societies since 1st January 1793.

PP 1833 VI Select committee on manufactures, commerce and shipping.

PP 1834 XXVIII Royal commission on the administration and practical reform of the poor laws.

PP 1836 XIV Select committee on the Port of London.

PP 1840 XI Select committee on the health of large towns.

PP 1840 XXII Royal commission on the handloom weavers.

PP 1840 XXIII Royal commission on the handloom weavers: reports from the assistant commissioners.

PP 1840 XXIV Royal commission on the handloom weavers: reports from the assistant commissioners.

PP 1843 XIII Royal commission on children's employment.

PP 1843 XIV Royal commission on children's employment, appendix to second report.

PP 1844 XVIII Royal commission on the state of large towns.

PP 1846 VII Select committee on district asylums.

PP 1847 XI Select committee on settlement and removal.

PP 1850 XVI Select committee of the House of Lords on parochial assessments.

PP 1852–53 XXVIII Return of the number of houses rated to the house tax.

PP 1854 XVII Select committee on poor removal.

PP 1856 XIII Select committee on masters and operatives (equitable councils of conciliation).

PP 1859 Sess. 2 VII Select committee on the irremovable poor.

PP 1860 XVII Select committee on the irremovable poor.

PP 1860 XXII Select committee on masters and operatives.

PP 1861 IX Select committee on poor relief.

PP 1862 X Select committee on poor relief.

PP 1864 LII Select committee on removal of paupers.

PP 1866 XXXIII Eighth report of the medical officer to the Privy Council.

PP 1867 X Select committee on poor relief.

PP 1867 XXXII Royal commission on trades unions.

PP 1867 LX Return relating to poor relief.

PP 1867–68 XIII Select committee on poor rate assessment.

PP 1867–68 XXXIX Royal commission on trades unions.

PP 1868–69 XXXI Royal commission on trades unions.

PP 1868–69 LIII Return of poor rates levied.

Secondary sources

Abrams, P., 1968, *The origins of British sociology 1834–1914*, University of Chicago Press, London and Chicago.

Address to the British and Foreign Bible Society ... by the journeymen bookbinders of London and Westminster, An, 1849, London.

Alexander, S., 1983, *Women's work in nineteenth-century London: a study of the years 1820–50*, Journeyman, London.

Alford, B.W.E., 1964, 'Government expenditure and the growth of the printing industry in the nineteenth century', *Economic History Review 2nd ser.*, 17, pp. 96–112.

Anderson, M., 1974, *Family structure in nineteenth-century Lancashire*, Cambridge University Press, Cambridge.

Anon., 1853, 'Charity, noxious and beneficent', *Westminster Review*, 59, pp. 62–88.

Anon., 1855, 'The charities of London', *Quarterly Review*, 97, pp. 407–50.

Appeal of the distressed operative tailors to the government, the aristocracy, the clergy and the public in general, 1850, J. Goodfellow, London.

Appeal of the journeymen bookbinders of London and Westminster to the committee, members, donors and subscribers of the British and Foreign Bible Society on the subject of cheap bibles, 1849.

Arnold, M., 1869, *Culture and anarchy*, Smith, Elder and Co., London.

Articles of the Friendly and United Society of Cordwainers, instituted at Westminster on 4 June 1792, pp. 82–90 in Aspinall, A. (ed.), 1949, *The early English trade unions*.

Articles of the Friendly Society of Journeymen Bookbinders of London and Westminster finally agreed to at Mitchell's rooms, Portsmouth Street, March 24th 1820, London.

Ashforth, D., 1976, 'The urban poor law' in Fraser, D. (ed.), *The New Poor Law in the nineteenth century*, Macmillan, London, pp. 128–48.

Ashton, T.S., 1959, *Economic fluctuations in England 1700–1800*, Clarendon, Oxford.

Aspinall, A. (ed.), 1949, *The early English trade unions*, Batchworth, London.

Atkins, P., 1990, 'The spatial configuration of class solidarity in London's West End 1792–1939', *Urban History Yearbook*, 17, pp. 36–65.

Atkinson, E., 1799, *An account of the rise and progress of the dispute between the masters and journeymen printers*, J. Ridgeway, London.

Bales, K., 1991, 'Charles Booth's survey of life and labour of the people in London 1889–1903' pp. 66–110 in Bulmer, M. *et al.*, *The social survey in historical perspective 1880–1940*, Cambridge University Press, Cambridge.

Baxter, G.W.R., 1841, *Book of the Bastilles*, John Stephen, London.

Beames, T., 1850, *The rookeries of London: past, present and prospective*, Bosworth, London.

Behagg, C., 1990, *Politics and production in the early nineteenth century*, Routledge, London.

Berg, M., 1985, *The age of manufactures 1700–1820*, Fontana, London.

Berg, M., 1993, 'Small producer capitalism on eighteenth-century England', *Business History*, 35, pp. 17–39.

Berg, M. and Hudson, P., 1992, 'Rehabilitating the Industrial Revolution', *Economic History Review 2nd ser.*, 45, pp. 24–50.

Berridge, V., 1978, 'Popular Sunday newspapers and mid-Victorian society' in Boyce, G., Curran, J. and Wingate, P. (eds), *Newspaper history from the seventeenth century to the present day*, Constable, London, pp. 247–64.

Berridge, V., 1986, 'Content analysis and historical research on newspapers' in Harris, M. and Lee, A. (eds) *The press in English society from the seventeenth to the nineteenth centuries*, Associated University Presses, London, pp. 201–18.

Bevan, G.P., 1880, 'The strikes of the past ten years', *Journal of the Royal Statistical Society*, 43, pp. 35–54.

Beveridge, W., 1909, *Unemployment: a problem of industry*, Longman, London.

Blankenhorn, D., 1985, '"Our class of workmen": the cabinet makers revisited' in Harrison, J. and Zeitlin, J. (eds), *Divisions of labour*, Harvester, Brighton, pp. 19–46.

Booth, C., 1902, *Life and labour of the people of London* (seventeen volumes), Macmillan, London.

Bosanquet, S.R., 1841, *The rights of the poor and Christian almsgiving vindicated*, James Fraser, London.

Bowley, A.L., 1900, 'The statistics of wages in the United Kingdom during the last hundred years (Part VI): wages in the building trades – English towns', *Journal of the Royal Statistical Society*, 63, pp. 297–314.

———— 1901, 'The statistics of wages in the United Kingdom during the last hundred years (Part VIII): wages in the building trade – concluded', *Journal of the Royal Statistical Society*, 64, pp. 102–11.

Bowley, A.L. and Wood, G.H., 1899, 'The statistics of wages in the United Kingdom during the last hundred years (Part V): printers',

Journal of the Royal Statistical Society, 62, pp. 708–15.

——— 1905, 'The statistics of wages in the United Kingdom during the last hundred years (Part XII): engineering and shipbuilding', *Journal of the Royal Statistical Society*, 68, pp. 563–614.

Boyer, G., 1990, *An economic history of the English Poor Law 1750–1850*, Cambridge University Press, Cambridge.

Brassfounders, braziers and coppersmiths manual containing ... the rules and regulations of the trade society, 1825, Cowie and Strange, London.

Briggs, A., 1967, 'The language of "class" in early nineteenth-century England' in Briggs, A. and Saville, J. (eds), *Essays in labour history*, Macmillan, London, pp. 43–73.

——— 1968, *Victorian cities*, Penguin, Harmondsworth.

Brooke, J.W., 1839, *The democrats of Marylebone*, W.J. Cleaver, London.

Brooks, C.E. and Hunt, T.M., 1933, 'Variations of wind direction in the British Isles since 1341', *Quarterly Journal of the Royal Meteorological Society*, 59, pp. 375–88.

Burgess, K., 1969, 'Technological change and the 1852 lock-out in the British engineering industry', *International Review of Social History*, 14, pp. 215–36.

Burn, J.D., 1858, *Commercial enterprise and social progress, or gleanings in London, Sheffield, Glasgow and Dublin*, Piper, Stephenson & Spence, London.

——— 1868, *A glimpse at the social condition of the working classes during the early part of the present century*, London.

Burn, W., 1861, *The first annual trade union directory*, London Trades Council, London.

Bythell, D., 1978, *The sweated trades: outwork in nineteenth-century Britain*, Batsford, London.

Cairncross, A.K. and Weber, B., 1956, 'Fluctuations in building in Great Britain 1785–1849', *Economic History Review 2nd ser.*, 9, pp. 283–97.

Campbell, R., 1747, *The London tradesman*, T. Gardner, London.

Cannadine, D., 1977, 'Victorian cities – how different?', *Social History*, 4, pp. 457–82.

——— 1980, *Lords and landlords: the aristocracy and the towns 1774–1967*, Leicester University Press, Leicester.

Caplan, M., 1978, 'The new poor law and the struggle for union chargeability', *International Review of Social History*, 23, pp. 267–300.

Capper, C., 1862, *The port and trade of London: historical, statistical, local and general*, Smith, Elder & Co., London.

Carlyle,T., 1840, *Chartism*, James Fraser, London.

Carpenter, M., 1851, *Reformatory schools for the children of the perishing and dangerous classes*, C. Gilpin, London.

Carter, H. and Lewis, R., 1990, *An urban geography of England and Wales in the nineteenth century*, Edward Arnold, London.

Chadwick, E., 1965, *Report on the sanitary condition of the labouring population of Great Britain*, Edinburgh University Press, Edinburgh (first edition 1842).

Chalmers, T., 1821–1826, *The Christian and civic economy of large towns* (three volumes), Chalmers and Collins, Glasgow.

Church, R.A., 1975, *The great Victorian boom*, Macmillan, London.

Clapham, J., 1916, 'The Spitalfields Acts 1773–1824', *Economic Journal*, 26, pp. 459–71.

Clout, H., 1991, *The Times London history atlas*, Times Books, London.

Cole, G.D.H. and Filson, A.W., 1951, *British working-class movements: select documents 1789–1875*, Macmillan, London.

Colquhoun, P., 1794, *Observations and facts relative to licensed ale houses in the City of London and its environs*, Henry Fry, London.

——— 1800, *Treatise on the commerce and police of the river Thames*, Joseph Mawman, London.

Committee of Manufacturers of London and its Vicinity 1814, 'The origin, object and operation of the apprenticeship laws', *The Pamphleteer*, 3, pp. 217–42.

Committee of Master Tailors, 1800, 'To His Grace the Duke of Portland, the Humble Memorial of the Committee of Master Tailors appointed to prosecute their journeymen for a combination to obtain an advance of wages' in Aspinall, A. (ed), *The early English trade unions*, pp. 33–5.

Cooney, E.W., 1955, 'The origins of the Victorian master builders', *Economic History Review 2nd ser.*, 8, pp. 167–76.

Cooper, C., 1850, *Papers respecting the sanitary state of part of the parish of St Giles in the Fields, London*, James Newman, London.

Cowherd, R., 1977, *Political economists and the English poor laws*, Ohio University Press, Athens, USA.

Crafts, N.F.R., 1982, 'Regional price variations in England in 1843: an aspect of the standard of living debate', *Explorations in Economic History*, 19, pp. 51–70.

——— 1985, *British economic growth during the industrial revolution*, Clarendon, Oxford.

Crafts, N.F.R. and Harley, C.K., 1992, 'Output growth and the British industrial revolution', *Economic History Review 2nd ser.*, 45, pp. 703–30.

Crafts, N.F.R., Leybourne, S.J. and Mills, T.C., 1989, 'Trends and cycles in British industrial production 1700–1913', *Journal of the Royal Statistical Society*, 152, pp. 43–60.

Crafts, N.F.R. and Mills, T., 1991, 'Trends in real wages in Britain 1750–1913', *Warwick Economic Research Papers*, 371, Department of Economics, University of Warwick, Warwick.

Creighton, C., 1965, *A history of epidemics in Britain*, Cass, London (first edition, two volumes, 1891–94).

Crompton, J.W., 1860, 'Report on printers' strikes and trades unions since January 1845', in *Trades Societies and Strikes*, National Association for the Promotion of Social Science, London, pp. 77–92.

Cronin, J., 1979, *Industrial conflict in modern Britain*, Croom Helm, London.

Cronjé, G., 1984, 'Tuberculosis and mortality decline in England and Wales, 1851–1910', in Woods, R. and Woodward, J. (eds), *Urban disease and mortality in nineteenth-century England*, Batsford, London, pp. 79–101.

Crossick, G., 1978, *An artisan élite in Victorian society: Kentish London 1840–80*, Croom Helm, London.

Crowther, M.A., 1983, *The workhouse system 1834–1929*, Methuen, London.

Davis, J., 1988, *Reforming London: the London government problem 1855–1900*, Clarendon, Oxford.

Day, J., 1838, *A few practical observations on the New Poor Law*, A. Redford, London.

Defoe, D., 1766, *The mercantile library of the complete English tradesman*, J. and A. Kelburn, London.

Dennis, R., 1984, *English industrial cities of the nineteenth century*, Cambridge University Press, Cambridge.

Denton, W., 1861, *Observations on the displacement of the poor by metropolitan railways and by other public improvements*, Bell and Daldy, London.

Derry, T.K., 1931–32, 'The repeal of the apprenticeship clauses of the statute of apprentices', *Economic History Review*, 3, pp. 67–87.

Dictionary of the Vulgar Tongue, 1971, Follett, Chicago (first edition, 1811).

District Visitor's Manual, 1840, General Society for Promoting District Visiting, London.

Dobson, C.R., 1980, *Masters and journeymen: a prehistory of industrial relations 1717–1800*, Croom Helm, London.

Dodd, G., 1843, *Days at the factories*, Charles Knight, London.

Driver, F., 1988, 'Moral geographies: social science and the urban environment in mid-nineteenth century England', *Transactions of the Institute of British Geographers, new series*, 13, pp. 275–87.

—— 1993, *Power and pauperism: the workhouse system 1834–1884*, Cambridge University Press, Cambridge.

Drummond, A.J., 1943, 'Cold winters at Kew Observatory 1783–1942', *Quarterly Journal of the Royal Meteorological Society*, 69, pp. 17–32.

Duffy, I., 1973, 'Bankruptcy and insolvency in London in the late eighteenth and early nineteenth century', D. Phil. Thesis, University of Oxford.

—— 1980, 'English bankrupts 1571–1861', *American Journal of Legal History*, 24, pp. 283–305.

Dunning, T.J., 1860a, 'Some account of the London Consolidated Society of Bookbinders', pp. 93–104 in *Trades Societies and Strikes*, National Association for the Promotion of Social Science, London.

—— 1860b, *Trades' unions and strikes: their philosophy and intention*.

Dyos, H.J., 1955–56, 'Railways and housing in Victorian London', *Journal of Transport History*, 2, pp. 11–21.

—— 1957, 'Urban transformation: a note on the object of street improvements in Regency and early Victorian London', *International Review of Social History*, 2, pp. 259–65.

—— 1967, 'The slums of Victorian London', *Victorian Studies*, 11, pp. 5–40.

—— 1977, *Victorian suburb: a study of the growth of Camberwell*, Leicester University Press, Leicester.

Dyos, H.J. and Aldcroft, D.H., 1974, *British transport: an economic survey from the seventeenth century to the twentieth*, Penguin, Harmondsworth.

Egan, P., 1821, *Life in London, or the day and night scenes of Jerry Hawthorn, Esq*, London.

Employer and the employed, being a few words on the disputes between the omnibus masters and their discharged servants, The, 1852, W.S. Johnson, London.

Engels, F., 1973, *The condition of the working class in England*, Lawrence & Wishart, London (first German edition, 1845).

Evans, D.M., 1845, *The City or the physiology of business*, Bailey, London.

—— 1848, *The commercial crisis 1847–1848*, Letts, Son and Steer, London.

Fielding, J., 1776, *A brief description of the cities of London and Westminster*, J. Wilkie, London.

Fischer, C.S., 1984, *The urban experience*, Harcourt Brace and Jovanovich, San Diego, USA.

Fisher, F.J., 1948, 'The development of London as a centre of conspicuous consumption in the sixteenth and seventeenth centuries', *Transactions of the Royal Historical Society*, 30, pp. 37–50.

Fletcher, J., 1844, 'The metropolis: its boundaries, extent and divisions for local government', *Journal of the Royal Statistical Society*, 7, pp. 69–85.

Flinn, M.W., 1974, 'Trends in real wages 1750–1850', *Economic History Review 2nd ser.*, 27, pp. 395–413.

Flint, K., 1987, *The Victorian novelist*, Croom Helm, London.

Foster, J., 1977, *Class struggle and the industrial revolution*, Methuen, London.

Fox, A., 1985, *History and heritage: the social origins of the British industrial relations system*, Allen and Unwin, London.

Fraser, D., (ed), 1976, *The New Poor Law in the nineteenth century*, Macmillan, London.

Fraser, H., 1981, *The coming of the mass market 1850–1914*, Macmillan, London.

Friedlander, D. and Roshier, R., 1966, 'A study of the internal migration in England and Wales part 1', *Population Studies*, 19, pp. 239–79.

Friendly Society of Ironfounders of England, Ireland and Wales, 1889, 414th monthly report.

Gaskell, P., 1833, *The manufacturing population of England*, Baldwin & Craddock, London.

Gast, J., 1802, *Calumny defeated, or a complete vindication of the conduct of the working shipwrights during the late disputes with their employers*, London.

Gavin, H., 1848, *Sanitary ramblings, being sketches and illustrations of Bethnal Green*, Churchill, London.

——— 1850, *The habitations of the industrial classes*, Society for Improving the Condition of the Labouring Class, London.

Gayer, A., Rostow, W. and Schwarz, A., 1953, *The growth and fluctuations of the British economy 1790–1850* (two volumes), Clarendon, Oxford.

Geary, R., 1984, *European labour protest 1848–1939*, Methuen, London.

George, M.D., 1927, 'The London coal–heavers: attempts to regulate waterside labour in the eighteenth and nineteenth centuries', *Economic Journal*, 2, pp. 229–48.

——— 1936, 'The Combination Laws', *Economic History Review*, 6, pp. 172–78.

——— 1966, *London life in the eighteenth century*, Penguin, Harmondsworth.

Gilbert, W., 1857, *On the present system of rating for the relief of the poor in the metropolis*, Association for Promoting the Equalization of the Poor Rate on an Equal Assessment over the Metropolitan District, London.

────── 1860, *Poor law reform – proceedings of the Metropolitan and County Association for the Equalization of the Poor Rate*, Judd and Glass, London.

Gilboy, E., 1934, *Wages in eighteenth-century England*, Harvard University Press, Cambridge, USA.

Gilding, R., 1971, *The journeymen coopers of East London*, History Workshop, Oxford.

Godwin, G., 1854, *London shadows: a glance at the "homes" of the thousands*, G. Routledge & Co., London.

Goodway, D.J., 1979, 'Chartism in London' Ph.D. thesis, University of London.

────── 1982, *London Chartism 1838–1848*, Cambridge University Press, Cambridge.

Gosden, P.H.J., 1961, *The friendly societies in England 1815–1875*, Manchester University Press, Manchester.

Grant, J., 1842a, *Lights and shadows of London life*, Saunders and Otley, London.

────── 1842b, *Pictures of popular people, or illustrations of human nature*.

Green, D.R., 1984, 'From artisans to paupers', Ph.D. Thesis, University of Cambridge.

────── 1988, 'Distance to work in Victorian London: a case study of Henry Poole, bespoke tailors', *Business History*, XXX, pp. 179–94.

Green, D.R. and Parton, A., 1990, 'Slums and slum life in Victorian England: London and Birmingham at mid-century' in Gaskell, M. (ed.), *Slums*, Leicester University Press, Leicester, pp. 17–91.

Grosley, P.J., 1772, *A tour to London or new observations on England and its inhabitants* (2 vols), Lockyer Davis, London.

Guy, W.A., 1845, *Unhealthiness of towns, its causes and remedies*, Charles Knight & Co., London.

Hall, P.G., 1962a, 'The east London footwear industry: an industrial quarter in decline', *East London Papers*, 5, pp. 3–22.

────── 1962b, *The industries of London since 1861*, Hutchinson, London.

Harris, J., 1994, *Private lives, public spirit: Britain 1870–1914*, Penguin, London.

Haynes, M., 1988, 'Employers and trade unions 1824–50', in Rule, J. (ed.), *British Trade Unionism 1750–1850*, Longman, London, pp. 237–70.

Head, E., 1848, 'Seventh and eighth reports from the select committee on settlement and poor removal', *Edinburgh Review*, 87, pp. 451–72.

Hennock, E.P., 1987, 'The measurement of urban poverty: from the metropolis to the nation 1880–1920', *Economic History Review, 2nd ser.*, 40, pp. 208–27.

—— 1991, 'Concepts of poverty in the British social surveys from Charles Booth to Arthur Bowley', in Bulmer, M. *et al.*, *The social survey in historical perspective 1880–1940*, Cambridge University Press, Cambridge, pp. 189–216.

Higgs, E., 1983, 'Domestic servants and households in Victorian England', *Social History*, 8, pp. 201–10.

Himmelfarb, G., 1971, 'Mayhew's poor: a problem of identity', *Victorian Studies*, 14, pp. 307–20.

—— 1984, *The idea of poverty: England in the early industrial age*, Faber and Faber, London.

Hobsbawm, E.J., 1960, 'Custom, wages and work-load in nineteenth-century industry' in Briggs, A. and Saville, J. (eds), *Essays in Labour History*, Macmillan, London, pp. 113–39.

—— 1984, *Worlds of labour*, Wiedenfeld and Nicolson, London.

Hohenberg, P. and Lees, L., 1985, *The making of urban Europe 1000–1950*, Harvard University Press, London.

Hollingshed, J., 1986, *Ragged London in 1861*, J.M. Dent, London (first edition 1861).

Hoppitt, J., 1987, *Risk and failure in English business 1700–1800*, Cambridge University Press, Cambridge.

Howe, E., 1943, *Newspaper printing in the nineteenth century.*

—— 1947, *The London compositor*, Oxford University Press, Oxford.

Howe, E. and White, H., 1948, *The London Society of Compositors: a centenary history (established 1848)*, Cassell, London.

Howell, G., 1902, *Labour legislation, labour movements and labour leaders*, Fisher Unwin, London.

Hudson, P., 1992, *The Industrial Revolution*, Edward Arnold, London.

Humphreys, A., 1977, *Travels into the poor man's country*, Caliban, Firle.

Humphries, J., 1977, 'Class struggle and the persistence of the working-class family', *Cambridge Journal of Economics*, 1, pp. 241–58.

Hunt, E.H., 1973, *Regional wage variations in Britain 1850–1914*, Oxford University Press, Oxford.

—— 1986, 'Industrialisation and regional inequalities: wages in Britain 1760–1914', *Journal of Economic History*, XLVI, pp. 935–66.

Hunt, F., 1986, 'Opportunities lost and gained: mechanization and womens' work in the London bookbinding and printing trades' in John, A. (ed.), *Unequal opportunities: women's employment in England 1800–1918*, Blackwell, Oxford, pp. 71–93.

Hyam, L., 1850, *The gentleman's illustrated album of fashion for 1850.*

Hyman, R., 1984, *Strikes*, Fontana, London.

Hyndman, H., 1892, *Commercial crises of the nineteenth century*, Swan, Sonnenstein and Co., London.

Inglis, K., 1971, *Poverty and the industrial revolution*, Hodder and Stoughton, London.

Jackson, R.V., 1992, 'Rates of industrial growth during the industrial revolution', *Economic History Review 2nd ser.*, 45, pp. 1–23.

James, H., 1989, *London stories*, Tabb House, Padstow.

Jeffereys, M. and Jeffereys, J.B., 1947, 'Wages, hours and trade customs of the skilled engineers', *Economic History Review*, 17, pp. 27–44.

Jenks, L., 1971, *The migration of British capital to 1875*, Nelson, London.

"J.H", 1844, 'The dwellings of the poor', *Illuminated Magazine*, 3, pp. 336–40.

Johnston, R.J., 1978, *Multivariate statistical analysis in geography*, Longman, London.

Jones, E., 1851–52, *Notes to the People* (two volumes), London.

Jones, G.S., 1971, *Outcast London*, Clarendon, Oxford.

Knight, C., 1841–44, *London* (6 volumes), London.

Knight, F.W., 1854, *The parochial system vs. centralization part II: effects of settlement and removal of the poor*, London.

Landers, J., 1993, *Death and the metropolis: studies in the demographic history of London 1670–1830*, Cambridge University Press, Cambridge.

Landes, D., 1983, *Revolution in time*, Belknap, Cambridge, USA.

Langton, J., 1984, 'The industrial revolution and the regional geography of England', *Transactions of the Institute of British Geographers, new series*, 9(2), pp. 145–67.

Lee, C.H., 1981, 'Regional growth and structural change in Victorian Britain', *Economic History Review*, 33, pp. 438–52.

————— 1984, 'The service sector, regional specialization, and economic growth in the Victorian economy', *Journal of Historical Geography*, 10, pp. 139–55.

————— 1986, *The British economy since 1700*, Cambridge University Press, Cambridge.

Lees, A., 1985, *Cities perceived: urban society in European and American thought 1820–1940*, Manchester University Press, Manchester.

Lees, L.H., 1979, *Exiles of Erin*, Manchester University Press, Manchester.

————— 1982, 'Strikes and the urban hierarchy in industrial towns, 1842–1901' in Cronin, J. and Schneer, J. (eds), *Social conflict and the political order in modern Britain*, Croom Helm, London, pp. 52–72.

Leeson, R.A., 1980, *Travelling brothers*, Granada, St Albans.

Lester, M., 1990, 'Insolvency and reform of English bankruptcy law 1831–1914', D. Phil. Thesis, University of Oxford.

Lhotky, J., 1844, *On cases of death by starvation*, John Oliver, London.

—— 1845, *Hunger and revolution*, Effingham Wilson, London.

Lindert, P.H. and Williamson, J.G., 1983, 'English workers' living standards during the industrial revolution: a new look', *Economic History Review 2nd ser.*, 36, pp. 1–25.

—— 1985, 'A reply to Crafts', *Journal of Economic History*, XLV, pp. 145–53.

Linebaugh, P., 1993, *The London hanged*, Penguin, London.

London Cabinet-Makers Union, 1811, *Book of Prices*.

Lovett, W., 1876, *The life and struggles of William Lovett in his pursuit of bread, knowledge and freedom*.

Low, S., 1850, *The Charities of London*.

—— 1862, *The Charities of London in 1861*.

Luckin, W., 1984, 'Evaluating the sanitary revolution: typhus and typhoid in London 1852–1900' in Woodward, J. and Woods, R. (eds), *Urban disease and mortality in nineteenth-century England*, Batsford, London, pp. 102–19.

Ludlow, J.T., 1850, 'Labour and the poor', *Frasers Magazine*, 41, pp. 1–18.

Lumley, W.G., 1858, 'On the present state of the administration of the relief to the poor in the metropolis', *Journal of the Royal Statistical Society*, 21, pp. 169–95.

Lushington, C.R., 1847, *The practice of the Mendicity Society by one who knows it well*, John Murray, London.

MacGill, G., 1858, *The London poor and the inequality of the rates raised for their relief*, Rymer, London.

Mackinnon, M., 1986, 'Poor Law policy, unemployment and pauperism', *Explorations in Economic History*, 23, pp. 299–36.

McLelland, 1987, 'Time to work, time to live: some aspects of work and the re-formation of class in Britain, 1850–1880' in Joyce, P. (ed.), *The historical meanings of work*, Cambridge University Press, Cambridge, pp. 180–209.

Mann, H., 1848, 'Statement of the mortality prevailing in Church Lane during the last ten years with the sickness of the last seven months', *Journal of the Royal Statistical Society*, XI, pp. 19–24.

Mariner, S., 1980, 'English bankruptcy records and statistics before 1850', *Economic History Review 2nd ser.*, 33, pp. 351–66.

Marshall, J., 1833, *A digest of all accounts*, Haddon, London.

Marshall, M., 1987, *Long waves of regional development*, Macmillan,

London.

Marx, K., 1954, *Capital*, Lawrence & Wishart, London (first edition, 1887).

Massey, D., 1984, *Spatial divisions of labour*, Macmillan, London.

Matthias, P., 1979, *The transformation of England*, Methuen, London.

Mayhew, H., 1968, *London Labour and the London Poor* (four volumes), Dover, New York (first edition 1861).

——— 1980–82, *The Morning Chronicle Survey* (six volumes), Caliban, Firle (vol. 1, 1980, vols 2, 3 and 4, 1981, vols 5 and 6, 1982; first published 1849–50).

Mearns, A., 1883, *The bitter cry of outcast London*, James Clark, London.

Meyrick, F., 1858, *The outcast and the poor of London*.

Mitchie, R.C., 1985, 'The London stock exchange and the British securities market, 1850–1914', *Economic History Review 2nd ser.*, 38, pp. 61–82.

Miles, W.A., 1839, *Poverty, mendicity and crime*, James Nisbet, London.

Mill, J.S., 1976, *Principles of political economy*, Augustus Kelley, Fairfield (first edition 1848).

Mitchell, B.R. and Deane, P., 1962, *Abstract of British historical statistics*, Cambridge University Press, London.

Moffatt, J.C., 1853, *Life of Thomas Chalmers*, Moore, Anderson and Co., Cincinatti, USA.

Moher, J., 1988, 'From suppression to containment: roots of trade union law to 1825' in Rule, J. (ed.), *British Trade Unionism 1750–1850*, Longman, London, pp. 74–97.

Moses, E., 1847, *Fashion's favourite or the mart of many*.

——— 1849, *The treasury of taste*.

——— 1850, *The pride of London*.

——— 1852, *The library of elegance*.

——— 1860, *The growth of an important branch of British industry: the ready made clothing system*.

Mudie, R., 1836, *London and Londoners, or a second judgement of 'Babylon the Great'*, Colburn, London.

Murray, J.F., 1843, *The world of London*, Blackwood, London.

Musson, A.E., 1954, *The Typographical Association*, Oxford University Press, London.

Nicholls, G., 1904, *A history of the English Poor Law*, P.S. King, London.

Noel, B., 1835, *The state of the metropolis considered*, James Nisbet, London.

Northcote Parkinson, C., 1948, *The trade winds: a study of British overseas trade during the French wars 1793–1815*, Allen and Unwin,

London.

Oliver, J.L., 1961, 'The East London furniture industry', *East London Papers*, 4, pp. 88–101.

———— 1964, 'Directories and their use in geographical enquiry', *Geography*, 49, pp. 400–9.

Oliver, W.H., 1964, 'The Consolidated Trades' Union of 1834', *Economic History Review 2nd ser.*, 17, pp. 77–95.

Olsen, D.J., 1979, *The growth of Victorian London*, Peregrine, London.

O'Neill, J., 1869, 'Fifty years experience of an Irish shoemaker in London', *St Crispin*, 1, pp. 241–323, and 2, pp. 14–123.

Origin, object and operation of the apprentice laws, 1814, London.

Orth, J.V., 1991, *Combination and conspiracy: a legal history of trade unionism, 1721–1901*, Clarendon, Oxford.

Owen, D., 1965, *English philanthropy, 1660–1960*, Oxford University Press, Oxford.

———— 1982, *The government of Victorian London 1855–1889: the Metropolitan Board of Works, the vestries and the City Corporation*, Harvard University Press, London.

Park, R.E., Burgess, E.W. and Mackenzie, R.D., 1967, *The City*, University of Chicago Press, Chicago, USA.

Parker, J., 1853, 'On the literature of the working classes', *Meliora*, 2, pp. 181–97.

Parry Lewis, J., 1965, *Building cycles and Britain's growth*, Macmillan, London.

Parssinen, T.M. and Prothero, I.J., 1977, 'The London tailors' strike of 1834 and the collapse of the Grand National Consolidated Trades' Union: a police spy's report', *International Review of Social History*, 22, pp. 65–107.

Pashley, R., 1852, *Pauperism and poor laws*, London.

Pattison, G., 1964, 'The East India Dock Company', *East London Papers*, 7, pp. 31–40.

Phelps Brown, H. and Hopkins, S., 1981, 'Seven centuries of building wages' in Phelps Brown, H. and Hopkins, S., *A perspective of wages and prices*, Methuen, London, pp. 1–31.

Place, F., 1972, *The autobiography of Francis Place* (ed. Thale, M.), Cambridge University Press, London.

Pollard, S., 1950, 'The decline of shipbuilding on the Thames', *Economic History Review 2nd ser.*, 3, pp. 72–89.

Potter, G., 1870, 'Strikes and lockouts from the workman's point of view', *Contemporary Review*, 15, pp. 32–54.

Power, M.J., 1978, 'Shadwell: the development of a London suburban community in the seventeenth century', *London Journal*, 4, pp. 29–46.

Price, R., 1980, *Masters, unions and men: work control in building and the rise of labour 1830–1914*, Cambridge University Press, Cambridge.

———— 1983, 'The labour process and labour history', *Social History*, 8, pp. 57–75.

Price Williams, R., 1885, 'The population of London', *Journal of the Royal Statistical Society* 48, pp. 349–432.

Prothero, I.J., 1966, 'London working-class Movements 1825–1848', Ph.D. Thesis, University of Cambridge.

———— 1969, 'Chartism in London', *Past and Present*, 44, pp. 76–105.

———— 1971, 'London Chartism and the trades', *Economic History Review 2nd ser.*, 29, pp. 202–19.

———— 1981, *Artisans and politics in early nineteenth-century London*, Methuen, London.

Rasmussen, S.E., 1960, *London: the unique city*, Penguin, Harmondsworth.

Rawson, R.W., 1843, 'Report of some inquiries into the condition and education of the poorer classes in the parish of Marylebone in 1838', *Journal of the Royal Statistical Society*, 6, pp. 44–8.

Read, D., 1976, 'The decline of St Monday 1766–1876', *Past and Present*, 71, pp. 76–101.

Reply of the journeymen bookbinders to remarks on a memorial addressed to their employers on the effects of a machine introduced to supercede manual labour, 1831.

Reply of the journeymen stuff hatters, 1834.

Reply to a letter from the committee of the Southwark Auxiliary Bible Society to the ... British and Foreign Bible Society, 1849.

Roberts, H., 1859, *The improvements of the dwellings of the labouring classes through the operation of government measures ... as well as individual efforts*, J. Ridgeway, London.

Rose, M., 1966, 'The allowance system under the New Poor Law', *Economic History Review 2nd ser.*, 19, pp. 607–20.

———— 1972, *The relief of poverty 1834–1914*, Macmillan, London.

———— 1976, 'Settlement, removal and the New Poor Law' in Fraser, D. (ed.), *The New Poor Law in the nineteenth century*, Macmillan, London, pp. 111–27.

———— 1981, 'The crisis of poor relief in England 1860–1890' in Mommsen, W.J. (ed.), *The emergence of the welfare state in Britain and Germany*, Croom Helm, London, pp. 50–70.

———— (ed.), 1985, *The poor and the city: the English Poor Law in its urban context, 1834–1914*, Leicester University Press, Leicester.

Rowntree, B.S., 1901, *Poverty: a study of town life*, Macmillan, London.

Rubinstein, W.D., 1977a, 'The Victorian middle classes: wealth, occupation and geography', *Economic History Review 2nd ser.*, 30, pp. 602–23.

—— 1977b, 'Wealth, élites and the class structure of modern Britain', *Past and Present*, 76, pp. 99–126.

—— 1981, *Men of property: the very wealthy in Britain since the Industrial Revolution*, Croom Helm, London.

—— 1992, 'The structure of wealth-holding in Britain 1809–39: a preliminary anatomy', *Historical Research*, 65, pp. 74–89.

—— 1994, *Capitalism, culture and decline in Britain 1750–1990*, Routledge, London.

Rudé, G., 1964, *The crowd in history, 1730–1848*, Wiley, London.

Rule, J., 1981, *The experience of labour in eighteenth-century industry*, Croom Helm, London.

—— 1986, *The labouring classes in early industrial England 1750–1850*, Longmans, London.

Rules and Orders of the Cabinet Makers Society, 1830, London.

Rules and Orders of the United Benevolent Sawyers ... instituted 18 December 1825, London.

'Rules of the Society of Journeymen Boot and Shoemakers', in Aspinall, A. (ed.), 1949, *The early English trade unions*, pp. 80–2.

Sabel, C. and Zeitlin, J., 1985, 'Historical alternatives to mass production: politics, markets and technology in nineteenth-century industrialisation', *Past and Present*, 132, pp. 133–76.

Samuel, R., 1977, 'Workshop of the world: steam power and hand technology in mid-Victorian Britain', *History Workshop Journal*, 3, pp. 6–77.

Saunders, J., 1844, 'A parting glimpse of St Giles', *Illuminated Magazine*, III, pp. 79–84.

Saunders, P., 1981, *Social theory and the urban question*, Hutchinson, London.

Schmeichen, J., 1984, *Sweated industries and sweated labour: the London clothing trades 1860–1914*, Croom Helm, London.

Scholliers, P. (ed.), 1989, *Real wages in nineteenth and twentieth-century Europe: historical and comparative perspectives*, Berg, Oxford.

Schumpeter, J. A., 1982, *History of economic analysis*, Allen and Unwin, London.

Schwarz, L.D., 1976, 'Conditions of life and work in London *c.* 1770–1820 with special reference to East London', Ph.D. Dissertation, University of Oxford.

—— 1979, 'Income distribution and social structure in London in the late eighteenth century', *Economic History Review 2nd ser.*, 32, pp. 250–59.

—— 1982, 'Social class and social geography: the middle classes in

London at the end of the eighteenth century', *Social History*, 7, pp. 167–85.

——— 1985, 'The standard of living in the long run: London 1700–1860', *Economic History Review 2nd ser.*, 38, pp. 24–41.

——— 1992, *London in the age of industrialisation: entrepreneurs, labour force and living conditions 1700–1850*, Cambridge University Press, Cambridge.

Scott, A.J. and Storper, M., 1984, *Production, work and territory: the geographical anatomy of industrial capitalism*, Allen and Unwin, London.

Shannon, H., 1935, 'Migration and the growth of London, 1841–91', *Economic History Review*, 5, pp. 79–86.

Shaw Lefevre, G. and Bennett, T., 1860, 'Account of the strike and lock-out in the building trades of London in 1859–60', in *Trades Societies and Strikes*, National Association for the Promotion of Social Science, London, pp. 52–76.

Sheppard, F., 1985, 'London and the nation in the nineteenth century', *Transactions of the Royal Historical Society*, 35, pp. 51–74.

Sheppard, F., Belcher, V. and Cottrell, P., 1979, 'The Middlesex and Yorkshire deeds registries and the study of building fluctuations', *London Journal*, 5, pp. 176–216.

Silberling, N.J., 1923, 'British prices and business cycles 1779–1850', *Review of Economic Statistics*, 5, pp. 223–61.

——— 1924, 'Financial and monetary policy of Great Britain during the Napoleonic Wars', *Quarterly Journal of Economics*, 38, pp. 214–33.

Simon, D., 1954, 'Master and servant' in Saville, J. (ed.), *Democracy and the Labour Movement*, Lawrence & Wishart, London, pp. 160–200.

Skyring, 1831, *Skyring's buildings prices*.

——— 1838, *Skyring's builders prices*.

——— 1845, *Skyring's builders prices*.

——— 1867, *Skyring's builders prices*.

Smiles, S., 1861, *Workmen's earnings, strikes and savings*, Murray, London.

Smith, A., 1974, *The wealth of nations*, Penguin, Harmondsworth.

Smith, J.T., 1817, *Vagabondiana, or anecdotes of mendicant wanderers through the streets of London*, London.

——— 1852, *The metropolis and its municipal administration*, London.

Soja, E., 1989, *Postmodern geographies: the reassertion of space and critical social theory*, Verso, London and New York.

Southall, H., 1988a, 'The origins of the depressed areas: unemployment, growth and regional economic structure in Britain before 1914', *Economic History Review 2nd ser.*, 41, pp. 236–58.

——— 1988b, 'Towards a geography of unionization: the spatial organization and distribution of the early British trade unions', *Transactions of the Institute of British Geographers, new series*, 13, pp. 466–83.

Southall, H., Gilbert, D. and Bryce, C., 1994, *Nineteenth-century trade union records*, Historical Geography Research Series, 27, c.

Spate, O.H.K., 1938, 'Geographical aspects of the industrial evolution of London till 1850', *Geographical Journal*, 92, pp. 422–32.

Stamp, J., 1916, *British incomes and policy*, King, London.

Statistical Society of London, 1840, 'Report of the committee of the Statistical Society of London on the state of the working classes in the parishes of St Margaret and St John Westminster', *Journal of the Royal Statistical Society*, 3, pp. 14–24.

—— 1848a, 'Investigation into the state of the poorer classes in St Georges in the East', *Journal of the Royal Statistical Society*, 11, pp. 193–249.

—— 1848b, 'Report of the committee of the council of the Statistical Society of London to investigate the state of the inhabitants and their dwellings in Church Lane, St Giles', *Journal of the Royal Statistical Society*, 11, pp. 1–18.

Stearns, P., 1974, 'Measuring the evolution of strike movements', *International Review of Social History*, 19, pp. 1–27.

—— 1975, *Lives of labour: work in a maturing industrial society*, Croom Helm, London.

Stevenson, J., 1977, *London in the age of reform*, Blackwell, Oxford.

—— 1992, *Popular disturbances in England 1700–1832*, Longmans, London.

Strang, J., 1858, 'The sewing machine in Glasgow and its effects on production, prices and wages', *Journal of the Royal Statistical Society*, 21, pp. 464–7.

Strang, W., 1845, *An address to the middle and working classes on the causes and prevention of the excessive sickness and mortality prevalent in large towns*, London.

Summerson, J., 1945, *Georgian London*, Pleiades, London.

Symmons, J.C., 1849, *Tactics for the times: as regards the condition and treatment of the dangerous classes*.

Taylor, B., 1983, *Eve and the new Jerusalem: socialism and feminism in the nineteenth century*, Virago, London.

Taylor, J.R., 1855, *Saturday half-holidays and the earlier payment of wages: collected correspondence*.

Thompson, E.P., 1967a, 'The political eduction of Henry Mayhew', *Victorian Studies*, 11, pp. 41–62.

—— 1967b, 'Time, work-discipline and industrial capitalism', *Past and Present*, 38, pp. 56–97.

—— 1968, *The making of the English working class*, Penguin, Harmondsworth.

—— 1973, 'Mayhew and the Morning Chronicle', in Thompson, E.P. and Yeo, E. (eds), 1973, *The unknown Mayhew*, Penguin, Harmondsworth, pp. 9–55.

Thompson, E.P. and Yeo, E. (eds), 1973, *The unknown Mayhew*, Penguin, Harmondsworth.

Thrift, N., 1977, 'The diffusion of Greenwich Mean Time in Great Britain', University of Leeds, Department of Geography working paper, 188.

Tilly, C., 1983, 'Flows of capital and forms of industry in Europe 1500–1900', *Theory and Society*, 12, pp. 123–49.

To his Grace the Duke of Portland, the Humble Memorial of the Committee of Master Tailors appointed to prosecute their journeymen for a combination to obtain an advance of wages (1800), in Aspinall, A. (ed.), 1949, *The Early English trade unions*, pp. 33–5.

Treble, J.H., 1979, *Urban poverty in Britain 1830–1914*, Batsford, London.

Tunzelman, G.N. von, 1979, 'Trends in real wages 1750–1850, revisited', *Economic History Review 2nd ser.*, 32, pp. 33–49.

Ure, A., 1835, *The philosophy of manufactures*, Charles Knight, London.

Vaughan, R., 1843, *The age of great cities*, Jackson and Walford, London.

Wadsworth, A.P., 1955–56, 'Newspaper Circulations 1800–1914', *Transactions, Manchester Statistical Society*, pp. 1–37.

Wages for making the various sorts of tin wares, proposed by the general meeting of the manufacturers, 1805.

Wakefield, E.G., 1831, *Households in danger from the populace*, Chalmers and Collins, Glasgow.

Waller, P.J., 1983, *Town, city and nation: England 1850–1914*, Oxford University Press, Oxford.

Wallerstein, I., 1989, *The modern world system*, Academic Press, London.

Ward, D., 1975, 'Victorian cities; how modern?', *Journal of Historical Geography*, 1, pp. 135–51.

—— 1980, 'Environs and neighbours in the "Two Nations": residential differentiation in mid-nineteenth century Leeds', *Journal of Historical Geography*, 6, pp. 133–62.

Warwick, R.E., 1855, *Observations on the laws of settlements, poor removals and the equalization of the poor rates*, Tirebuck, London.

Webb, R.K., 1955, *The British working class reader 1790–1848*, Allen and Unwin, London.

Webb, S.J. and Freeman, A., 1912, *The seasonal trades*, Constable, London.

Webb, S.J. and Webb, B., 1920, *The history of trade unionism*, Longmans, London.

—— 1929, *English local government: English poor law history, Part 2: the last hundred years*, Longmans and Green, London.

Weber, A.F., 1899, *The growth of cities in the nineteenth century*, Macmillan, New York.

Weight, G., 1840, 'Statistics of the parish of St George the Martyr, Southwark', *Journal of the Royal Statistical Society*, 3, pp. 50–71.

Weir, W., 1842, 'St Giles, past and present' in Knight, C. (ed.), *London*, vol. 3, pp. 266–7.

Weld, C.R., 1843, 'On the condition of the working classes in the inner ward of St George's parish, Hanover Square', *Journal of the Royal Statistical Society*, 6, pp. 17–27.

Weyland, 1884, *These fifty years: being the jubilee volume of the London City Mission*, London City Mission, London.

Wilkes, J., 1816, *An address on behalf of the distressed poor in the northern half of the metropolis and especially of the watch and clock manufacturers within the parish of St Luke.*

Williams, K., 1981, *From pauperism to poverty*, Routledge and Kegan Paul, London.

Williams, R., 1975, *The country and the city*, Paladin, St Albans.

Williamson, J.G., 1980, 'Earnings inequality in nineteenth-century Britain', *Journal of Economic History*, 40, pp. 457–75.

—— 1985, *Did British capitalism breed inequality?*, Allen and Unwin, London.

Wirth, L., 1964, *On cities and social life*, University of Chicago Press, Chicago, USA.

Wohl, A.S, 1977, *The eternal slum: housing and social policy in Victorian London*, Edward Arnold, London.

—— 1983, *Endangered lives: public health in Victorian Britain*, Dent, London.

Wright, T., 1867, *Some habits and customs of the working classes*, Tinsley, London.

—— 1868, *The great unwashed*, London.

Wrigley, E.A., 1967, 'A simple model of London's importance in changing English society and economy 1650–1750', *Past and Present*, 37, pp. 44–70.

Yeo, E., 1973, 'Mayhew as a social investigator' in Thompson, E.P. and Yeo, E. (eds), *The unknown Mayhew*, Penguin, Harmondsworth, pp. 56–109.

Young, A., 1772, *A six week's tour through the southern counties of England and Wales*, Strahan, London.

Index